PUBLICATIONS OF THE BUREAU OF BUSINESS
AND ECONOMIC RESEARCH
UNIVERSITY OF CALIFORNIA, LOS ANGELES

Previously published in this series:

THE NATURE OF COMPETITION IN GASOLINE DISTRIBUTION
AT THE RETAIL LEVEL
by Ralph Cassady, Jr., and Wylie L. Jones (1951)

THE PACIFIC COAST MARITIME SHIPPING INDUSTRY, 1930–1948
VOLUME I: AN ECONOMIC PROFILE
by Wytze Gorter and George H. Hildebrand (1952)

THE ROLE OF MERGERS IN THE GROWTH OF LARGE FIRMS
by J. Fred Weston (1953)

THE PACIFIC COAST MARITIME SHIPPING INDUSTRY, 1930–1948
VOLUME II: AN ANALYSIS OF PERFORMANCE
by Wytze Gorter and George H. Hildebrand (1954)

THE MEXICAN PETROLEUM INDUSTRY, 1930–1958
by J. Richard Powell (1956)

THE PERSECUTION OF HUGUENOTS AND FRENCH ECONOMIC
DEVELOPMENT, 1680–1720
by Warren C. Scoville (1960)

"DISGUISED UNEMPLOYMENT" IN UNDERDEVELOPED AREAS
by Yong Sam Cho (1963)

THE DEVELOPMENT OF THE SPANISH TEXTILE INDUSTRY, 1750–1800
by James Clayburn La Force, Jr. (1965)

ECONOMIC DEVELOPMENT AND EXPORT GROWTH
by Robert E. Baldwin (1966)

COMPETITION AND OLIGOPSONY
IN THE DOUGLAS FIR LUMBER INDUSTRY

PUBLICATIONS OF THE
BUREAU OF BUSINESS AND ECONOMIC RESEARCH
UNIVERSITY OF CALIFORNIA, LOS ANGELES

COMPETITION AND OLIGOPSONY IN THE DOUGLAS FIR LUMBER INDUSTRY

BY

Walter J. Mead

UNIVERSITY OF CALIFORNIA PRESS
BERKELEY AND LOS ANGELES
1966

UNIVERSITY OF CALIFORNIA PRESS
BERKELEY AND LOS ANGELES

CAMBRIDGE UNIVERSITY PRESS
LONDON, ENGLAND

PRINTED IN THE UNITED STATES OF AMERICA

TO MY WIFE

Acknowledgments

In preparing this study, I have enjoyed enthusiastic cooperation from federal agencies and also from private industry. In
response to request, private business records were usually made
available for limited use. The behavior of buyers in the market for
federal timber could not have been understood and identified without the willing cooperation of operators in this market. It should
be perfectly obvious that persons are rather sensitive about inter-
personal and interfirm relationships in a market characterized by
fewness. Yet, in the process of extensive interviews, operators were
willing to discuss their experience. All discussions were prefaced
by the guarantee that the privacy of such information would be
preserved; that is, that individual and firm names would not be
identified unless information is based upon public sources.

With no suggestion of spreading the responsibility for errors
that may be contained in this analysis, I would like to express my
deep appreciation to the people, numbering in the hundreds, who
have extended their cooperation. As research was conducted over
a period of several years and required extensive interviews from
coast to coast and even in the Deep South, it is not possible to identify all the people who have made significant contributions. I cannot, however, neglect to mention a few whose encouragement and
assistance made this book possible. At Crown Zellerbach Corporation, Mr. Clarence W. Richen and his able staff of professional
foresters (refugees from the teaching profession) have literally
been my teachers in forestry over a period of time antedating this
study. I am grateful to Mr. L. R. Moyer of the Frank Lumber Co.
for many penetrating discussions, sometimes lasting well beyond
the midnight hour. Substantial assistance was also given by Mr. T.
K. Oliver of Timber Products Co.; Mr. George Flannagan of Elk
Lumber Co.; Mr. Aaron Jones of Seneca Sawmill Co.; Mr. Denby
Mackie of Timberlane Lumber Co.; Mr. William Dean, editor of
Random Lengths; and Mr. Irvin Luiten of Weyerhaeuser Co.
Valuable criticism and suggestions were given by Dr. Marion Claw-
son of Resources for the Future, Inc., formerly director of the

Bureau of Land Management. Tireless assistance and valuable
consultation were contributed by Dr. Carl A. Newport, chief of
the Division of Forest Economics Research of the Pacific Northwest Forest and Range Experiment Station, United States Forest
Service; by Mr. Thomas Glazebrook, Timber Management Division of the Forest Service; and by Mr. George Hartman of the
Bureau of Land Management. To my professional colleagues who
gave encouragement and read parts of the manuscript, I offer grat-
itude. They include Professor John Zivnuska at the University of
California, Berkeley; Professors Corwin Edwards and H. T. Koplin
at the University of Oregon; Professor Robert F. Lanzillotti at
Michigan State University; and Professors K. N. Rao and William
F. Kennedy at the University of California, Santa Barbara.

Financial assistance has been provided from several sources. The
Bureau of Business and Economic Research, UCLA, has provided
continuous financial support since the project was initiated in 1958.
In addition to financial support, the patient counsel and encouragement of Bureau Director Ralph Cassady, Jr., is most appreciated.
The Agricultural Experiment Station at Berkeley, California,
provided a helpful grant for released time. In this connection, services and consultation from Dean Henry Vaux and Professor John
A. Zivnuska of the School of Forestry, University of California,
Berkeley, were of great assistance. The Pacific Southwest Forest
and Range Experiment Station at Berkeley also provided some
financing for released time. Resources for the Future, Inc., provided both expense financing and a released-time grant that considerably accelerated research progress. Finally, the Research Committee at the University of California, Santa Barbara, continuously
made research-expense grants available. Even my acknowledged
debts are obviously numerous.

W. J. M.

University of California
Santa Barbara

Contents

[xi]

TABLES

FIGURES

Introduction

The United States lumber industry is frequently cited by economists to illustrate a real world approximation to the model of
pure competition. Indeed, at the output level, with its 16,000 mills
and nearly the same number of firms producing homogeneous
products, the lumber industry shows a remarkably close correspondence between the real world and the theoretical model. We find
that individual firms, even the largest, face a perfectly elastic demand curve for their lumber, and that the profit rate is no higher
than that hypothesized by the competitive model. But at the timber
input level, the industry deviates widely from the model of pure
competition in which factor supply functions have infinite elasticity. Because geographical markets for timber resources are narrowly circumscribed and the supply function for timber is relatively inelastic, a change in the level of output by a firm influences
the price of timber resources. Consequently, there is interdependence among firms in any timber market. Thus, the timber market
is oligopsonistic rather than competitive.

The behavior of firms as buyers of timber is in sharp contrast
with the behavior of firms as sellers of lumber. The former, reflecting an oligopsonistic structure, includes implicit and explicit collusion among buyers, whereas the latter reflects a competitive
structure and shows virtually no evidence of collusion.

Performance of the lumber industry is mixed and leaves much to
be desired. At the timber input level in the Douglas fir region there
is a wide price disparity between competitive and noncompetitive
timber sales, and large firms have a significant degree of market
power in the national forest timber markets. This market power is
manifest in a significantly lower average cost for national forest
timber purchased by large firms relative to small firms. The
market-power aspect of performance follows directly from the oligopsonistic structure of the timber market. Other evidence on
performance at the output level raises substantial doubts whether

for federal timber in the Douglas fir region. As geographical markets for timber input are narrowly circumscribed, competition is restricted to relatively few buyers. In this oligopsonistic structure, the conduct of competitors is subjected to intensive analysis, and noncompetitive behavior is identified.

The limited tools of analysis available for the study of performance are used in an attempt to appraise the performance record of the lumber industry. We are concerned with performance at the product output level and the timber resource management level. In addition, performance of buyers of national forest timber resources is subjected to detailed analysis. Positions of market power in the timber resource market are examined. Finally, the relationship between structure and behavior on the one hand, and final performance results on the other, are discussed and appraised to the limit allowed by the present tools of analysis.

DEFINITION OF THE LUMBER INDUSTRY

When we speak of the lumber industry we refer, at the output level, to the softwood sector of the total lumber-manufacturing industry. Softwood lumber represents approximately 80 percent of all lumber production, with hardwood lumber accounting for the remainder. The plywood industry is excluded from this definition of the lumber industry. While plywood utilizes the same raw material and is also a close competitor with softwood lumber in the construction market, an entirely different production technology is involved, and plywood is thought of as a separate industry. Similarly, the composition-board industry is excluded from this concept of the lumber industry. Composition board utilizes sawdust, planer shavings, wood flakes, and sometimes bark, all part of the residual from lumber or plywood production.

Geographically, primary emphasis in this study is given to the Douglas fir region. The traditional geographical limits of this region are defined by the West Coast Lumbermens Association as "the 19 counties in Western Oregon and the 19 counties of Western Washington which lie between the crest of the Cascade Mountains and the Pacific Ocean."[5] The same definition is employed by the United States Forest Service.[6] Within the Douglas fir region, Douglas fir is the principal species, but west coast hemlock, Sitka spruce,

---

5 *Statistical Yearbook, 1959–1960*, West Coast Lumbermens Association (Portland, Ore., 1962), p. i.

6 *Timber Resources for America's Future*, U.S. Department of Agriculture, Forest Service, Forest Resources Report no. 14 (Washington, 1958), p. 6.

and western red cedar are also common species of the area. Our primary interest is not in Douglas fir lumber as a species, but rather in the softwood lumber industry that is centered in the geographical area defined as the Douglas fir region.

Logic would favor inclusion of the redwood region of north-western California within the Douglas fir region. Contiguous to the important southwestern Oregon producing area, it is a major producing source of softwood lumber (see table 1). For most pur-poses, the northwestern California area is considered part of the same industry, centered in the Douglas fir region. Statistical in-formation, however, is not readily available beyond the standard definition of the Douglas fir region. Therefore, owing to both con-vention and convenience, the standard definition is employed.

The Douglas fir region, with 1.8 percent of the total United States area[7] and 4.5 percent of the nation's forest land area, holds 37 percent of the remaining softwood sawtimber volume,[8] and accounts for about 30 percent of national softwood lumber pro-duction. Containing the largest stand of old-growth timber in the United States, it is regarded as a major center of the lumber in-dustry for the nation. Other important geographical areas may also be identified. The western pine region is made up of all or parts of twelve Western states, excluding the Douglas fir region and the California redwood area. This large area produces about 36 percent of all United States softwood lumber. The twelve states in the southern pine lumber-producing region account for about 21 percent of total softwood lumber production. Further, in recent years imports of softwood lumber, mainly from British Columbia, have become significant. In 1963 imports amounted to about 5 billion feet, or 18 percent of national production.

There is no strict geographical definition of the lumber industry in this analysis. For some purposes, the entire softwood lumber industry is the relevant industrial classification. For other purposes, relatively homogeneous subareas of the Douglas fir region are the appropriate basis of analysis. Much of the detailed analysis is de-voted to competition in the auction markets for federal timber. For this purpose, rather small geographical areas called "working circles" become the relevant geographical market. It is convenient to conduct the latter analysis within the limits of the Douglas fir region.

---

[7] Excluding Alaska and Hawaii.
[8] *Timber Resources for America's Future,* p. 555.

TABLE 1
SOFTWOOD LUMBER PRODUCTION, UNITED STATES AND REGIONAL, 1954-1964

Year	Total U.S.		Douglas fir region		California redwood region		Western pine region[a]		Southern pine region[b]		Other	
	Volume[c]	Percent	Volume[c]	Percent	Volume[c]	Percent	Volume[c]	Percent	Volume[c]	Percent	Volume[c]	Percent
1954	29.3	100	9.3	31.7	2.7	9.2	8.0	27.3	7.3	24.9	2.0	6.8
1955	29.8	100	9.6	32.2	2.7	9.1	8.8	29.5	7.4	24.8	1.3	4.4
1956	30.2	100	8.7	28.8	3.0	9.9	9.0	29.8	7.7	25.5	1.8	6.0
1957	27.1	100	7.9	29.2	2.5	9.3	8.0	29.5	6.6	24.3	2.1	7.7
1958	27.4	100	8.4	30.7	2.7	9.9	8.5	31.0	6.4	23.4	1.4	5.1
1959	30.7	100	9.1	29.6	2.9	9.4	9.9	32.2	6.7	21.8	2.1	6.8
1960	26.7	100	8.0	30.0	2.3	8.6	9.2	34.5	5.6	21.0	1.6	6.0
1961	26.1	100	7.7	29.5	2.2	8.4	9.0	34.5	5.6	21.5	1.6	6.1
1962	26.8	100	8.0	29.8	2.2	8.2	9.5	35.4	5.7	21.3	1.4	5.2
1963	27.8	100	8.3	29.8	2.1	7.6	10.1	36.3	6.0	21.6	1.3	4.7
1964	29.5	100	9.0	30.5	2.2	7.5	10.6	35.9	6.3	21.4	1.4	4.7

a The western pine region includes eastern Washington, eastern Oregon, California (except the redwood region), Nevada, Idaho, Montana, Wyoming, Utah, Colorado, Arizona, New Mexico, and part of South Dakota.
b The southern pine region includes Virginia, North Carolina, South Carolina, Florida, Georgia, Tennessee, Alabama, Mississippi, Arkansas, Louisiana, eastern Oklahoma, and eastern Texas.
c In billions of board feet.

SOURCES: Developed from West Coast Lumbermens Association, *Statistical Yearbook, 1963* (Portland, Ore., 1965); Thomas E. Hamilton, *Production, Prices, Employment and Trade in Pacific Northwest Forest Industries*, Pacific Northwest Forest and Range Experiment Station, U.S. Forest Service (Portland, Ore., 1965); Lumber Survey Committee, *National Survey of Lumber Demand and Supply*, quarterly issues.

There is both a national lumber market and, owing to relatively high transportation costs, regional concentrations for lumber distribution. The southern pine lumber-producing area markets lumber in a rather restricted area. In 1960, 78.1 percent of all southern pine lumber shipments were limited to the twelve producing states within the southern pine area. Only 3.8 percent of this region's production was destined for states lying west of the Mississippi River, and 1.8 percent was channeled to export. The balance, 16.3 percent, was shipped to states east of the Mississippi River and north of the southern pine region, but not including the New England states.

The distribution area for the Douglas fir region and the western pine region is relatively unrestricted. In 1960 shipments from both regions were sent to every state in the nation. The principal destinations are similar for Douglas fir and western pine shippers. They consist, first, of the three West Coast states, and, second, of the populous Midwestern and Eastern states. Texas is also an important market for lumber from both regions.[9] Thus, Douglas fir region production competes with southern pine only where transportation costs allow. The market data suggest a high degree of substitutability among various species. Cross elasticities of demand among species for many uses would be quite high.

The important public policy issues to which it is hoped this study will make a contribution include (1) concentration of timberland ownership in private hands, and (2) distribution of timber from the large public ownerships, principally the Department of Agriculture (Forest Service) and the Department of Interior (Bureau of Land Management).

---

[9] Data on lumber shipments are from "Distribution of Lumber Shipments," reports provided by the West Coast Lumbermens Association, the Western Pine Association, and the Southern Pine Association.

PART I

Demand, Supply, and Cost Issues

Although my primary objective in this study is to explore the relationship between the structure of an industry, the conduct of competitors in it, and final performance results, certain background analysis must be developed. Specifically, information is needed about the economies of scale in lumber production in order to judge whether cost-of-production factors require large-scale plants and firms, or, on the other hand, favor small-scale operations suitable for conditions of atomistic competition. Information about the elasticity of demand and supply for both lumber and timber is also needed.

In chapter 1 I will seek to identify the optimum plant size and the optimum firm size in lumber production, and to generalize about the shape of the short-run average cost curve for suboptimal levels of output. In chapter 2 the demand functions for lumber and timber are examined. The objective is to generalize about elasticity of demand. In chapter 3 analysis is shifted to supply conditions, and the objective is to identify the supply elasticity for both the raw material, timber, and the final product, lumber.

CHAPTER 1

Economies of Scale in Lumber Production

As part of the basic data prerequisite to an analysis of competition, the competitive position of plants and firms of various sizes must be known. Further, it is desirable to have some comprehension of the behavior of production costs for various output levels. In this chapter I therefore attempt to identify the optimum plant size, the optimum firm size, and the shape of the short-run average cost curve for suboptimal and superoptimal levels of production.

The analysis rests upon four kinds of evidence. First, I examine the record of plant and firm survival over a period of years to determine whether there is a clear tendency for a specific size class to survive the rigors of competition. Second, I draw on engineering estimates of optimum plant size. Third, on the basis of an examination of a multitude of operating sawmills and familiarity with the profit-maximizing problem, I explore deductively the fundamental conditions that determine cost behavior. On this a priori basis I attempt to identify both the optimum plant size and the optimum firm size for lumber production. Fourth, the shape of the single-plant short-run average cost curve is estimated after a detailed examination of firm accounting records and of the probable behavior of cost items for alternative levels of output. Following conventional practice, I assume that factor prices remain constant as a firm or a plant expands or contracts output, that selling costs are constant, and that the technological framework remains fixed. My analysis, based on conditions found in the Douglas fir region, is not necessarily applicable to other production regions.

THE SURVIVOR APPROACH

The "survivor technique" for estimating optimum plant and firm size is based on the proposition that an efficient plant or firm must

respond to a multitude of forces converging in the market. The
total of such forces is extremely complex. Proven ability to survive
and prosper under a complex of forces is the best indicator of
overall efficiency. The leading advocate of the survivor technique
is George Stigler, who holds that an "efficient size of firm, on this
argument, is one that meets any and all problems the entrepreneur
actually faces: strained labor relations, rapid innovation, government regulation, unstable foreign markets, and what not. This is,
of course, the decisive meaning of efficiency from the viewpoint
of the enterprise."[1] Stigler examines the alternative methods of
estimating optimum size and concludes that the survivor technique avoids the principal problems associated with direct com-
parisons of actual costs for firms of different sizes, the comparison
of rates of return on investment, and engineering estimates. He
argues that the survivor technique is more direct, simpler, and
"more authoritative." By the latter he means that it wears the
stamp of approval granted by the marketplace.

The survivor technique, however, is not without its problems. A
record of survival indicates the result of operations not only within,
but also beyond, the competitive rules of the game. One runs the
risk of presenting the laurel of distinction to a size class of firms
operating in violation of free-market principles. Thus, a firm sur-
viving owing to a substantial position of market power, perhaps
supported by artificial barriers to entry which preclude effective
competition, may ineffectively utilize scarce resources. Further, as
Leonard Weiss has suggested, "small firms may survive and grow
because of their ability to exploit monopsonistic positions in local
labor markets or to circumvent the law."[2] This criticism, however,
is more a caution against careless application of the survivor technique than a criticism of the technique itself. If a careful examination of the behavior of a given industry accompanies appraisal of
optimum size, then the survivor technique would seem to retain
its superiority over alternative approaches. Finally, in view of its
hazards, this technique is likely to yield more reliable estimates
of optimal plant size than of optimal firm size.

Before proceeding with an analysis of survival, care must be
taken in selecting the period of time to be studied. A period of
rapid growth accompanied by high and even increasing levels of

---

[1] George J. Stigler, "The Economies of Scale," *Journal of Law and Economics*, I
(Oct., 1958), 56.
[2] Leonard W. Weiss, "The Survival Technique and the Extent of Suboptimal
Capacity," *Journal of Political Economy*, LXXII (June, 1964), 246.

profitability should be avoided because all but the completely inept would survive and prosper. Such a period in the lumber industry is covered in the ten years from 1941 to 1951. During this time the All Commodities Wholesale Price Index increased 102 percent, but lumber prices exactly doubled this percentage change, increasing by 204 percent. A satisfactory base for analysis is the period since 1952 in which lumber prices varied with cyclical conditions, but followed a virtually horizontal trend. At the same time, labor costs and quasi rents accruing to timber resource owners increased sharply. Profits of nontimber-owning firms were correspondingly strained. Between 1952 and 1962 the number of operating sawmills in the Douglas fir region declined by 50 percent, as 500 mills ceased operations. This period, therefore, offers a satisfactory span of time over which we may examine the record of survival by plant size and firm size, if care is taken to consider the effect of timber ownership (and consequent receipt of capital gains from timber ownership) as well as the evidence of large-firm market power.

Optimum plant size.—Excellent data concerning the survival record based on plant size are available from 1952 through 1962. Data on number of plants, volume of production, and percent of total production by four size classes are shown in table 2. During this period, lumber production from the Douglas fir region declined about 22 percent. Production from the penultimate size class of mill, however, increased by 36 percent. All other size classes show a reduction in output, although for the largest size class an 11 percent decline in output was less than the reduction registered for the entire region. The two size classes producing less than 80,000 board feet per eight-hour shift show substantial declines in both number of mills and output, with the largest decline registered for the smallest size class. The penultimate group also shows that the average output per mill expanded during this time. Thus, 6 percent fewer mills produced 36 percent greater output within the 80,000 to 119,000 board feet per eight-hour day size class. This result may be due in part to expansion into multishift operations.

The percent of total output accounted for by each of four plant size classes in the Douglas fir region is also shown in table 2. The distribution by percent of output automatically adjusts for the downward trend in lumber production found during this period of time. An extremely clear trend is shown from the penultimate size class. This mill size expanded its share of total regional lumber production from 14 to 25 percent, and the trend is unbroken by any periodic reverse movement. The largest size class also increased

TABLE 2
Distribution of Lumber Output in the Douglas Fir Region by Plant Size, Based on Association Data, In Selected Years

Size class	Capacity[a]	Ratio 1962 to 1952		1962			1960			1958		
		Nb	Output[c]	Nb	Output[c]	Percent of total output	Nb	Output[c]	Percent of total output	Nb	Output[c]	Percent of total output
Small	Less than 40	.33	.30	202	546	7	291	633	8	291	726	9
Medium small	40-79	.62	.57	128	1,394	17	154	1,441	18	150	1,435	17
Medium large	80-119	.94	1.36	77	2,031	25	89	2,044	25	90	2,000	24
Large	120 or more	.90	.89	86	4,106	51	80	3,911	49	89	4,278	50
Total[d]		.50	.78	493	8,077	100	614	8,029	100	620	8,439	100

Size class	Capacity[a]	1956			1954			1952		
		Nb	Output[c]	Percent of total output	Nb	Output[c]	Percent of total output	Nb	Output[c]	Percent of total output
Small	Less than 40	371	908	10	388	1,052	11	608	1,819	18
Medium small	40-79	202	2,046	23	204	2,299	25	207	2,445	24
Medium large	80-119	82	1,718	20	76	1,433	15	82	1,497	14
Large	120 or more	84	4,087	47	111	4,499	49	96	4,603	44
Total[d]		739	8,759	100	779	9,283	100	993	10,364	100

a In thousands of board feet per eight-hour day.
b Number of plants.
c In millions of board feet.
d Total production does not equal the sum of production in all size classes, as mills having less than 10 million feet annual production are excluded.
Source: Developed from data supplied by West Coast Lumbermens Association.

its share of total output. The trend in this case, however, is not without its reverse movements. In two instances the largest size class declined in percent of total output. These data suggest that the most efficient plant size is in the 80,000 to 119,000 (or perhaps to 140,000) board feet per eight-hour day size class.

Opposite movements are shown for the two smaller size classes. Mills producing less than 40,000 board feet per eight-hour day show a clear and unbroken loss in market share, declining from 18 percent of the total output in 1952 to only 7 percent in 1962. The medium-small size class (40,000 to 79,000 board feet per eight-hour day) shows a sizable decline in market share from 24 to 17 percent. The decline, however, is not uninterrupted. The data strongly indicate that the smallest size class is not an effective competitor under market conditions that prevailed from 1952 through 1962. The same conclusion may be drawn for the medium-small size class, but with a somewhat lower degree of certainty.

The data on size classes presented above are based on rated capacity for an eight-hour day. In fact, some of the mills included in each category produced substantially more than their rated capacity by virtue of two-shift or even three-shift operations. This measurement difficulty can be overcome by examining size classes based on annual production. Suitable data on this basis are provided by the Directory of the Forest Products Industry. The record from 1954 through 1963 is shown in table 3, which has the advantage of providing a breakdown of the largest of the four size classes shown in table 2. The largest group included half of the total regional output. Comparable data, however, are available only since 1954. From this base through 1963 a clear expansion has occurred in the size class producing between 40 and 59 million feet per year. This size class expanded output 137 percent from 1954 through 1963. Similarly, but without the same degree of clarity, an expansion occurred in the 20 to 39 million feet per year size class. In all other size classes a substantial drop in production volume occurred. The most distinct decline, in both number of mills and volume of production, occurred in the very large mills, those producing in excess of 80 million feet per year.

Directory data for the very small mills are incomplete; the smallest size shown is 10 million feet per year. This level of output corresponds to about 45,000 board feet per eight-hour day, assuming one-shift operations and 220 working days per year. Thus, the very small size class shown in table 2, based upon capacity per eight-hour day, is not shown in table 3. The omission is of little consequence,

TABLE 3

DISTRIBUTION OF LUMBER OUTPUT IN THE DOUGLAS FIR REGION BY PLANT SIZE, BASED ON DIRECTORY DATA, IN SELECTED YEARS

Size Class[a]	Ratio 1963 to 1954	Ratio 1963 to 1958	1963 Nb[b]	1963 Annual output[c]	1963 Percent of total Output	1958 Nb[b]	1958 Annual output[c]	1958 Percent of total Output	1954 Nb[b]	1954 Annual output[c]	1954 Percent of total Output
10-19	d	.85	55	764	9	63	902	11	d	d	d
20-39	1.07	1.17	63	1,727	21	52	1,472	17	55	1,610	17
40-59	2.37	1.52	39	1,888	23	27	1,242	15	16	794	9
60-79	.74	.82	10	661	8	11	810	10	13	898	10
80-99	.25	.54	1	90	1	2	168	2	4	355	4
100 or more	.20	.25	1	113	1	3	449	5	4	552	6
Total regional production[e]	.90	.99		8,374			8,439			9,283	

a Annual production in millions of board feet.
b Number of plants.
c In millions of board feet.
d Data unavailable.
e The sum of production in all size classes does not equal total production, as mills having less than 10 million feet annual production are excluded.

SOURCE: Developed from data in annual issues of *Directory of the Forest Products Industry* (Seattle: Miller Freeman Publications).

however, since the analysis (based on daily capacity) rather clearly establishes the inability of the smallest size class to survive in competitive markets.

The analysis presented in table 3 is consistent with the previous findings. The optimum mill size appears to be in the 80,000 to 119,000 board feet per eight-hour shift class (medium-large mills), or, on an annual basis and more narrowly defined size classes, 40 to 59 million feet per year production schedule. Thus, mills producing between 80,000 and 119,000 feet per eight-hour shift, operating on a two-shift basis and working 220 days per year, would produce between 35 and 53 million feet per year.

Table 3 sheds additional light on the very large size class, because a further breakdown is shown for the largest group. Mills having at least a 120,000 board feet per eight-hour shift capacity and working two shifts 220 days per year would produce at least 53 million board feet per year. Although this group is not subdivided in table 2, it is subdivided into four different classes in table 3. Table 2 suggests that the largest size class has a fair degree of survivability, but when this class is further subdivided a marked difference is found between the new size classes. The findings of table 2 may be interpreted as follows: within the largest size class producing 120,000 board feet or more per eight-hour shift, only those mills approaching the lower limit of this class interval show an ability to survive in competition. Consequently, the upper limit of the optimum size class is 140,000 board feet per eight-hour capacity. Such a mill would employ approximately seventy-five people on a one-shift basis; it is, therefore, a relatively small plant.

Similarly, the mills in the 40,000 to 79,000 board feet per eight-hour shift group may include some having an excellent survival record in the upper range of the class interval. Mills yielding 80,000 board feet per day may produce 35 million feet per year on a two-shift basis. Table 3 shows that the group producing from 20 to 39 million feet per year expanded output from 1954 to 1963, and at an even faster rate in the 1958–1963 period.

Again, the findings from table 2 may be reinterpreted. Overall, the data seem to support the following conclusion: the most efficient plant size based upon survivability appears to include mills of the 60,000 to 140,000 board feet per eight-hour day group. Or, from table 3, based upon annual production and smaller class intervals, it appears that the optimum mill size is within the range of 20 to 59 million feet per year. The annual data and the eight-hour daily capacity data provide consistent estimates of optimum plant size.

The data analyzed are not without shortcomings. The major problem arises from the fact that lumber mills are not homogeneous, and there is no way of establishing more homogeneous subclasses. The major classes of lumber mills may be identified as grade recovery mills and dimension mills. The grade recovery mills at one time dominated the lumber industry. Producing a multitude of grades and types of lumber, they are characterized by a relatively high "average realization" on lumber production (high average value per thousand board feet of lumber production). In order to achieve this end, labor is used more extensively and log input more intensively. In contrast, the dimension mill produces lumber of 2-inch minimum thickness. Emphasis is placed on a higher level of output per man-hour at the expense of lower average realization value per unit of output. Some dimension mills, called "stud mills," produce only two-by-fours 8 feet long and concentrate on maximizing output and minimizing labor input. The data examined do not allow a distinction by the categories discussed above. As dimension mills tend to be somewhat smaller than the older-style grade recovery mills, the data also indicate that mill types have shifted from grade recovery to dimension mills. Nevertheless, our conclusions hold. It is still true that the very large and the small mills have not survived the rigors of competition, whereas the medium and medium-large mills have survived and have expanded their share of total output. The reasons for this expansion may include a shift in the basic type of milling activity.

Optimum firm size.—Discussion of the optimum firm size raises the question: Is there any evidence in survival data that multiplant firms are more efficient than single-plant firms? The data available to answer this question are somewhat conflicting. From 1958 to 1963 the number of multiplant firms operating in the Douglas fir region declined from twenty-five to twenty-two.[3] At the same time, lumber production declined a modest 4 percent. Over this period of time, the number of separate plants operated by multiplant firms increased from eighty to eighty-nine. Fourteen of these additional plants, however, are accounted for by the Georgia Pacific Corporation merger activity in the South. Of the primarily Western mills there was a slight decline from eighty-eight to eighty-five in the number of plants operated by multiplant mills.

---

3 *Forest Industries*, 1964 Yearbook and Buyer's Guide, vol. 91, no. 2 (May 29, 1964).

Lumber production by firm size in 1958 and 1963 shows a clear expansion in the small-firm category yielding 40 to 59 million feet per year (see table 4[4]). All but five of the forty-seven firms in this category were single-plant firms. Each of these five operated two plants. Table 4 also shows a substantial expansion in production by the two largest size classes where total firm production is at least 250 million feet per year. All eight companies in this category for 1963 are multiplant firms. The six large, multiplant firms of 1958 operated an average of 9.25 plants per firm, but, in 1963, the eight largest firms operated an average of 8 plants per firm.

Whereas the analysis of optimum plant size based on the survivor technique yields conclusive results, the same technique applied to firm data is rather inconclusive. In view of this situation, any further judgment on optimum firm size is deferred until the third point in the analysis, which is based on deductive reasoning.

THE ENGINEERING APPROACH

Optimum plant size.—The second source of evidence relative to optimum plant size is based on personal interviews with engineers primarily engaged as consultants in sawmill design. The professional training of these men leads to an emphasis on such tech-

TABLE 4

DISTRIBUTION OF LUMBER OUTPUT IN WESTERN UNITED STATES BY FIRM SIZE, IN SELECTED YEARS

Size class[a]	Ratio output 1963 to 1958	1963		1958	
		Number of firms	Annual output[b]	Number of firms	Annual output[b]
10-19	0.82	122	1,734	147	2,106
20-39	0.85	100	2,719	113	3,209
40-59	1.42	47	2,758	41	1,949
60-79	1.12	20	1,327	19	1,190
80-99	1.08	6	543	6	505
100-249	0.92	15	2,198	15	2,399
250-499	1.28	4	1,089	3	853
500 or more	1.37	4	3,150	3	2,303

a Annual production in millions of board feet.
b In millions of board feet.

SOURCE: Developed from data in annual issues of *Directory of the Forest Products Industry* (Seattle: Miller Freeman Publications).

---

4 Table 4 refers to firms operating primarily in the eleven Western states, whereas tables 2 and 3, concerned with plant size, are restricted to the Douglas fir region. This distinction in geographical area is necessary because several important firms in the Douglas fir region have substantial operations in the western pine region as well.

nological factors as headsaw capacity and coordinate capacities of
other production-line equipment. No attempt was made to develop
information on optimum firm size from this source. Information
on plant size was obtained entirely by personal interviews with
three design engineers associated with firms deeply involved in
sawmill designing.[5] This question was asked: "If you were requested to design a dimension sawmill to most profitably convert
logs into lumber in the Douglas fir region, what range of eight-hour
daily capacity would you aim for?" After considerable discussion
intended to clarify the question, the following answers were obtained from the three interviewees, respectively: 50,000 to 80,000
board feet per eight-hour shift; 60,000 to 75,000 board feet per
eight-hour shift, on a two-shift basis; and 60,000 to 85,000 board
feet per eight-hour shift.

In each instance the answers were given in terms of an initial
capacity. It was recognized that output normally expands beyond
initial and designed capacity as a "balancing process" takes place,
with bottlenecks eliminated at various stages of production. While
the engineering estimates of optimum plant size are somewhat less
than the optimum plant size indicated by survival data, the two
approaches may be consistent when normal growth takes place.
The engineering approach tells us something about the optimum
scale for a plant that is yet to be constructed, whereas survival data
indicate optimum size for plants that have survived not only competition, but also the shakedown process, in the first few months
or years of operation. It is quite conceivable, therefore, that the
engineers' estimates of the initial optimum scale are consistent
with survival data when the latter indicate a somewhat larger optimum size.

THE DEDUCTIVE APPROACH

Significant insights concerning economies of scale for both plants
and firms in the lumber industry may result from a deductive line
of reasoning. We will first explore the nature of lumber production
at the plant level.

Optimum plant size.—Half a century ago Sir Henry Clay wrote:
"Whenever the material worked is not uniform in quality, or
cannot be graded or treated in bulk, then the large-scale methods

---

[5] The engineering approach based on a written questionnaire was employed by
Joe S. Bain, "Economies of Scale, Concentration, and the Conditions of Entry in
Twenty Manufacturing Industries," *American Economic Review*, XLIV (March,
1954), 15–39.

. . . will not apply."[6] Here the field is the small firm. This early insight may be even more valid as automation succeeds mechanization. The principal raw-material input for a lumber mill is logs, and logs are heterogeneous. No two logs are the same, and the difference is significant. In this aspect the lumber industry is unlike most other manufacturing industries. For example, in the pulp industry no two wood chips flowing into the digester are the same, but the difference is not significant. Some chips contain portions of knots, but these can be screened out at a later stage in the production process.

In lumber production, where differences between logs are ignored in order to maximize output and minimize labor cost per unit of time, there is a substantial decline in average value of lumber output. When logs pass through a band-saw headrig, the sawyer visually examines each log and adjusts it on the carriage before making his initial cut. The log is reexamined and rotated as cutting proceeds. As the raw material flows on through the production process, critical decisions are made about successive alternative cuts. One may identify three basic stages in the process of converting a log to lumber. First, at the headrig, decisions on thickness are made by the sawyer.[7] Second, at the edger, decisions on width are made by the edgerman. Third, at the trim saws, decisions on length are made by the trimmerman.

By current technology all decisions are made on the basis of a quick visual inspection. The mechanical or chemical tests useful in such industries as pulp production and oil refining are not applicable in the lumber industry. In lumber milling a saw operator examines the raw material, and by pressing buttons or by pulling a lever he renders his decision. The decisions he makes affect the average value realized from lumber production. The decisions that must be made are both complex and profit sensitive. Two kinds of interdependence result from production-line decision making. Interdependence vastly increases the complexity of the profit-maximizing problem. First, the values of two or more pieces of lumber resulting from any given cut made at any of the three stages of production are interdependent. When a 2-inch-thick unedged cant comes before the edgerman in a dimension sawmill he may cut it into two-by-fours, two-by-sixes, two-by-eights, two-by-tens,

---

[6] Henry Clay, *Economics for the General Reader* (London: Macmillan, 1916), p. 34.
[7] Decision making at this point is more critical for grade recovery mills than for dimension mills.

two-by-twelves, or any combination of widths. But these items have different unit values, depending on market conditions. When any single cut is made, two pieces are created which may be of different values (per thousand board feet), and may also differ in total value from the original cant. Second, interdependence exists between the average value of lumber output, on the one hand, and cost of production, on the other. The greater the effort exerted to obtain higher average values through closer examination of the raw material and resawing, the higher will be the labor cost per unit of output.

I have attempted to demonstrate that the lumber industry requires complex decision making at the production-line level, with critical consequences for ultimate profitability for the firm. The complexity and the profit-sensitivity features, as described above, may not be unique among manufacturing industries. One would be hard pressed, however, to find another line of manufacturing in which all the important stages in production are characterized by these two critical features.

Having established the complexity and the profit-sensitivity features of production-line decision making in the lumber industry, we may now inquire into the position of the decision maker, the hourly paid production-line worker. Except in the very small mills, the owner-manager is virtually never the decision maker, as the sawyer, the edgerman, or the trimmerman. In only rare instances in the lumber industry are these critical decision makers in a profit-sharing position. Their incentive to maximize milling profits is given only by the "instinct of workmanship," or the realization that their jobs depend upon at least a minimum level of profitability for the firm. While there is undoubtedly a general desire to give a "day's work for a day's pay," there are some substantial negative features that must be identified in a realistic appraisal of the decision-making situation.

Two dominant characteristics may be identified: (1) a "don't know" condition, and (2) a "don't care" condition. While the degree of knowledgeableness of the sawyer, the edgerman, and the trimmerman varies widely, the recognized complexity of the decision-making situation would lead one to the generalization that most production-line decision makers do not know which of the many alternatives confronting them will maximize profits for the firm. They must appraise several variables and render a decision requiring competence in mathematics and economic relationships.

The educational qualifications of the production-line decision makers seldom exceed a high school education and are frequently less. Therefore, given the complexity of the decision-making requirement, one should not expect a high level of performance in this profit-sensitive position.

In addition to the "don't know" situation that prevails widely, there is also the "don't care" situation, which is encountered less frequently. This situation, which in the extreme extends to open antagonism against the firm, was brought out clearly in a human relations survey recently conducted by a lumber-manufacturing and timber-owning concern. Each employee of the firm was asked to respond to certain questions, one of which was, "What do you think of the company?" The pointed reply of one anonymous employee was, "Give me a match!" While this reaction would perhaps rarely be encountered and probably could quickly be identified when encountered, an apathetic attitude toward company profits is probably more widespread. Firms in the lumber industry have made only infrequent use of the profit-sharing device to increase employee interest in company profits.

Given the complexity and profit sensitivity of production-line decision making, together with widespread "don't know" and less common "don't care" situations, what may be inferred about the economies of scale owing to plant size and firm size in lumber production? Under present technology, visual inspection of the raw material continues to be a necessity. Electronic scanners in conjunction with computer decision making are not yet available. Assuming that the owner-manager has more knowledge about the alternatives that maximize profits than do his employees, and further that he has a higher level of motivation (incentive), the performance of production-line decision making can be improved by closer owner-manager supervision. To the degree that the profit-motivated owner is separated from production-line decision makers, profits may be expected to deteriorate. The larger the plant, the greater the difficulty of communication between the profit recipient and the production-line decision maker. While the ability of owners to supervise a multitude of production-line decision makers varies widely, we would expect the quality of supervision to be subject to sharply diminishing returns at high levels of output. This deductive-reasoning conclusion is consistent with both engineering estimates and survival data on optimum plant size.

Optimum firm size.—The deductive approach to the economies of scale issue may be extended to the multiplant firm. As two or more lumber-manufacturing plants are operated within a single firm, some of the authority of the person whom Papandreou[8] identified as "the peak coordinator" is delegated to subordinates. If the peak coordinator is the owner, and subordinates are neither owners nor recipients of profit shares, then the incentive to maximize profit is less direct. A measure of the "don't care" situation is introduced into supervision. If the firm is a large one and consists not only of several lumber-manufacturing plants, but veneer, plywood, pulp and paper, and other enterprises as well, then communication between the peak coordinator and production-line decision makers is further removed. In addition, the large firm takes on the handicaps of a bureaucracy. Decisions on major capital investments must pass through several management levels and committees charged with allocating scarce capital among many competing investment opportunities.

The problems of a bureaucracy are characteristic of all large-scale enterprises and must be offset by economies of scale from other sources. It is conceivable that in lumber manufacturing the diseconomies of the bureaucracy, together with the diseconomies of more distant and detached supervision of critical production-line decision making, may be offset by substantial economies of scale from other sources. But the lumber-manufacturing industry does not offer any apparent offsetting economies from multiplant operations. National advertising based on brand names is of little importance in the lumber industry. The accompanying product differentiation which Joe Bain identifies[9] as a major advantage of established firms and the most important barrier to entry is again of no significance in the lumber industry. Finally, the process of lumber wholesaling is so highly developed and highly competitive that very few residual benefits would be available to a firm establishing its own lumber-wholesaling function.

The above considerations suggest that no obvious economies of large-scale operations are available to offset the deductively indicated diseconomies of multi-plant operations. We are, therefore, led from this deductive line of reasoning to the conclusion that the optimum firm size is not multiplant but rather single-plant, and

8 Andreas G. Papandreou, "Some Basic Problems in the Theory of the Firm," in Bernard F. Haley, ed., *A Survey of Contemporary Economics* (Homewood, Ill., 1952), II, 191.

9 Joe S. Bain, *Barriers to New Competition* (Cambridge: Harvard University Press, 1956), p. 216.

that the single plant of optimum size, in turn, is not likely to exceed 140,000 board feet per eight-hour shift, or about 60 million feet per year.

Our conclusions with reference to optimum firm size are at variance with one type of information developed from firm-survival data. Table 4 shows that a substantial expansion in output for the two largest classes of firms did, in fact, occur. We must now reconcile this empirical data with our deductive conclusions.

One fault of the survivor technique, as indicated earlier, is that survival is the complex result of many forces, including some beyond the competitive rules of the game. Where large firms enjoy a significant advantage owing to market power, survival evidence would be discounted as an indicator of optimal firm size. At a later point (Part III) it is shown that large firms do, in fact, enjoy a significant market power position in the market for federal timber resources. This fact contributes to the survivability of large firms. Second, all eight firms in the two largest size classes for 1963 shown in table 4 are substantial owners of private timber, much of it purchased at historically low cost. For example, in 1900 the Weyerhaeuser interests acquired 900,000 acres of timberland in the Douglas fir region from Northern Pacific at a cost of 6 dollars per acre. The Bureau of Corporations estimated that, in terms of the probable log yield, the price was only 10 cents per thousand board feet.[10] In contrast, the weighted average price paid for all national forest timber purchased in the Douglas fir region from 1959 to 1962 was about 24 dollars per thousand board feet. Of course, the Weyerhaeuser Company has borne the cost of taxes, management, carrying charges, and so forth, over the years. These charges substantially increase the cost of timber acquired in 1900. Nevertheless, the annual cost of timber to Weyerhaeuser must be insignificant relative to timber cost to competitors who must purchase free market timber at current prices. The good judgment and foresight of Weyerhaeuser founders and other firms in a similar position substantially distorts the meaning of survival data. In measuring efficiency in lumber production, then, one measures not only the desired quality, but also the effect of timber ownership and oligopsony power on survivability. For these considerations, I am inclined to discount that part of the conflicting evidence bearing on optimum firm size which appears to show significant expansions for large lumber-producing firms. The data presently

---

[10] Ralph Hidy *et al., Timber and Men* (New York: Macmillan, 1963), p. 213.

available, however, do not permit an unequivocal conclusion on optimum firm size.

At this point it would be desirable to show graphically the derived minimum cost (optimum size) range for plants and firms. But the preceding analysis has concentrated attention on optimum size and gives little insight into the shape of the cost function. The final step in identifying economies of scale, therefore, requires directing attention to cost behavior at alternative output levels.

COST ESTIMATION APPROACH: SHORT-RUN AVERAGE COST FUNCTION

When inquiring about the shape of the short-run average cost function for various levels of output in lumber production, there are certain problems one must be aware of. First, the lumber industry is characterized by wide variation in quality of raw-material input into lumber mills. Within the capacity range of milling machinery, production costs vary inversely with log size, principally the diameter, and directly with the standard deviation of the diameter. Thus, a cost study based on statistically derived functions, such as the Yntema study of the steel industry, may show the mixed result of alternative levels of output and variation in size of log input on production costs.[11] Accurate data describing log input are rarely available to enable corrections to be made for variation in the input factor. Second, operating objectives of different mills vary widely. Some mills seek high grade and value recovery, thus necessitating higher labor cost. Others emphasize high production with low labor input. Costs of production normally vary directly with the average value per unit of lumber output (the average realization per thousand board feet). But high cost of production does not necessarily indicate inefficiency. Again, these developments may lead to confusion in a statistical cost study.

Other methods of deriving a cost function are available.[12] The cost-estimating procedure used here has its own problems and a high probable error. It does, however, yield estimates of sufficient accuracy for my purposes. The accounting records of two firms have been subjected to detailed analysis. The study begins with recorded costs for a present stage of operations and attempts to estimate the behavior of unit cost for levels of output in addition

---

[11] T.N.E.C. Papers (pamphlets and charts submitted by United States Steel Corporation to the Temporary National Economic Committee), Vol. I (1940).

[12] *Cost Behavior and Price Policy*, National Bureau of Economic Research (New York, 1943), pp. 90–109.

to the current level. The first mill subjected to cost analysis, identified as mill A, had an eight-hour daily capacity of 108,000 board feet. Mill A operated on a two-shift basis and averaged 240 operating days per year. Its total output for the year subjected to cost study, 1958, was 52 million board feet. Thus, mill A may be classed within the range of the optimum mill size. Cost estimates were made in conferences with the plant manager and the chief accountant following detailed study of present costs. These estimates were for a single 8-hour shift and for three short shifts per day consisting of 7.5 hours each. The short-shift basis allows 1.5 hours per day "down time" for necessary daily maintenance. Thus, moving from two shifts totaling 16 hours to three short shifts totaling 22.5 hours (2.8 shifts) required an additional 6.5 hours of operating time. In conference with the manager and the accountant, an item-by-item study of costs was conducted. In each instance it was made clear that only incremental costs associated with an expansion of output (or in the event of a reduction in output, cost savings realized) were desired.

The findings of the cost estimates for mill A under alternative shifts are shown in table 5. Examination of these data shows that some costs, for example, property taxes, are independent of output levels. Other costs, including some power costs, vary exactly with output. Still others show a mixed effect and change with output, but less than proportionately. No attempt was made to estimate the effect on average unit cost of increasing output beyond the volume shown for 22.5 hours of operation per day or for reduction below the 8-hour level. Management was strongly of the opinion, however, that further attempts to increase output would incur substantial unit cost increases. Similar sharp cost increases were expected for operations at less than a single 8-hour shift. The average total unit cost estimates given in table 5 are plotted in figure 1.

Similar cost estimates were made for mill B which was currently producing at a "curtailed output," 85 percent of its rated capacity per 8-hour day. The rated capacity of mill B was 123,000 board feet. Thus, mill B is also within the optimum mill size. The findings for mill B are given in table 6 and are also plotted in figure 1. While the absolute costs of production for mill B are significantly higher than for mill A, our primary interest is in the shape of the cost function and not in its absolute level.[13]

---

[13] Mill B has permanently ceased operations, presumably because of its higher costs of production.

TABLE 5
Estimates of Costs at Various Levels of Output, Mill A

Basic data	One 8-hour shift per day	Two 8-hour shifts per day[a]	Three 7.5-hour shifts per day
Total annual output[b]	26,013	52,026	71,200
Number of employees			
Sawmill	36	64	96
Yard	40	78	103
Office	20	24	25
Total	95	166	224
Average hourly wage for 1,920 hours per year	$2.53	$2.56	$2.60

Cost item	One 8-hour shift per day	Two 8-hour shifts per day[a]	Three 7.5-hour shifts per day
Labor	$ 461,470	$ 815,923	$1,118,208
Supplies, expenses, and repairs			
Sawmill, pond, green chain	16,027	29,140	38,750
Stacking, unstacking, dry chain	1,300	2,601	3,640
Dry kilns	5,440	9,880	13,840
Transfers	6,250	12,500	17,100
Planing mill	10,300	18,730	25,630
Storing	520	520	520
Lumber—general	8,870	16,130	22,600
Total	$ 48,707	$ 89,501	$ 122,080
Power			
Sawmill, pond, green chain	6,760	13,007	17,880
Dry kilns	20,320	36,940	51,716
Planing mill	5,980	11,970	16,400
Lumber—general	570	1,040	1,420
Total	$ 33,630	$ 62,957	$ 87,416
Overhead			
Capital consumption	180,000	188,644	195,000
Insurance	6,745	6,745	6,745
Property taxes	16,865	16,865	16,865
Related payroll taxes	45,890	81,145	111,205
General administration	77,000	102,052	110,000
Total	$ 326,500	$ 395,451	$ 434,815
Grand total	$ 870,307	$1,363,832	$1,762,519
Cost per thousand board feet	$ 33.45	$ 26.20	$ 24.75

[a] Present operating level.
[b] In thousands of board feet.

The empirical findings of the short-run average cost function clearly suggest that economies of scale are present through two shift operations and probably into three short shifts. Higher levels of output are expected to increase costs sharply. Managers of most plants operating on a one-shift basis, when asked about the wisdom

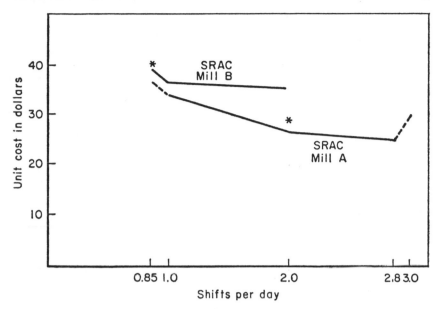

Fig. 1. Short-run average total unit cost estimates for mills A and B under alternative shifts. Broken-line segments are based on managerial opinion of general trend. Asterisk indicates present level of output. Other points on the short-run average cost (SRAC) line are based on cost estimates. Shifts per day, shown on the horizontal axis, emphasize the principal source of output variation in the short run.

of two- or three-shift operations in view of the probable lower unit costs, rationalized their present position in terms of the difficulty of acquiring additional logs to supply a second or third shift. This "difficulty" may be reinterpreted in terms of a higher unit cost for log input. For the purpose of this cost study, I assumed that raw-material costs were constant for various levels of output. Hence, higher raw-material costs are not shown in the cost estimates. Some operators also pointed out that their "average realization" (average revenue) would decline with the addition of the second or third shift of operations. Others were fearful of a decline in over-run.[14] This view is consistent with the analysis contained in my third approach to the optimal plant and optimal firm size. It is not the result of a negatively sloping firm demand curve, but rather is due to the inexpansibility of management where sec-

[14] Overrun is the relationship between board feet of lumber output (a lumber scale) and board feet of log input (a log scale). The principal determinant of overrun is log size. Overrun varies inversely with log diameter.

TABLE 6

ESTIMATES OF COSTS AT VARIOUS LEVELS OF OUTPUT, MILL B

Basic data	Curtailed output, 8 hours per day[a]	One 8-hour shift per day	Two 8-hour shifts per day
Total annual output[b]	24,787	29,250	55,650
Number of employees	122	142	284

Cost item	Curtailed output, 8 hours per day[a]	One 8-hour shift per day	Two 8-hour shifts per day
Manufacturing			
Wages	$ 509,438	$ 594,600	$1,189,200
Social security	20,375	23,780	47,570
Industrial insurance	11,458	13,300	25,500
Gas, oil, lubrication	9,610	10,571	21,142
Supplies and repairs	66,200	66,200	132,400
Lumber inspection	2,365	2,365	4,730
Log scaling	11,965	14,100	27,300
Maintenance	27,376	30,200	75,500
Power	8,333	8,333	10,100
Purchased water	6,970	6,970	12,909
Hauling and loading	16,490	19,500	37,600
Miscellaneous	924	1,090	2,100
Total	$ 691,504	$ 791,009	$1,586,051
Overhead			
Administration salaries	83,519	83,519	88,519
Social insurance	3,805	3,805	4,005
Insurance	15,178	15,178	15,178
Capital consumption	52,103	52,103	60,103
Property taxes	26,371	26,371	26,371
Supplies and expenses	1,640	1,640	1,640
Fire protection	3,410	3,410	3,410
General administration	88,848	88,848	108,848
Total	$ 274,874	$ 274,874	$ 308,074
Grand total	$ 966,378	$1,065,883	$1,894,125
Cost per thousand board feet	$ 39.00	$ 36.40	$ 34.00

a Present operating level.

b In thousands of board feet.

ond- or third-shift operations are subject to less careful supervision by the profit-motivated peak coordinator. As indicated earlier, however, this factor is of negligible importance for stud mills, of slight importance for dimension mills, and of considerable significance for grade recovery mills.[15]

---

15 If reliable information were available on the loss in average realization owing to the inexpansibility of management factor, the loss in average realization for second- and third-short-shift operations might be treated as a cost and combined with

SUMMARY

In summary, the evidence on plant size strongly suggests that the medium and medium-large range is optimal. This range varies from 60,000 to 140,000 board feet eight-hour capacity and employs seventy-five people or less. It has an upper limit of 280,000 board feet on a two-shift basis. Clearly, very small mills (less than 40,000 feet per eight-hour rated capacity) are not effective competitors. Similarly, very large plants appear to be inefficient. The complexity and profit-sensitive character of production-line decision making lead to relatively small-scale operations in lumber production. Evidence on optimum firm size is inconclusive.

Our findings on the short-run average cost function indicate that two-shift and perhaps three-short-shift operations for stud and dimension mills are likely to be the most profitable unless precluded by external diseconomies resulting from higher-cost timber input. For grade recovery mills, where high average realization (average revenue) is sought, three-shift operations would appear to be unreasonable, and even two-shift operations may be precluded for reasons of external diseconomies and/or "falldown" in grade recovery.

---

the short-run average cost data shown in figure 1. For mill A, the cost reduction moving from two- to three-shift operations amounts to $1.45 per thousand board feet. It is quite likely that average realization would decline for a grade recovery mill in an amount equal to or in excess of this cost reduction. Hence, it would appear improbable that three-shift operations would be optimal for a grade recovery mill.

CHAPTER 2

Elasticity of Demand
for Lumber and Timber

A thorough analysis of the structure, behavior, and performance of an industry requires prior knowledge derived from analysis of economies of scale. This analysis has been provided in chapter 1. In addition, appraisal of competition requires a prior knowledge of demand and supply elasticities for the principal input items as well as the industry's output. These subjects are discussed in chapters 2 and 3. Chapter 2 provides an analysis of the demand function for lumber in the United States and the demand for timber in the Douglas fir region. While this study is concerned with the Douglas fir lumber industry for most analytical purposes, the market for lumber is national, and there is a high degree of substitutability between lumber produced in the Douglas fir region and lumber from other regions. Indeed, for some species and for some purposes, perfect substitution exists.

The method of analysis for demand elasticity provides two approaches to the objectives: deductive analysis and inductive analysis. From the deductive point of view, we will begin by setting forth propositions from economic theory which help to identify the elasticity coefficients. We then proceed from the general to the particular and draw conclusions relating to the elasticity of lumber and timber demand. While the first approach is generally deductive, it is not purely so; empirical data are drawn upon where appropriate to substantiate a point. No attempt is made to identify a precise elasticity coefficient from the deductive analysis. Rather, elasticity may be classified generally as (1) elastic, (2) unitary elasticity, or (3) inelastic. The second approach is inductive. A recent econometric analysis of price elasticity of demand for lumber is reviewed, and the findings are related to the deductive approach.

[32]

THEORETICAL PROPOSITIONS
INDICATIVE OF DEMAND ELASTICITY

The following four propositions are drawn from economic theory relevant to the elasticity of demand.

The time dimension.—Elasticity of demand is greater as the time factor lengthens after a price change. A time lag in adjusting consumption to a price change is the consequence of four inherent conditions: (1) The spread of knowledge of a price change requires time. Items continuously purchased by professional buyers have a shorter time lag than items infrequently purchased by consumers. (2) Habits attach buyers to particular sellers and brands. Disengagement requires the passage of time. This point applies to professional as well as to nonprofessional customers. For example, architects become accustomed to using standard products for standard jobs. (3) Regulatory factors inhibit rapid adjustment. Building codes must be amended to allow new uses of products. Regulations of such governmental agencies as the Federal Housing Administration and the Veterans Administration must occasionally be adjusted to facilitate a change in product use. (4) Finally, durability delays adjustment. When the price of a durable good is increased, resentful users may keep their present equipment in service longer if durability permits. Further, advance information on a price increase may be leaked to consumers who may make advance purchases. Both events require the passage of time before a "normal" pattern of consumption is restored, with the time period being longer for more durable goods.

Substitutability.—The greater the (1) suitability and (2) availability of substitutes for factor X in the production process, the greater is its price elasticity of demand. If factor X has a good substitute, factor Y, then a small increase (decrease) in the price of X will be associated with a relatively large decrease (increase) in the quantity of X demanded, and will further be associated with an increase (decrease) in the quantity demanded of substitute factor Y. In order to understand the relationship of substitution to the price elasticity of the demand for X, both suitability and availability of substitute factors must be considered.

Suitability of substitution is denoted by the magnitude of the elasticity of substitution between any two factors of production. This concept measures the degree by which a factor is substituted for another as a result of a small change in its price when (1) supplies of factors are perfectly elastic at established prices, and (2) product output is held constant. A high value for this elasticity indicates the factors are good technical substitutes.

Availability may be demonstrated by an example. Suppose factor Y is a highly suitable substitute for X. If Y has a highly inelastic supply function, then it would not be an effective substitute for X. Conceptually, one would conclude that because the elasticity of substitution is high, the demand for factor X would be relatively elastic. But a quantitative analysis would show a relatively inelastic demand.

The importance of substitution suitability among factors may be graphically clarified within the framework of production isoquant theory. In figure 2, *a*, line *II* indicates how two factors may be combined to produce a given output. Thus y_6 of factor Y and x_1 of factor X produce the same output as y_1 of factor Y and x_7 of factor X. Isoquant curve *II* is comparatively straight, indicating that factors X and Y are good technical substitutes and therefore have a high elasticity of substitution.

In figure 2, *b*, *c*, the solid lines represent supply curves for factors X and Y. These curves relate the quantity of a factor that will be offered for sale at a given price. At price p_5 in figure 2, *c*, y_3 of factor Y will be supplied. As a large price increase for factor Y at price p_5 would not substantially increase the quantity of Y offered, this curve is inelastic at that price. At price p_3, a small price change would substantially affect the quantity of factor Y offered. Therefore, this curve is elastic at price p_3. As the next chapter shows, these curves approximate the supply curves for timber and lumber.

From figure 2, *b*, *c*, isocost curve *AA* is constructed in figure 2, *a*, relating the amounts of X and Y which may be purchased at a given cost. This isocost curve is relatively flat to the left of point *J* because a small decrease in the amount of Y used, say from y_3 to y_2 (fig. 2, *c*), is associated with a reduction in the price of Y from p_5 to p_4. With available money, x_4 of factor X at price p_1 can be purchased as shown in figure 2, *b*. Likewise the curve is very steep to the right of point *J* because more of X can be purchased only at very high prices. In order to increase purchases of X from x_4 to x_6 (fig. 2, *a*), no Y can be bought as all available money is expended on X. Isoquant curve *II* and isocost curve *AA* intersect at *J*, indicating the equilibrium quantities for producing the indicated level of output. At that combination of factors X and Y, the output is produced for least cost.

If the supply curve for X shifts upward so that the price is

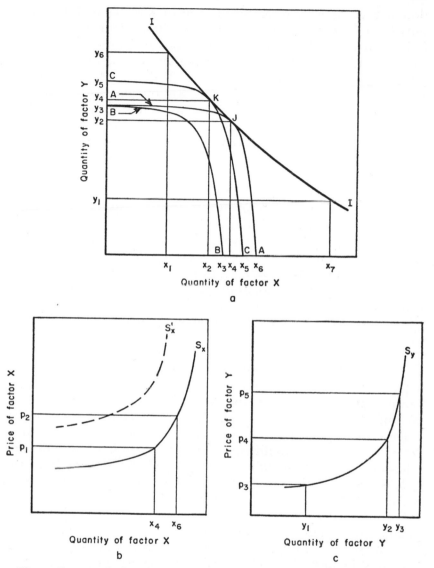

Fig. 2. Factor substitution.

doubled for any given quantity supplied (see curve S'_x in fig. 2, *b*), then for the same cost only quantities of X and Y along isocost curve *BB* can be purchased. If output were to be maintained, then isocost curve *CC* would be relevant, and least-cost inputs for this output would be established at *K*. In this example, despite the doubling of the price of X, the amount of X demanded decreased only from x_4 to x_2. Therefore, the elasticity of demand for factor X is low because alternative factors are not available despite being suitable substitutes. Excepting a hypothetical situation in which absolutely fixed proportions are required, a factor price reduction (increase) will always result in substitution and additional (reduced) use of the lower cost factor. The more substitutable other factors are for factor X, the most elastic is the price-demand function for factor X. Therefore, economic theory suggests that substitutability (both suitability and availability) be examined in order to classify the demand for a factor of production. Substitutability applies to product demand as well as to factor demand, though the technique for demonstrating substitution in response to product price changes would be different.

Elasticity of demand for subsequent products.—The more elastic the demand for final or subsequent products, the more elastic the demand for a factor utilized in producing the former. In discussing substitutability, we assumed that final product output was constant. Here we will analyze the effect of lower factor prices on the output of products and therefore on the demand for factors of production.

This analysis may be illustrated by supply and demand curves for product A, which uses factors X, Y, and Z. In figure 3, *a*, *b*, the supply curve *S* represents the marginal cost of producing an additional unit of product A. It rises because of the law of diminishing returns. At a sufficiently low price, such as p_0 in figure 3, *a*, no amount of product A will be produced because all firms will have ceased operations. Two different demand curves have been drawn. The demand curve *DD* in figure 3, *a*, is inelastic; the one in figure 3, *b*, is elastic. Both markets are in stable equilibrium at price p_3 and at quantity supplied and demanded q_1.

Consider the effect of a price reduction for factor X. The final product supply curve will fall (marginal cost will decline) for each level of output owing to two adjustments. First, the supply curve falls to *S'* because the bundle of factors needed to produce A at each level of output costs less. Second, the curve further falls to *S"* as factor X is substituted for the more expensive factor Y, according to the preceding proposition.

The effect of this price decline on the demand for factor X depends, among other forces, upon the elasticity of the final product demand curve. In the market with the inelastic demand (fig. 3, *a*), the quantity of A increases only to q_2. In figure 3, *b*, the quantity of A increases to q_3 because of the high demand elasticity for prod-

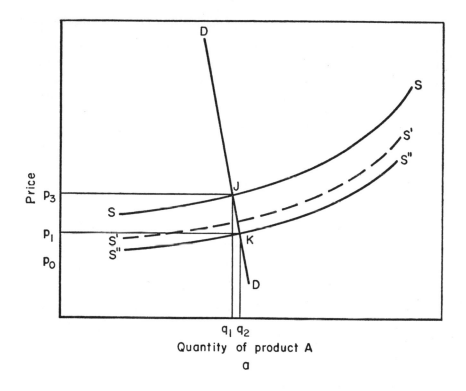

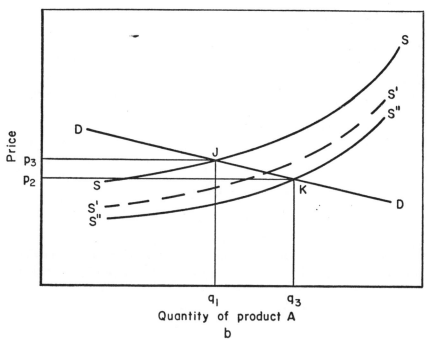

Fig. 3. Effect of changes in factor prices on demand for factors of production.

uct A. At output q_3 more of factor X is demanded than at output q_2.
Thus, the elasticity of demand for a factor is greater, the larger
the elasticity of demand for its subsequent products.

Importance of item in final product price.—For items in derived
demand, the importance of the item in the total cost of the finished
product influences price elasticity of demand for a factor. Stigler's
formulation of this point is: "As a rule, the elasticity of demand for
a productive service will be smaller the smaller the proportion of
total cost this service occasions, given the possibility of substituting
other inputs."[1] Given the following restrictive assumptions—pure
competition prevails, the marginal rate of substitution of factor X
for other productive services in the production of A is zero, and
the final product demand curve has zero elasticity—*ceteris paribus*
the effect of a given percent change in the price of input factor X
on the price of final product A is represented by $P_x \cdot R = P_A$,
where P_x is the percent change in the price of input factor X, R is
the ratio of the cost of factor X embodied in product A to the total
cost of product A, and P_A is the percent change in the price of final
product A. If the ratio R is small, then a relatively large reduction
in the price of X will produce a relatively small reduction in the
price of A. The increased quantity of X demanded may then be
very small. If the demand for A is highly elastic, the resulting increase in the quantity of X demanded becomes larger. Where substitution among factors is possible, the elasticity of demand for a
factor will be higher than indicated above. In figure 3, the importance of this relationship is illustrated by the distance between
S and S'. If the ratio R is large, a price decrease will significantly
lower the supply curve for that product, as indicated in this example.

The next specific problem is to estimate the price elasticity of
demand, first for lumber, and then for timber. No attempt is made
in this deductive approach to give a numerical estimate of elasticity. Rather, elasticity is identified in three categories: (1) elastic, (2)
unitary elasticity, or (3) inelastic demand.

DEDUCTIVE ESTIMATE OF PRICE ELASTICITY
OF DEMAND FOR LUMBER

Probably the most important determinants of demand elasticity
are availability and suitability of substitutes for lumber. Since ap-

---

[1] George J. Stigler, *The Theory of Price* (rev. ed.; New York: Macmillan, 1952),
p. 191.

proximately three-fourths of all lumber production[2] is used in the construction industry, substitutability in this end use is our main concern. The possibilities of substitution between lumber and other building materials are quite extensive. For example, floor joists traditionally have been constructed of wood. In recent years, however, cement slabs, though generally regarded as less desirable than wood, have made substantial inroads in residential building because cement-slab construction costs less than wood construction. Where mass-construction builders aim for minimum-cost housing, a slight change in the ratio of lumber cost to cement cost in floor construction may be expected to lead to shifts in use. Similarly, lumber used in siding faces competition from such products as stucco, brick, plywood, and aluminum.

The qualities to be considered in a choice among products include not only cost, but desirability, durability, and maintenance costs. Again, however, when cost-conscious builders observe a change in the ratio of lumber costs to alternative siding materials, some shift in usage should be expected. Further, roof sheathing and subflooring face close competition from plywood. Although a relative change in material cost would result in substitution, the dominant factor is not material cost, but labor cost. More labor is required to install roof sheathing and subflooring made of lumber, compared with plywood. Therefore, in some uses, a wage increase for carpenters adds more to the installed costs of lumber than of plywood. We are not concerned here, however, with the elasticity of substitution between labor and lumber.

In the three examples given above, substitutability is a persistent possibility. In other lumber uses, substitutes are less appropriate. For example, there are no good substitutes for studs (2 x 4's, 8 feet long) in framing a house. The closest substitutes are concrete block and a combination of cement and brick. Some attempts have been made to introduce steel studs. Use of the first two substitutes is common in commercial construction but relatively undesirable and uncommon in residential construction. A price change in studs would therefore be expected to produce a more modest shift in usage. But, when a decision is made to shift from wood to alternative framing materials, a substantial reduction in wood usage takes place. Henry Vaux, in his inductive study of California housing requirements for lumber, concludes that "structures without a

---

[2] *Lumber Industry Facts, 1960–61*, National Lumber Manufacturers Association (Washington, 1962), p. 37.

wood frame require only fifty to sixty percent as much structural lumber as wood frame dwellings."[3]

More examples of substitutability could be given. Although very little is known about coefficients of substitution, it is apparent that substitutes for lumber in construction do exist and that the ease and the desirability of substitution differ widely among the several possible uses of lumber in construction. Extensive substitution away from wood has, in fact, taken place in recent years. Table 7 shows a 44.5 percent reduction in lumber use per dwelling unit from 1920 to 1953. Substitution for lumber is widespread among the major categories of lumber use and constitutes a persistent trend over the several years shown in table 7. Part of the decline in lumber usage per dwelling unit is due to a change in style and a reduction in the size of houses since 1920. According to Forest Service estimates, the average size of houses has declined 28 percent over the same span of time. Using the Forest Service size index, the average amount of lumber used per dwelling unit of constant size is computed for the years shown. From 1920 to 1953, total lumber use declined 22.8 percent after adjustment for the decline in housing size. This latter estimate may be treated as an indicator of substitution away from lumber.

Substitution from lumber to competing building materials apparently has vastly accelerated since 1950. Over the thirty-one-year period from 1920 to 1950 the average annual reduction in lumber usage per dwelling unit of constant size was 0.5 percent per year. In sharp contrast, from 1950 to 1953 the shift away from lumber was at the annual rate of 3.0 percent.

The observed decline in lumber use for residential construction may be due to changes in taste, to the introduction and availability of new competing products, to the improvement of established products, to the upward trend in wage rates, or to other causal forces. If the decline of lumber used in dwelling units of constant size is to be accounted for by substitution resulting from price changes, one would expect to find supporting evidence in continuously higher lumber prices relative to prices of competing building materials.

Prices of select building materials are available beginning with 1927. A long-term increase in the ratio of lumber prices to other

3 Henry J. Vaux, "An Economic-Statistical Analysis of Lumber Requirements for California Housing," *Hilgardia*, XIX (March, 1950), 483.

building materials, shown in figure 4, is indeed present through 1951. Furthermore, very rapid increases in the ratio occurred in the thirteen years from 1939 to 1951. Thus, relative price behavior is consistent not only with the long-run substitution away from lumber, but with the accelerated rate of substitution shown for 1950 to 1953. We would expect to find substitution lagging behind the causal price change. The very rapid increase in lumber prices occurring during the 1940's may therefore have stimulated substitution, which continued not only into 1953, but has persisted through

TABLE 7

Lumber Use per Dwelling Unit in Selected Years Between 1920 and 1953
In board feet per dwelling unit

Component	Year				
	1920	1930	1940	1950	1953
Foundations	1,700	1,350	1,300	1,100	900
Floors	4,300	3,700	3,300	2,550	1,950
Ceilings	975	825	800	750	800
Roofs	2,800	2,250	2,550	2,600	2,400
Exterior walls	2,500	2,350	2,100	1,750	1,600
Interior walls	2,950	2,300	1,700	1,500	1,500
Millwork	2,600	1,950	1,400	1,050	950
Accessories[a]	1,075	675	750	400	400
Total	18,900	15,400	13,900	11,700	10,500
Index of lumber use per dwelling unit (1920 = 100)	100.0	81.5	73.5	62.0	55.5
Index of size of dwelling unit (1920 = 100)	100.0	86.0	80.5	72.0	72.0
Average lumber use per dwelling unit of constant size (in board feet)	18,900	17,907	17,267	16,250	14,583
Index of average lumber use per dwelling unit of constant size (1920 = 100)	100.0	94.7	91.4	86.0	77.2

a Includes detached garages and miscellaneous other accessories.

Sources: Lumber use by component: Stanford Research Institute, *America's Demand for Wood, 1929–1975* (Tacoma, Wash.: Weyerhaeuser Timber Co., 1954), p. 35. Index of size of dwelling unit: U.S. Department of Agriculture, Forest Service, *Timber Resources for America's Future*, Forest Resources Report no. 14 (Washington, 1958), p. 382.

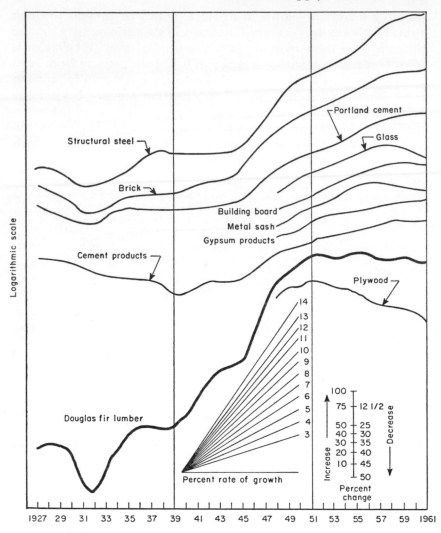

Fig. 4. Price trends for Douglas fir lumber compared with those for competing building materials (semilog scale, 3-year moving average).

SOURCES: For Douglas fir lumber, 1926–1948: U.S. Department of Commerce, Office of Business Economics; 1949–1962: U.S. Department of Commerce, *Business Statistics*, 1953, 1955, 1959, 1963 editions. For portland cement and structural steel: 1947–1956: U.S. Department of Commerce, *Construction Volume and Costs, 1915–1956* (Washington, 1958); 1957–1962: Housing and Home Finance Agency, *Housing Statistics*, Annual Data (May, 1964). For all other building materials: 1926–1960: Housing and Home Finance Agency, *Housing Statistics*, Historical Supplement (Oct., 1961); 1961, 1962: Housing and Home Finance Agency, *Housing Statistics*, Annual Data (May, 1964).

the decade of the 1950's and up to the present. Finally, with the introduction of new building materials such as aluminum, and the improvement of established products such as cement, the technical possibility of substitution has increased.

Any judgments offered about the availability of substitutes as reflected in their elasticity of supply must be somewhat superficial, as the primary interest of this study is centered on competitive conditions. The important substitute products appear to be plywood, cement, concrete block, brick, stucco, and aluminum. Certainly none is highly supply elastic with respect to price. All except plywood require nonreproducible resources in their production. While vast supplies of clay are used in brick production, they differ in quality and accessibility and hence involve increasing costs. On the basis of availability of critical raw materials, one would expect the most inelastic items to be aluminum and concrete, yet the output of both has increased sharply in recent years. Cement production in 1962 was 80 percent above the 1947 figure, and aluminum was up 75 percent.[4] Obviously, neither item has been confronted with an inflexible supply ceiling. Secular trends, however, do not establish a degree of price elasticity. Plywood is in an interesting position since its critical raw material is shared with lumber. Within the limits of product substitution between lumber and plywood, there is no problem of resource availability because any lumber price increase that resulted in a shift in demand from lumber to plywood would, at the same time, make raw material available for a similar shift. On the basis of the foregoing discussion, it may be concluded that supply elasticity coefficients for products that may be substituted for lumber would not significantly limit the effectiveness of substitutability. Substitute products appear to be both suitable and available.

Because the principal use of lumber is derived from the demand for housing and other building construction, the elasticity of demand for lumber is influenced by the importance of lumber in the total cost of construction and by the elasticity of demand for construction. In a recent study of residential construction costs in New Haven, Connecticut, Joseph Zaremba found that "lumber comprises about fifteen percent of total house costs, the percentage decreasing as house price increases."[5] Suppose that the supply of

---

[4] *Business Statistics*, U.S. Department of Commerce (Washington, 1963), pp. 164, 188.

[5] Joseph Zaremba, *Economics of the American Lumber Industry* (New York: Robert Speller, 1963), p. 110.

lumber is reduced for any number of possible reasons. Because the demand curve for lumber is not perfectly elastic, the price of lumber will rise. If the price of lumber rises, the average cost of residential and other construction will rise. Ignoring the possibility of substitution for the moment, and assuming that the demand for housing is price inelastic, construction costs will increase by an amount determined by the importance of lumber in the total cost of construction. Thus, if the cost of lumber accounts for 15 percent of the total cost of construction, as suggested in the Zaremba study, then a 10 percent increase in lumber cost would increase residential construction cost by 1.5 percent. Relaxing the inelastic demand for housing assumption, the greater the demand elasticity, the larger will be the reduction in quantity of lumber demanded. Introducing the possibility of substitution between lumber and alternative building materials, the reduction in quantity of lumber demanded would be slightly larger. Therefore, an initiating reduction in lumber production followed by a price increase will generate not only a substitution effect in construction but also a rather minor construction demand effect, both of which contribute to a decline in the quantity of lumber demanded at higher prices.

From the scanty evidence, we must draw a conclusion. The dominant factor surveyed is the possibility of substitution among building materials in response to changes in the price of lumber. The relatively small importance of lumber in total construction costs, together with a probable price inelastic demand for residential construction, contributes little toward an elastic demand condition. Therefore, the sum of the evidence suggests that, whereas some substitution is to be expected in response to long-run price movements, the demand for lumber is within the inelastic range, and a given percentage increase (decrease) in the price of lumber is associated with a smaller percentage decrease (increase) in the quantity demanded. Although the elasticity of demand is greater as the time period for adjustment is lengthened, the conclusion given above is intended to reflect the full time-adjustment effect. Whatever the coefficient of demand elasticity for lumber, such elasticity has probably increased in recent years because new substitutes for lumber have been developed.

ECONOMETRIC EVIDENCE

The deductive approach to elasticity estimation may be supplemented by evidence based on an econometric analysis of demand and supply functions for lumber. In a comprehensive econometric

study, I. I. Holland discusses the demand for and supply of softwood lumber over the thirty-one-year period from 1915 through
1950, excluding the World War II years 1942 through 1946. The
results of his two-equation model are:[6]

$$\text{Demand: } Y_1 = 15 + 0.021Y_2 + 0.35Z_1 - 25Z_2$$
$$\qquad\qquad\quad (0.036) \quad (0.091) \quad (8.6)$$
$$\text{Supply: } \quad Y_2 = 150 + 8.6Y_1 - 2.4Z_2$$
$$\qquad\qquad\qquad (1.0) \quad (0.64)$$

where Y_1 is the price per thousand board feet of softwood construction lumber in dollars, Y_2 is per capita shipments of softwood construction lumber in board feet, Z_1 is per capita expenditures for
new construction including maintenance and repair in dollars, and
Z_2 is per capita production of portland cement in barrels. The Y
variables are endogenous, and the Z variables are exogenous. The
numbers in parentheses beneath the regression coefficients are
their respective standard errors. All regression coefficients, except
the coefficient of Y_2, are significant at the 1 percent confidence
level. Interest in demand elasticity, however, centers in this variable. Not only is the coefficient of Y_2 not significantly different from
zero, but its sign is the opposite of what would be expected based
on economic theory. Holland concludes that his findings "would
suggest that the elasticity of demand for lumber has been infinitely
elastic over the period of the study."[7] Since this statement is contrary to a priori evidence on price-quantity behavior, Holland re-
jects his econometric findings with respect to the price-quantity
relationship.

In the demand equation, however, lumber price rather than
quantity was made the dependent variable, because suitable prices
of substitute commodities were not generally available.[8] In order
to test the more conventional relationship, Holland algebraically
transposed the variables Y_1 and Y_2 and recalculated his regression
coefficients. The results reversed the findings with respect to elasticity. The findings then suggested that "the elasticity of demand
for lumber over the period of the analysis has been completely inelastic, and price flexibility infinite."[9] This conclusion was also
held untenable in view of contrary a priori evidence. Discarding his

[6] I. I. Holland, "Some Factors Affecting the Consumption of Lumber in the United
States with Emphasis on Demand" (unpublished Ph.D. dissertation, University of
California, Berkeley, 1955), p. 152.

[7] *Ibid.*, p. 157.

[8] *Ibid.*, p. 155.

[9] *Ibid.*, p. 157.

econometric evidence concerning the price-quantity relationship, Holland drew the following intuitive conclusion: "The demand elasticity for this commodity probably lies in a narrower range between these extremes (prefectly elastic or perfectly inelastic), the exact elasticity depending upon particular circumstances and specific construction use." At another point he wrote: ". . . it does not seem reasonable to reject the *a priori* specification of a low demand elasticity on the basis of the results worked out so far."[10]

Because the econometric analysis at present available is very unsatisfactory, the deductive analysis of demand elasticity developed in the preceding section is accepted. The analysis of competition in the Douglas fir lumber industry contained in this study is therefore based on the conclusion that the lumber demand function is within the inelastic range.

DEDUCTIVE ESTIMATE OF PRICE ELASTICITY OF DEMAND FOR TIMBER

A judgment about the shape of the demand curve for timber is also needed. Applying the propositions derived from economic theory, we may again draw generalized conclusions. The possibility of substitution is much more limited. A very minor degree of substitution is possible between log input and labor input, and between log input and capital intensity. The possibility of greater capital intensity in response to higher log prices is limited to (1) a narrower saw kerf that would produce more lumber and less sawdust; (2) more precisely engineered saws to produce straighter cuts, the latter allowing reduced waste in the process of planing; and (3) a higher degree of utilization resulting from such innovations as end- and edge-gluing. The first two capital intensity possibilities are limited by technology. Higher log prices theoretically would stimulate technological improvements. But the relationship is indirect, irregular, and slow. The third possibility may be somewhat more responsive to the value of the raw material being used, but the possible net gains in physical output again are quite small. Because substitution between log input and capital intensity appears to be unpromising, attention is concentrated on the possibility of substitution between log input and labor input.

The substitution issue may be phrased as follows: given an increase (decrease) in the price of timber, to what extent can producers adjust their production technology by substituting labor

---

10 *Ibid.*, p. 158.

TABLE 8

RELATIONSHIP BETWEEN EMPLOYMENT, LABOR COST, AND STUMPAGE PRICES, 1947–1963

Year	Stumpage price for Douglas fir timber (in dollars per thousand board feet)a	Average hourly earnings, sawmill employees, Douglas fir region (in dollars)b	Employment in logging and sawmills, Oregon (in thousands)c	Lumber production, Oregon (in millions of board feet)d	Employment per million board feet of annual lumber production (computed)
1947	9.90	1.53	61.0	7,102	8.58
1948	19.90	1.66	67.0	7,842	8.54
1949	11.10	1.68	59.1	7,185	8.23
1950	16.40	1.77	65.6	8,239	7.96
1951	25.40	1.93	70.4	8,219	8.57
1952	25.80	2.03	67.3	9,037	7.45
1953	20.20	2.08	63.6	8,423	7.55
1954	16.20	2.10	59.0	8,851	6.66
1955	28.90	2.17	62.7	9,181	6.83
1956	37.70	2.24	57.5	8,361	6.88
1957	26.20	2.25	49.3	6,895	7.15
1958	21.80	2.27	45.7	7,545	6.06
1959	36.80	2.38	48.0	8,222	5.84
1960	32.00	2.49	44.3	7,549	5.87
1961	27.60	2.55	39.1	7,366	5.31
1962	24.80	2.56	39.4	7,712	5.10
1963	27.90	2.64	39.0	7,991	4.88

a U.S. Forest Service, *The Demand and Price Situation for Forest Products 1963*, Miscellaneous Publication no. 983 (Washington, Nov., 1964).

b Western Wood Products Association, *Statistical Yearbook, 1963* (Portland, Ore., 1965).

c State of Oregon, Department of Employment, Division of Research and Statistics.

d West Coast Lumbermens Association, *Statistical Yearbook, 1952* (Portland, Ore., 1953); *Statistical Yearbook, 1955–56* (Portland, Ore., 1957); Western Wood Products Association, *Statistical Yearbook, 1963* (Portland, Ore., 1965).

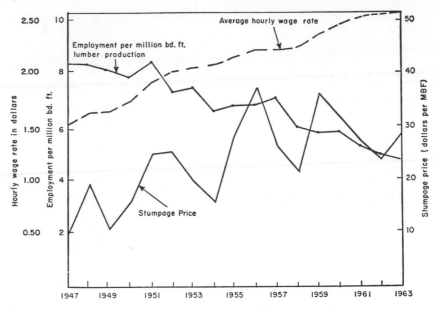

Fig. 5. Relationship between employment, labor cost, and stumpage.

SOURCES: Wage rate: Western Wood Products Association, *Statistical Year-book, 1963* (Portland, Ore., 1965). Employment: State of Oregon, Department of Employment, Division of Research and Statistics. Stumpage price: U.S. Forest Service, *The Demand and Price Situation for Forest Products, 1963,* Miscellaneous Publication no. 983 (Washington, Nov., 1964).

for logs (logs for labor)? The apparent answer is that the possibilities for profitable substitution are quite limited. While there is no doubt that with slower production speed and more careful (labor-consuming) examination of the raw material, the flow of "waste" material into the burner or chipper could be reduced in quantity, the present high degree of utilization does not permit significant further improvement. An insight into this relationship may be gained through examination of the post–World War II record. During this period the price of stumpage increased sharply, as shown in table 8 and figure 5. Stumpage prices increased 182 percent while the price of labor increased only 73 percent. With this increase in raw-material cost relative to labor cost, we would expect to find some evidence of a relative increase in labor use per unit of output. Satisfactory data for rigorously testing this hypothesis are not available. There are data from which employment per unit of lumber production may be ascertained. Contrary to the response expected from the relative price trends, the employment of labor declined persistently from 1947 to 1963. Employment per million board feet of lumber production in 1963 was only 57 percent of the 1947 level.[11] The trend in employment per unit of output is reasonably well described by a straight line, although stumpage prices increased very sharply, by 281 percent, from 1947 to 1956 and declined 26 percent from 1956 through 1963.

In the absence of reliable data on the relationship between log input into lumber mills and lumber output, we cannot prove the absence of substitution between log input and other factors of production in response to a significant change in timber prices. We would not, however, intuitively expect a meaningful degree of substitution, and the limited empirical information available does not indicate the kind of substitution that existing price trends would lead one to expect. In the absence of the important substitutability element, the first approximation must be that the demand for timber is highly inelastic.

Data collected and published by the West Coast Lumbermens Association (WCLA) show that for the year 1962 the cost of stumpage amounted to about 16 percent of the total cost of finished lumber ready for shipment at the lumber mill.[12] As of 1962 the average realization on West Coast lumber shipments is given by the WCLA at 73 dollars per thousand board feet.[13] From these data it may be calculated that in 1962 stumpage cost amounted to about 12 dollars for every thousand board feet of lumber produced. In 1962 the average wholesale lumber price per thousand board feet for large buyers was 110 dollars. For this market, stumpage cost is about 10 percent of the total cost of lumber.[14]

Lumber usage accounts for about 80 percent of total log usage represented by lumber and veneer-plywood. The ratio of stumpage

---

[11] The dominant factor producing the secular decline in employment per unit of output would appear to be substitution between labor and capital, stimulated by rising wage rates and technological change. Arrow and others have estimated through statistical measures that a 1 percent increase in wages relative to the price of capital in the lumber industry will increase the capital-labor ratio by .86 percent. Regression analysis has established that 91 percent of the variation in the capital-labor ratio can be explained by such relative price movements (Kenneth Arrow *et al.*, "Capital Labor Substitution and Economic Efficiency," *Review of Economics and Statistics*, XLIII [Aug., 1961], 227).

[12] *Statistical Yearbook, 1961–1962*, West Coast Lumbermens Association (Portland, Ore., 1964), p. 8.

[13] "Industrial Facts," West Coast Lumbermens Association (Portland, Ore., May, 1964), p. 8.

[14] This ratio corresponds with an estimate based on a study of stumpage and appraisal practices (Sidney Weintraub, "Price-Making in Forest Service Timber Sales," *American Economic Review*, XLIX [Sept., 1959], 629).

cost to total cost of plywood (⅜-inch base) is approximately the same as for lumber i.e., (1 to 10). Thus, if for any reason a 10 percent increase occurs in the price of timber, the effect on competitive prices for lumber and plywood would be only 1 percent at a maximum. As previously estimated, lumber demand is in the inelastic range with respect to price. We will now assume the demand for plywood to have the same degree of elasticity. But, our estimate of lumber demand elasticity was based on the traditional *ceteris paribus* assumption, including a constant price for plywood. Plywood is the closest substitute for lumber. As we analyze the elasticity of demand for timber, we must eliminate substitution between lumber and plywood because these substitute products utilize the same raw material, timber. If this elimination is made for both lumber and plywood, then the price elasticity of demand for lumber would become even lower (highly inelastic) than previously indicated. If the demand for lumber and plywood taken together is inelastic, if the cost of stumpage is only 10 percent of the cost of lumber in consumer markets, and if substitution between logs and other factors of production in the manufacture of lumber and plywood is negligible, then it follows that the demand for stumpage must be highly inelastic.

Summary

The theoretical determinants of demand functions have been identified and deductively applied in order to estimate the general shape of the demand functions for lumber and timber. In addition, the highly unsatisfactory findings of an econometric analysis of the demand for lumber have been examined. The conclusion follows that the demand for lumber with respect to price is within the inelastic range. The dominant factor contributing a degree of elasticity is the possibility of substitution between lumber and alternative available building materials. The closest substitute for lumber is another wood product, plywood.

Deductive examination has also led to the conclusion that demand for timber is highly inelastic. When lumber and plywood are combined as the two principal products processed from timber, the price elasticity of timber's final products is more inelastic than for lumber alone, as the combination eliminated the relationship of substitutability between lumber and plywood. Further, because there is no close substitute for logs in the manufacture of lumber, and the cost of stumpage is a small part of the total cost of lumber in the consumer market, it may be concluded that the demand for timber is highly inelastic.

CHAPTER 3

Elasticity of Supply for Timber and Lumber

Analysis of competitive relationships in the markets for lumber and timber requires prior knowledge of the general shape of supply and demand curves. The preceding chapter is concerned with demand elasticity, and we now turn to a deductive analysis of supply elasticity. First, propositions developed from economic theory relevant to supply elasticity will be set forth. Such propositions are guides to research in that they indicate operational conditions corresponding to various elasticity conditions. Second, utilizing the relevant theory, we will identify deductively the industry supply functions for timber in the long run and various interpretations of the short run. Third, again proceeding from relevant theory, and having prior determination of cost functions in lumber production, we will attempt to deductively determine the shape of the supply function for lumber under specified conditions. Econometric evidence will also be reviewed. We are concerned only with sustainable increases in the supply of timber and lumber offered for sale in response to a price increase, not with a quantity increase that is an offset for reduced production in a preceding period or that must be offset by a future reduction in output.

THEORETICAL PROPOSITIONS INDICATIVE OF SUPPLY ELASTICITY

The following guidelines for estimation have been developed from economic theory:

Capital theory.—A timber resource is partly a stock resource and partly a flow resource. At any point in time there is a known inventory of timber, the growing stock. In the Douglas fir region, a large part of the growing stock consists of old-growth timber. The merchantable inventory may be liquidated at a faster or slower rate. The economic theory governing its rate of liquidation is given by capital theory. The optimum rate of resource use is the rate that "maximizes the present value of the flow of (expected) net revenues."[1] Thus, if present stumpage (standing timber) prices increase relative to anticipated future prices, one would expect that profit-motivated owners of merchantable timber would increase their liquidation rate, that is, increase their current quantity supplied. A reversal of the present-future price relationship should produce the opposite effect.

But growing stock is both the product and the "factory." Timber is a reproducible resource (a flow resource). As such, a decision to invest in additional production is a conventional investment decision, and its analysis is based on estimated future net income, discounted at an appropriate interest rate and compared with the value of present resources that must be committed to the investment. Whether stock resource or flow resource, capital theory governs. Any price-induced change in the growing-stock liquidation rate is excluded from this investigation of price elasticity of supply on the ground that any such price effect is not sustainable. We are concerned entirely with the flow aspect of timber resources.

The time factor.—Elasticity of supply is greater as the time period is lengthened. Within the limits of the short run, expansion in output occurs as a result of already established firms expanding output in response to an excess of marginal revenue over marginal cost. In the long run, where the period of time is sufficiently long to expand the physical plant, new producers may enter the industry, and existing producers may expand their present facilities.

Short-run supply curve.—Given certain common assumptions, the short-run supply curve of an industry is obtained by horizontally summing the short-run marginal cost curves of individual firms in the industry. The common assumptions are: (1) There are no external economies or diseconomies, pecuniary or technological. (2) The motive of economic behavior is short-run profit maximization. (3) Competitive conditions prevail in the final product market. (The individual firm demand curve is perfectly elastic.) (4) The individual firm cost functions for factors of production utilized in the industry are determinate. Cost functions for factors utilized by individual firms are determinate (*a*) under competitive conditions in factor markets, (*b*) when a monopsony faces many

---

[1] S. V. Ciriacy-Wantrup, *Resource Conservation* (Berkeley and Los Angeles: University of California Press, 1952), p. 77.

sellers, and (*c*) in a workably collusive factor market. The cost functions facing individual firms are indeterminate (*a*) when a noncollusive oligopsony buys from many sellers, (*b*) under noncollusive bilateral oligopoly, and (*c*) under noncollusive bilateral monopoly.

The shape of the short-run marginal cost curve for the firm and the short-run supply curve for the industry is also influenced by the availability of alternative uses in the short run to which the firm's resources may be shifted. The greater the availability of production alternatives for given manufacturing facilities and for given raw materials, the greater will be the elasticity of supply for products and raw materials, respectively. In the short run, production may be stopped when price is below average variable cost. Given a decline in final product prices, a firm may have alternatives that are more attractive than closing down. If the variable resources committed to a firm may be readily transferred to another use that is more profitable than the first use, firms may quickly shift such resources away from the first industry. Where this is a realistic possibility, the tail of the industry supply curve may be highly elastic. The price level at which alternative employment of a firm's resources becomes relevant would be indicated by the short-run average variable cost curve if variable costs are computed on the basis of the alternative or opportunity cost principle. In this event, costs would reflect the value of resources in their next-best alternative use.

Further, within any given industry, individual firms differ in efficiency and even in their respective combinations of productive services. Therefore, the level of short-run average variable costs varies among firms in the same industry. It follows that some loss-minimizing firms will be forced to cease production in response to a price decline sooner than their more efficient competitors. Thus, when an industry includes firms that differ widely in efficiency (as measured by the relative level of average variable costs), the tail end of the industry supply curve may again become highly elastic.

The theory of the firm assumes that entrepreneurs are knowledgeable concerning relationships between their objectives and their alternatives. If producer knowledge of production and market alternatives is perfect, supply elasticities may be relatively high. Thus, as technology or relative prices change and bring about a shift in profitability from product A to product B, production will be more responsive if knowledge is of a high order.

Barriers to entry.—In the long run, the industry supply curve will be more elastic if barriers to entry are minimal. As profitability in the subject industry becomes relatively attractive, thereby inducing entry of new firms, such entry will be reflected in a shift to the right in the upper segment of the industry supply curve. The higher the barriers to entry, the more inelastic is the long-run supply curve.

DEDUCTIVE ESTIMATE OF PRICE ELASTICITY OF TIMBER SUPPLY

Supply elasticity coefficients may differ for any given product or resource at various points on the quantity scale. This is more likely to hold true for natural resources subject to stock constraints. It is obvious that if there is abundant "idle capacity" such as prevailed in the mid-1930's, a small price increase can bring forth a relatively large increase in supply of timber and lumber. When full employment prevails, the same relative price increase would not produce a similar quantity increase. We must therefore specify the point on the quantity scale under discussion. The economic conditions that serve as a setting for this exploration of supply elasticity are those that prevailed from 1950 through 1962. This was a period of high-level economic activity and average economic growth; it included three minor recessions.

To begin an analysis of supply elasticity for timber, timber resources must be classified into groups relatively homogeneous in management objectives. For this purpose, a three-way classification is sufficient: (1) publicly owned, (2) privately owned by large firms, and (3) other privately owned. In 1962, 56 percent of all timber harvested in the Douglas fir region came from private timber ownership (see table 9). The remaining 44 percent came from public ownership, of which 30 percent originated with the Forest Service. Timber in private ownership has been and continues to be cut at a faster rate than publicly owned timber. If some private timber is being harvested at unsustainable rates, a decline in timber harvest from the private sector must be expected. From 1953 to 1962, a decline in both the absolute and relative log production from private ownership was evident. In 1953, 83 percent of the region's log production came from private sources. The private share declined to 56 percent by 1962. At the same time, log production from public sources increased both absolutely and relatively. The absolute changes are nearly compensating, so that total log production from the Douglas fir region in 1953 was almost identical with that in 1962. A Forest Service study estimates that by 1990 production from private timberlands in the Douglas fir region will account for

TABLE 9

Log Production by Source, Douglas Fir Region, 1953–1962

Year	Private and other Volume[a]	Private and other Per-cent	State Volume[a]	State Per-cent	Bureau of Land Management Volume[a]	Bureau of Land Management Per-cent	National forest Volume[a]	National forest Per-cent	Indian lands Volume[a]	Indian lands Per-cent	Total production[a]
1962	6,206,511	56	460,142	4	1,084,495	10	3,318,300	30	121,939	1	11,191,387
1961	5,664,555	59	464,779	5	864,011	9	2,543,287	26	122,238	1	9,658,870
1960	6,937,737	64	425,628	4	814,421	8	2,523,880	23	116,323	1	10,817,999
1959	6,554,724	59	403,265	4	938,929	8	3,176,775	28	112,475	1	11,186,168
1958	5,860,728	63	402,189	4	727,191	8	2,250,722	24	77,494	1	9,318,324
1957	7,101,029	75	b		578,388	6	1,750,372	18	64,602	1	9,494,391
1956	9,395,308	79	b		521,284	4	1,945,071	16	119,230	1	11,980,893
1955	9,996,665	83	b		b	..	1,917,060	16	181,689	1	12,095,414
1954	8,730,961	81	b		b	..	1,904,398	18	117,562	1	10,752,921
1953	9,119,196	83	b		b	..	1,792,235	16	121,938	1	11,033,369

a In thousands of board feet.

b Data, not identified separately, are included in "Private and other."

Source: U.S. Forest Service, Forest Survey Reports, published annually by Pacific Northwest Forest and Range Experiment Station, Portland, Ore.

52 percent of the total timber output, with public lands providing the remainder.[2]

The profit maximization assumption.—The first determinant of supply elasticity to be considered is the ownership pattern and the management objectives (profit maximizing or other) followed by a given ownership. The stated objectives of government agencies are relatively detached from economic factors. The objectives of the Forest Service are, first, to produce the maximum sustainable yield of timber and, second, to harvest this amount annually: "The objective is to manage each working circle so that it will produce a maximum sustained yield of the products it is best suited to grow. This can be accomplished by selecting a rotation which coincides with the culmination of mean annual increment for the desired products and then regulating the cut so as to achieve, as soon as practicable, the annual or periodic removal of the proper volume."[3] Thus, the calculation of the physical volume that can be harvested annually is based upon silvicultural considerations and not upon an economic rotation period. The annual cut objective is identified as the "allowable cut" rather than the sustained yield capacity. If a working circle is well stocked with readily accessible balanced age classes and if markets are reliable, the allowable cut will equal the sustained yield capacity.[4]

The Forest Service, periodically under criticism for failure to market the full allowable cut, has made its marketing policy clear. Secretary of Agriculture Orville L. Freeman wrote as follows: "We want to market the full allowable cut from every National Forest working circle and to give priority to development of the working circles where there is substantial demand and heavy mill capacity. We feel the Forest Service has been making good progress in this respect. . . . We want better adherence to previously announced timber sale schedules regardless of upward and downward swings in the lumber market. The Forest Service is being requested to make special efforts to do so in the future."[5] This statement indicates an intention to market an amount of timber annually based

---

2 *Timber Trends in Western Oregon and Western Washington,* Pacific Northwest Forest and Range Experiment Station, U.S. Forest Service Research Paper PNW-5 (Portland, Ore., 1963), p. 95.

3 "Forest Service Handbook," U.S. Forest Service, sec. 2412.1.

4 *Ibid.*

5 Letter from Secretary of Agriculture Orville L. Freeman to Senator Wayne Morse, April 17, 1962 (on file with U.S. Forest Service, Region 6 headquarters, Portland, Ore.).

on previous calculations, instead of dependence on economic factors.

Forest Service policy has historically been based upon an intent to harvest the allowable cut. The Chief of the Forest Service has expressed the historical objectives: "For almost twenty years, an objective of National Forest management has been the development of cutting at the full allowable rate on each National Forest working circle. Although we have not reached this goal we have been making steady progress toward it."[6]

The allowable cut has been steadily increased in recent years. In explaining these increases, Cliff made clear a six-point basis for readjusting the allowable cut objectives: (1) Timber inventories have been revised to reflect higher standards of utilization. Thus, resources have been shifted from the submarginal to the supramarginal classification. (2) Improvements in logging techniques have opened up new areas of difficult terrain and low-quality timber stands previously considered inoperable. (3) The technical process of computing the allowable cut has been adjusted by reducing the safety factors. The accumulation of knowledge concerning forest management has produced more reliable estimates of factors affecting the allowable cut determination. (4) New data on growth and mortality in mature uncut stands show sources of growth not previously included in technical calculations of the allowable cut. (5) The period of regeneration has been reduced owing to such factors as advance reforestation, stand improvement, and sale area betterment. (6) Some areas previously set aside for recreation and scenic purposes have been included in growth and harvest calculations.[7] These points are significant for their lack of market considerations. There is no reference to the price of timber in deriving the allowable cut, except that price increases bring timber from the submarginal to the supramarginal category.

The operational objectives of the Bureau of Land Management with reference to annual timber sales are similar to those of the Forest Service. The BLM manual states: "Lands shall be managed for permanent forest production and the timber on these lands sold, cut and removed in conformity with the principle of sustained yield. . . . Within the limitations imposed by the demand

---

6 Letter from Edward P. Cliff, chief, U.S. Forest Service, to Orville L. Freeman, May 7, 1962 (on file with U.S. Forest Service, Region 6 headquarters, Portland, Ore.).

7 Statement of Edward P. Cliff before Senate Commerce Committee Hearing, June 15, 1962 (mimeographed), pp. 10–11.

for timber, the appropriations available for making sales, sound forest management and multiple use conservation principles, the full sustained yield allowable cut shall be offered for sale annually in each master unit."[8] Thus, the sustained-yield objective and the annual allowable cut calculation are also basic to BLM timber sales objectives. Demand for timber, however, is an item deserving some consideration. The Bureau of Land Management allows variations within the sustained-yield calculation. Under the constraint that timber sales over a five-year moving average do not exceed the allowable cut calculation, the BLM handbook contains the following instructions: "Timber sales in any one year in a master unit may exceed the sustained-yield capacity as determined by Secretarial order so long as the running average obtained during a reasonable period is below the sustained-yield capacity of the master unit (Chief Counsel's opinion). In carrying out this opinion, it will be the policy to use a five-year moving average."[9]

If the regulations governing Forest Service and Bureau of Land Management timber sales are followed, the timber volume sold by these two federal agencies will be price inelastic, especially when the period of analysis extends to five years. The governing authority concerning quantity is not price, but rather the sustained-yield capacity calculation and the allowable cut calculation, both based upon silvicultural rather than price considerations.

The supply of timber offered by the federal agencies may, however, be somewhat more responsive (on a sustainable basis) to price than official policy statements would indicate. The annual allowable cut from national forests in the Douglas fir region steadily increased from 2,187 million board feet in 1954 to 2,987 in 1962, an increase of 37 percent in eight years. Table 9 shows very large increases in actual sales of timber by both the Forest Service and the BLM. Much of this increase is accounted for by a successful effort to catch up with the allowable cut. Some of the increase in the allowable cut is due to failure to harvest this cut over many previous years. But part of the increase in allowable cut is also due to its recalculation under new concepts of sustainable yield and new standards of log merchantability. Lower-grade logs have become merchantable. This is an economic event stimulated by price

---

[8] *BLM Manual*, U.S. Department of the Interior, Bureau of Land Management, Vol. VIII, sec. 2.7.3.
[9] "Timber Sale Procedure Handbook," U.S. Department of the Interior, Bureau of Land Management, pp. 1–2.

increases. Thus, the sustainable supply of public timber must show some positive quantity response to price.

The elasticity of timber supply from privately owned resources varies from ownership to ownership. The large timberland-owning firms in the Douglas fir region, which expect to be in business continuously, have a very long time horizon for decision making. The annual cutting practices of such large timberland-owning firms as Weyerhaeuser Company and Crown Zellerbach Corporation are based upon sustainable cutting considerations that do not differ widely from practices followed by the Forest Service. The principal difference is that the rotation period basic to the allowable cut is somewhat shorter in industrial forest holdings as compared with federal timber ownerships. Presumably, the lower rotation period for private enterprise reflects the profit motivation. If based on correct calculations, it indicates that the discounted net value of timber resource investments is higher for rotation periods shorter than those used by the federal agencies. Further, private firms should be somewhat more responsive to price-induced changes in standards of merchantability.

About all that can be said regarding the small, private ownerships is that the time horizon should be shorter for them than for either public or large private ownerships. Since the normal rotation period for timber in the Douglas fir region is approximately equal to the human life expectancy and is longer than the residual expectancy of adult owners, and since there is no reliable free market for timberland and growing stock, one would expect small private owners to place a relatively greater value on present values, that is, to use a higher discount rate for future income. A high discount rate virtually precludes planting additional timberland as a quantity response to higher stumpage prices. Other degrees of intensive forest land management which delay output and income would also tend to be inelastic with respect to price. If the small operators are well informed, they may be expected to respond, as do large private owners, to price-induced changes in the standards of merchantability. But, in any event, the quantity increase owing to a movement of logs from submarginal to supramarginal status is not great.

In the foregoing discussion the pattern of timber resource ownership and management objectives by ownership group has been examined. The conclusion indicated is that, insofar as management objectives by ownership group are concerned, the sustainable supply of timber is likely to be somewhat more elastic for private relative to public ownerships.

The time factor.—As a second consideration in identifying timber supply elasticity, a clear distinction should be made by time periods. The price-output relationship embodied in a supply curve is normally discussed in terms of a dichotomy, the long run or the short run. A large number of short runs, however, may be identified, depending on which productive services are fixed in a given decision-making situation. The usual dual classification is not suitable for our purposes. Rather, four different "runs" where the output response to the price variable has different characteristics are identified. The short run consists of three periods: (1) less than one year, (2) one to thirty years, and (3) thirty to fifty years. The long run for timber production is defined as from fifty to eighty years in the Douglas fir region.

1) Restricting the analysis to relatively high-level economic activity, the only source of a sustainable net increase in log production within a period of time less than one year is through redefinition of the submarginal log. If the price of stumpage should double, some logs formerly having no positive value and treated as culls or "weed species" would become supramarginal. Such material, however, contains little usable volume and is not extensive; therefore it cannot result in a significant increase in annual production. While some increase in quantity would occur within the less-than-one-year short run, the supply curve must be considered highly inelastic.

2) In the short run consisting of one to thirty years, again omitting from consideration the vast excess capacity situation such as prevailed in the mid-1930's, some net increase in timber production could result from the introduction of more advanced timber management practices. As in the less-than-one-year short run, additional production must come from more effective utilization of existing "plant" capacity. This period of time allows logging roads to be constructed in advance of logging needs, in turn permitting the following advanced timber management practices: (a) *Existing* second-growth timber stands in appropriate age classes may be thinned, producing a small increase in annual production. (b) Mature timber not previously under intensive management may be prelogged. This process removes small-diameter timber in a separate logging operation prior to clear-cutting. By this means, small timber normally destroyed in the clear-cutting operation is utilized. (c) Mature old-growth timber held in inventory for later cut-

ting may be salvage-logged for "dead and down" timber. Some of this timber, depending on the species, would be partly or entirely lost through decay. Again, a small net increase in volume may be realized. (*d*) Higher stumpage prices would also lead to efforts to protect more valuable timber from losses owing to fire, disease, and insect infestation. If such protective measures are taken, it may be assumed that some success would be achieved and annual average timber production would be increased. In addition, the modest gain claimed for the less-than-one-year short run would also be effective in the one-to-thirty-year short run. Yet the net increase in volume of production related to a price increase would remain quite modest. The elasticity of supply in this short run must be identified as clearly inelastic.[10]

3) Within the thirty-to-fifty-year short run, it is possible to achieve some additional net increase in volume of timber production as a result of thinning timber in the thirty-to-fifty-year age class which was planted in response to a stumpage price increase. Nonstocked and understocked timberland exists in the Douglas fir region. A large increase in stumpage prices might be expected to stimulate some additional reforestation, and, beginning at approximately thirty years of age, a small increase in log production may occur as a result of second-growth thinning. The residual trees would grow at a faster rate while volume removed in periodic thinning operations would be expected to have a net economic value. The increase in volume would again be modest for two reasons. First, timber harvested from thinning production is of small diameter and therefore contains relatively little volume. Second, it is questionable that even a 100 percent increase in stumpage price would stimulate much additional reforestation. Some thinning is already being practiced. Decision makers would need to be convinced that additional thinning is profitable at the higher stumpage prices and that the more favorable price-cost relationship will persist. Profitability would need to be demonstrated in terms of a relatively attractive discounted net return on a reforestation investment. The timber supply curve would probably gain

---

[10] On the basis of a regression analysis, Teeguarden concludes that "total (public and private) sawlog output in the Central Sierra [region of northern California] was highly correlated with [lumber] price movements" (Dennis E. Teeguarden, *The Lumber Industry in the Central Sierra Nevada Region*, California Agricultural Experiment Station, Bulletin 811 [April, 1965], p. 41). Teeguarden's findings, based on year-to-year variations in prices and quantity of log production, measure cyclical variation, whereas I am concerned with sustainable supply.

some additional elasticity within the thirty-to-fifty-year short run, but it would remain classified as inelastic.

4) The long run is normally defined as a period of time long enough to expand plant capacity. For growing timber in the Douglas fir region, the required period varies between fifty and eighty years. This rotation period is employed by some of the large timber companies in calculating their allowable cut. It is the period extending from a point in time at which one crop is clear-cut to the point where a new forest crop is available for harvest as merchantable timber. A higher stumpage price (a more favorable cost-price relationship) expected to persist for an extremely long period of time may generate additional investment in the planting of presently nonstocked or understocked timberland, thereby increasing log production in the long run. These gains in output are in addition to those enumerated above for shorter periods.

The Forest Service has made a detailed study of the long-run relationship between price and output based upon stated management assumptions. From this study, it has concluded that, if average-quality timberland were managed for continuous sawlog production, if an even-age silvicultural system were followed with intensive management including thinning and prompt reforestation of cutover land, if all timber were managed under close professional supervision with a complete road network available, and if losses from fire and other menaces were held to a negligible level, an approximate 100 percent increase in stumpage value would bring forth an approximate 14 percent increase in annual timber output.[11] These conditions are ideal, and it is unlikely that they could be attained. Although there are more unknowns than answers in the long-run problem, I am quite certain that the long-run timber supply curve does not approach an elastic condition; instead, it is likely to be relatively inelastic. Thus, whereas elasticity increases as the "run" is increased, it varies only from highly inelastic, in the less-than-one-year short run, to a relatively inelastic condition in the long run. The reader should be reminded that we have given no consideration to unsustainable increases in production by drawing on growing stock in response to a current price increase. Further, the analysis is restricted to the Douglas fir region.

Alternative factor employment.—A third factor that may influence the supply curve of timber is the possibility of alternative use of forest land. In the short run, a decline in the value of stumpage

11 *Timber Trends in Western Oregon and Western Washington,* p. iv.

(current and prospective) would lead to conversion of timberland to another use if relatively profitable alternatives existed. The possibilities of shifting timberland to agricultural and grazing use in the Douglas fir region are limited.[12] Most commercial forest land is in mountainous country, and economically feasible shifting apparently has been exhausted. Throughout the United States there is evidence of a reversal of the long trend that has shifted forest land to agricultural uses. A recent survey of the nation's timber resources concludes that "for the last several decades, the area returned to forest seems to have exceeded the area cleared."[13] From 1945 to 1953 the area classified as commercial forest land increased from 461 to 485 million acres.[14] Although some forest land is being converted to residential areas, the net movement in recent years is clearly in the other direction. Whereas some land may have a profitable alternative commercial use, "more commonly, forest land cannot be shifted economically into agriculture or other pecuniary use, although it often does have high value for recreation use."[15]

When land is shifted to a wilderness use, commercial harvest of forest products is normally forbidden. Similarly, land transferred to the national park system is dedicated to recreation and scientific uses: "The cutting or removal of any live or dead vegetation for the sole purpose of use, sale or exchange, except as specifically authorized, violates the fundamental purpose of the parks as expressed in the basic laws and regulations relating to them." The specifically authorized exceptions are limited to cutting "necessary to protect and maintain the vegetation and to permit safe use and full enjoyment of the parks by the people."[16]

It is not clear that there exist profitable alternative commercial uses of timberland to which privately held land might be transferred. Further, there is no reason to believe that transfers to recreational use are price responsive. If timberland has no significant

---

[12] A Senate staff report on lumber industry problems begins with the following observation: "America's forest lands are mainly confined to those parts of the United States where soil is unfit for farming" ("The Small Independent Firm's Role in the Forest Products Industry," U.S. Senate, Report of the Select Committee on Small Business, 86th Cong., 1st sess. [Washington, 1959], p. 9).

[13] *Timber Resources for America's Future*, U.S. Department of Agriculture, Forest Service, Forest Resources Report no. 14 (Washington, 1958), p. 126.

[14] *Ibid.*, p. 125.

[15] Charles H. Stoddard, *The Small Private Forest in the United States* (Washington: Resources for the Future, 1961), p. 21.

[16] Letter on national park policy from Harthon L. Bill, chief, Resources Management and Visitor Protection, National Park Service, July 9, 1964.

price-responsive profitable alternative uses, then the costs of "tree farming" may be very small when viewed as opportunity or alternative costs. One of the essential and peculiar features of timber "manufacture" is that the "manufacturing" process continues, though not at maximum efficiency, even when all human efforts are withdrawn. Timber grows wild. The payment of annual property taxes is necessary to retain a given private ownership, but not to continue timber growth. Thus, property taxes do not constitute a social cost of growing timber.

The principal cost of holding timber resources for additional growth is the imputed interest cost. But interest must be calculated on the net conversion value of timber (stumpage value) and is given as the foregone income from the next-best alternative use of the values committed to timber growth. If stumpage prices decline, the net conversion value also declines. Correspondingly, the imputed interest charge is reduced. Even when a timberland owner elects to harvest his timber and thereby withdraw his capital, natural regeneration in the Douglas fir region will normally set the timber-"manufacturing" process in motion again, free of charge, but not necessarily with maximum efficiency.

The necessary social cost of growing timber at submaximum levels is approximately nil. It follows that when stumpage prices decline, or when anticipated prices decline, production will not be stopped. The tail of the supply curve, which normally is truncated when average variable costs are no longer covered by product prices, has no positive cost terminal point. The timber supply function remains inelastic at low stumpage prices.

Barriers to entry.—A fourth factor relative to the elasticity of timber supply is closely related to the third. Free entry into an industry introduces more elasticity into supply functions, and barriers to entry are responsible for less elasticity. Entry conditions, however, refer to long-run supply functions, whereas exit from the industry may take place in a relatively short period of time. Barriers to entry of the type identified by Bain[17] are significant. Product differentiation barriers are nonexistent. But economies of scale are important, and absolute cost advantages are prohibitive. Entry is meaningful only if land not currently used for growing timber is converted to tree farming. Knowledge of the most efficient scale for timber-growing operations is inadequate, and additional

---

[17] Joe S. Bain, *Barriers to New Competition* (Cambridge: Harvard University Press, 1956), chaps. 3–5.

research has been called for.[18] The meager evidence available suggests that under conditions prevailing in the southern pine region, at least 10,000 acres would be the required minimum for a sustained-yield unit.[19] Stoddard summarizes the available information: "The bulk of the small holdings considered uneconomic for systematic management contain less than 5,000 acres."[20] But efficient management requires more than minimum acreage. The land area must be "blocked up"; that is, the land resources must be geographically compact rather than scattered. Land would have to be converted from another use, probably agriculture. It is highly improbable that 10,000 acres of contiguous land not at present in timberland use could be found in the Douglas fir region and purchased at land values that would permit profitable tree farming. Entry into timber production should not, therefore, be considered a realistic possibility under present or probable future conditions. Entry would not contribute elasticity to a probably inelastic long-run timber supply curve. Existing firms may acquire some submarginal farmland not currently in timberland use. But the quantity available in the Douglas fir region is very small.

Knowledge of production alternatives.—A fifth factor, inadequate knowledge of production alternatives, further contributes to long-run supply inelasticity in timber production. Perfect knowledge of one's alternatives in timber production requires knowledge of events many years, even decades, into the future. The element of uncertainty is so crucial that even managements of large timber companies do not know whether it is profitable to invest a sum of money to reforest timberland, to pay property taxes on timberland for the entire rotation period, and to forego alternative interest income in order to realize an ultimate value in mature and merchantable timber fifty to eighty years later. In the absence of knowledge of profitability associated with tree farming, we would not expect a small change in current stumpage prices to produce a significant effect in the long-run supply curve. Within the one-to-thirty-year short run the future is, of course, more certain. Correspondingly, intensive management practices may rest upon a more precise estimate of profitability. Knowledge of alternatives is quite inadequate in the timber industry as compared

---

[18] See Marion Clawson, "Economic Size of Forestry Operations," *Journal of Forestry*, LV (July, 1957), 521–526.

[19] *Forest Credit in the United States* (Washington: Resources for the Future, April, 1958), p. 17.

[20] *Op. cit.*, p. 53

with other industries, and hence lack of knowledge would further indicate an inelastic supply curve.

The deductive evidence, supported in part by data, indicates clearly that the supply curve for timber is relatively inelastic, whether we think in terms of the long run or of one of the short runs identified above. The shorter the run, however, the more inelastic the supply function.

A graphic model may be constructed showing the supply curve of national forest timber. The model may be extended to include Bureau of Land Management sales, as supply conditions are virtually identical. No attempt is be made to show a graphic model of the private timber supply curve, as private stumpage sales are a relatively minor part of the total timber supply actually traded. No statistical records of stumpage sales from privately owned timber are available. Estimates provided by Mason, Bruce, and Girard, the largest firm of consulting foresters operating in the Douglas fir region, indicate that approximately 200 million board feet of timber are sold annually in stumpage form from all privately owned timber stands in the region. This amounts to about 2 percent of all regional log production. Some private timber is sold or exchanged in log form. Some stumpage has been sold by Georgia Pacific Corporation on an irregular basis. Railroad holdings and the Hill family interests are regular suppliers of timber on a sustained-yield basis. Finally, a small but unknown amount of stumpage is sold from farmer-owned commercial forest resources.[21]

The supply model for federal timber is shown in figure 6. Supply curve S represents the less-than-one-year short run, and S' represents the one-to-thirty-year short run. Timber is offered for sale at the appraised price. Any quantity up to the allowable cut OQ will be offered at the appraised price OP. Thus, the supply curve up to the allowable cut is perfectly elastic at the appraised price. Current legislation does not permit sales of federal timber below the appraised price. For prices bid above the appraised price point E, the supply curve varies depending upon the period of time under

---

21 In other regions, "farmer and miscellaneous private" sources account for a major timber reserve and annual supply. Whereas only 7.2 percent of the net volume of softwood sawtimber is in nonpublic and nonforest industry ownership in the Douglas fir region, in California, 26.8 percent, and in the South, 53.0 percent of the volume is found in this sector (*Timber Resource Statistics for the Pacific Northwest*, Pacific Northwest Forest and Range Experiment Station, U.S. Forest Service Resource Bulletin PNW-9 [Portland, Ore., 1965], p. 7; *Timber Trends in the United States*, U.S. Department of Agriculture, Forest Service, Forest Resources Report no. 17 [Washington, 1965], pp. 155–157).

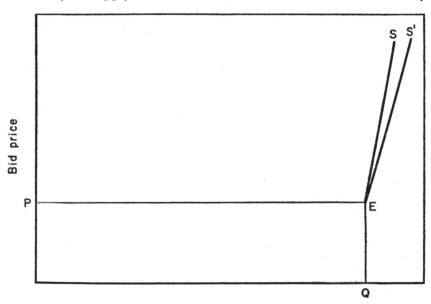

Quantity per unit of time

Fig. 6. Model for federal timber supply.

consideration. Within a time period of less than one year, the sustainable increase in quantity in response to higher prices is very small. Hence, in the less-than-one-year short run, the supply curve of national forest timber becomes *PES*. The supply curve sector *ES* is highly inelastic, and quantity supplied is approximately equal to the allowable cut, *OQ*.

In a longer period of time from one to thirty years, some additional small increase in the quantity of timber offered may occur as a function of price conditions. Therefore, the supply curve segment *ES'* shows a slightly higher degree of elasticity, still within the inelastic category. In the short run defined as one to thirty years, the supply curve of national forest timber is given by the line *PES'*.

DEDUCTIVE ESTIMATE OF PRICE ELASTICITY OF LUMBER SUPPLY

To identify the shape or elasticity of the short-run and long-run supply curves for lumber, the approach is primarily deductive, although econometric evidence is appraised. The relevant economic theory identified earlier is applied to the lumber situation. The factors examined are: (1) the firm short-run marginal cost function, (2) the importance of external pecuniary diseconomies, (3) the effect of barriers to entry, (4) the possibility of alternative uses for productive services committed to lumber production, and (5) the knowledgeability factor among lumber mill management.

The firm short-run marginal cost function.—This discussion presupposes that individual firm managements know their cost functions. A firm that is part of a noncollusive oligopsony or a noncollusive bilateral monopoly is faced by indeterminate factor supply curves. Theoretical cost functions for alternative levels of resource input cannot be determined. The discussion must, therefore, be concerned with other market structures where supply functions are determinate.

As noted earlier, under competitive conditions and in the absence of external diseconomies the industry short-run supply curve is obtained by horizontally summing individual firm marginal costs above the point of intersection with firm average variable cost. The essential feature of the supply curve for lumber, however, is that external pecuniary diseconomies are quickly encountered when firms attempt to expand output. The industry supply curve therefore, cannot be thus obtained. If the market provides an incentive for lumber mills to expand output, and this incentive is the result of a general increase in demand for lumber, then all firms enjoy the same favorable circumstances and all have an incentive to expand output, though in varying degree. As all firms attempt to expand output, they immediately encounter the inelastic supply curve for timber identified in the preceding section. Additional bidding for free market timber results in a substantially higher price of timber, but only a modest increase in quantity. The problem is portrayed graphically in figure 7, *a*.

Suppose that the demand curve for housing has shifted to the right, bringing with it a comparable increase in demand for building materials, including lumber and plywood. As the demand curve for lumber shifts to the right, it intersects the supply curve at a higher, but, for the moment, unknown point. Assume that lumber prices move from P_0 to P_1. Initially, this would cause individual firms to attempt an expansion in output along their marginal cost curves from Q_2 to Q_3, as shown in figure 7, *b*. As previously demonstrated, the short-run average cost curve is downward sloping, becoming relatively flat between one and three shifts. As the timber supply curve is inelastic in any time period, firms, as a group, are unable to move to Q_3, and, instead, substantial cost increases are incurred. This is reflected in an upward shift in the short-run aver-

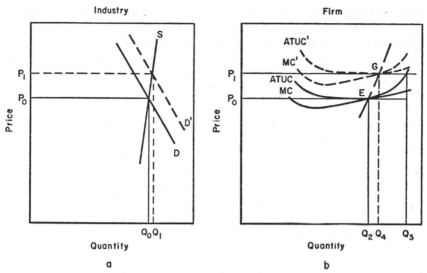

Fig. 7. Cost and demand model for lumber firms.

age cost curve and the marginal cost curve to $ATUC'$ and MC'.
A new intersection of marginal cost and price is obtained, indicating output Q_4. Points E and G may be connected with a line that
may be identified as a "quasi supply" curve. The industry supply
may now be obtained by horizontally summing all quasi supply
curves.

Output expansion requires increased input of all factors of production. The supply curves of labor and capital are sufficiently
elastic so that external diseconomies from these two sources would
not appear to be significant. The limiting factor of production is
the sawlog supply. Earlier we explored the possibility of substitution between labor and/or capital and logs and concluded that the
marginal rate of substitution was low; therefore, significant substitution is not an important factor.

The previous analysis of the supply curves for timber was concerned primarily with the supply of publicly owned timber because, in the Douglas fir region, most stumpage offered in the free
market is from public ownership. This section is concerned with
the supply curve of lumber. Private timber supplies are relevant
because lumber enters the open market whether it is cut from
public or private timber. It was previously concluded that the
supply of public timber is inelastic. The sustainable supply of
"captive" timber (owned in fee by the milling firm) may be slightly

more elastic, but is still within the inelastic category. The somewhat higher elasticity would be due to the profit motive operative
within the private sector, but would be restrained by other considerations in the public sector. The elasticity of timber supply
from public and private sources, within the framework of an attempt to identify the elasticity of lumber supply, here concerns the
short run period of one to thirty years. Consideration of a temporary increase in supply resulting from unsustainable reductions in
growing stock is excluded from the analysis.

Barriers to entry.—Conditions of entry into lumber manufacturing may affect the elasticity of lumber supply in the long run.
A later analysis (see chap. 6) establishes that barriers to entry into
lumber milling are relatively low. The only serious restriction on
entry concerns the ability to obtain logs. Although entry of new
firms stimulates competition for timber, it does not necessarily
produce an increase in the timber supply. The timber supply is,
therefore, limiting. Except for the possibility of shifting log supplies between lumber use and alternative factor uses the sustainable supply function for lumber cannot be significantly greater
than that of timber, which has been identified as relatively inelastic.

Alternative factor employment.—At this point, the possibility
of alternative uses for resources normally committed to lumber
production may be introduced. There are only two important uses
of logs: lumber and veneer-plywood production. In the long run,
shifts can and do occur. The persistent shift in the past two decades
has been from lumber to veneer-plywood production in response
to relatively more profitable utilization in the latter product. In
regard to price elasticity of lumber supply, the peculiar condition
is that the dominant forces causing changes in lumber prices also
cause similar changes in plywood prices. The primary use of both
products is building construction. The other important price-de-
termining force is log supply limitation, and this, of course, affects
both uses. Therefore, the possibility of alternative factor employment for logs does not introduce any important degree of lumber
supply elasticity.

The knowledgeability factor.—The final point concerns the state
of management knowledge in the industry. To the extent that
management is well trained and perceptive, minor price changes
may lead to quick output reactions by profit-seeking entrepreneurs.
The so-called profit squeeze occurring since lumber prices reached
high levels in the early 1950's has produced some striking illustra-
tions of progressive and highly profitable management. In general,

however, lumber-mill operators have shown relatively little interest in the modern science of management. Their particular talent has historically been based on a small-scale machine shop inventive and innovative ability, not on knowledge of marketing, finance, or even sophisticated production management. Lumber-mill management talent differs markedly, for example, from its counterpart in the electronics and chemical industries. A career of lumber-mill management does not beckon a Harvard Business School graduate. Extensive interviews revealed relatively little interest in such modern decision-making techniques as linear programming. This situation prevails in spite of the fact that there are a multitude of log types that may be converted by a variety of processes into a host of alternative wood products. Important production decisions involving many variables are typically made "by the seat of the pants." Zaremba, writing critically about the United States lumber industry as a whole, observes: "The level of managerial ability is exceedingly low and lumber operators are not very progressive."[22]

There is wide variation between the least efficient and the most efficient firms. Quality of management appears to be the most important variable accounting for the dispersion. Although the point is a relatively minor one, the observed lack of a well-trained management group in lumber milling would suggest some output inflexibility with respect to price changes.

In summary, the above deductive analysis indicates that the long-run lumber supply curve is inelastic, and that the principal factor responsible for this conclusion is the inelastic supply curve for timber. At the same time, the short-run marginal cost curve for the individual lumber mill is highly elastic in those instances where the log supply function is known and additional logs may be obtained at constant prices.

ECONOMETRIC EVIDENCE

In his econometric studies, I. I. Holland produced a two-equation supply-demand model. Econometric estimates of a supply function for lumber are likely to be more reliable than demand estimates because the supply function should be relatively stable. The supply equation developed two significant variables, the endogenous variable Y_2, per capita shipments of softwood lumber, and the exogenous variable Z_3, average cost of manufacturing softwood lumber.

---

[22] Joseph Zaremba, *Economics of the American Lumber Industry* (New York: Robert Speller, 1963), p. 196.

The equation (see p. 45, above) indicates that an increase of 1 dollar in the price of softwood lumber is associated with an increase in per capita lumber shipments of 8.6 board feet. Using average values for Y_1 (average annual price of softwood construction lumber) and Y_2, and holding Z_3 constant, the arc elasticity of supply can be computed for a 1-dollar price change. Supply elasticity is $+1.7$. Thus, the econometric evidence indicates that the softwood lumber supply function is elastic, in contrast with the inelastic supply function suggested by deductive analysis. Can these two answers be reconciled?

The econometric analysis is based on annual data and therefore on year-to-year changes in price, shipments, and manufacturing cost. In contrast, the deductive analysis ignores year-to-year variations and attempts, instead, to identify the sustainable increases in lumber production which would occur as a result of price increases. Thus, the two approaches do not yield comparable estimates of supply elasticity. The econometric analysis provides useful information on supply behavior with respect to price which is not comparable with either the short-run or the long-run supply functions developed from economic theory. In the theoretical concept, the supply function is sustainable as it responds to price changes.

Summary

The attempt to identify the general shape of the supply functions for timber and for lumber has been restricted to sustainable supply increases related to price increases. Deductive analysis reveals that the supply function for timber is highly inelastic in the less-than-one-year short run. Elasticity is increased modestly as the period of time under consideration is increased. Each of two additional short runs, the one-to-thirty-year short run and the thirty-to-fifty-year short run, allows additional factors to be variable. Finally the fifty-to-eighty-year long run is a production period of sufficient length to allow output from expanded "plant" capacity. Although the elasticity of supply increases with the time period, even in the long run the supply of timber must be considered relatively inelastic.

In examining the elasticity of supply for lumber, the primary method of analysis was deductive, although econometric evidence was reviewed. The firm short-run marginal cost curve is believed to be elastic over a wide range. This condition does not produce an elastic industry supply curve, however, as external pecuniary diseconomies are encountered. The relatively inelastic timber supply was found to be the dominant factor resulting in an inelastic lumber supply. The possibility of shifting logs from other uses (veneer-plywood production) in response to a lumber price increase was held to be of minor importance, as the forces causing a lumber price increase are likely to bring about a parallel increase in the price of plywood. The possibility of expanded production through more intensive use of labor and capital in conjunction with fixed log input is believed to be unimportant. The supply function for lumber, while more elastic than that for timber, is still in the inelastic range.

PART II

The Structure of the Industry

Industry structure refers to the arrangement of parts and the relationship among the several parts of the whole industry. Edward S. Mason, in defining market structure in his preface to Carl Kaysen and Donald F. Turner, Antitrust Policy *(Cambridge: Harvard University Press, 1959), speaks of "those permanent, or slowly changing, competitive limitations of which a firm must take account in formulating its own policies. The most important of these limitations are the number and size distribution of buyers and sellers in the market, the conditions of entry of new firms, and the extent of product differentiation, including geographical dispersion." We are concerned here with the constituent parts and their pattern of organization within the industry. The definition of industrial structure and the method of research employed to analyze structure must be interpreted in terms of the research objectives. The structure of the industry is analyzed because it may indicate a degree of competition. The research objective is to determine to what extent the conduct or behavior of competitors and the final performance of an industry may be predicted from knowledge of structure.*

Structure is analyzed at three levels: resource ownership and acquisition, lumber production, and wholesale distribution of lumber. As an analytical tool, concentration ratios are employed to study industry structure. Concentration ratios show the share of a total market accounted for by a few large operators.

Chapter 4 provides an analysis of concentration in timber resource ownership and the trend of concentration, and also takes up the structure of the federal timber markets and relevant geographical markets. In chapter 5 the degree of concentration in lumber production and its trend over time, for both the nation as a whole and the Douglas fir region in particular, are examined. Chapter 6 is concerned with the conditions of entry into the lumber industry as a dimension of structure, as well as the importance of product differentiation in the lumber market.

CHAPTER 4

Economic Concentration in Timber Resource Ownership and Acquisition

---

In perfect competition, "each economic unit is so small relative to the market that it exerts no perceptible influence on the prices of the things it buys and sells."[1] At the other extreme, a monopoly has only one seller in a given market. Between these two polar extremes, neither of which exists as a pure form in the private and nonpublic utilities sectors of the United States economy, there are various degrees of "workably competitive" and oligopolistic industries. In an oligopoly, "a firm bases its market policy in part on the expected behavior of a few close rivals."[2] If the few large producers perform in such a way as to obtain the objectives that competition is supposed to obtain, the oligopoly may be termed "workably competitive." It is generally assumed that an industry composed of more than a few sellers, where no one seller, or likely combination, is large enough to enforce a sustained price increase by reducing output, is an effectively competitive industry. Such an industry, however, may not be workably competitive.

The concern of this chapter is the concentration of economic power at the first of three market levels in the Douglas fir lumber industry: (1) resource ownership and acquisition, (2) lumber production, and (3) wholesale lumber distribution. Conclusions about the degree of economic concentration in timber resource ownership and its trend over time depend upon the use of concentration ratios, which refer to the share of a given market accounted for by a few of the largest sellers in that market. In the context of

---

1 George J. Stigler, *The Theory of Price* (New York: Macmillan, 1947), p. 21.
2 *Ibid.*, p. 226.

[77]

timber resource concentration, the numerator of a concentration ratio is the summation of timberland (acres) owned by the "big few," and the denominator is the total ownership by all firms in the industry.

HISTORIC AVERSION TO CONCENTRATED TIMBER RESOURCE OWNERSHIP

The degree of concentration in timber resource ownership has concerned thoughtful men during several periods of United States economic development. In 1913, the Federal Bureau of Corporations made an extensive national study of timberland ownership. In his letter of transmittal covering the bureau's report, Herbert Knox Smith, commissioner of corporations, wrote:

There are many combinations in other industries whose formation is complete. In the lumber industry, on the other hand, the Bureau finds now in the making a combination caused, fundamentally, by a long standing public policy. The concentration already existing is sufficiently impressive. Still more impressive are the possibilities for the future. In the last forty years concentration has so proceeded that 195 holders, many inter-related, now have practically one-half of the privately owned timber in the investigation area (which contains 80 percent of the whole). This formidable process of concentration, in timber and in land, certainly involves grave future possibilities of impregnable monopolistic conditions, whose far reaching consequences to society it is now difficult to anticipate fully or to over estimate.[3]

The investigation area to which the study refers accounts for 80 percent of the land area of the United States; it is not the Douglas fir region. The Bureau of Corporations study drew the following conclusions:

1. The concentration of a dominating control of our standing timber in a comparatively few enormous holdings, is steadily tending toward a central control of the lumber industry.

2. There is vast speculative purchase and holding of timberland far in advance of any use thereof.

3. There is an enormous increase in the value of this diminishing natural resource, with great profits to its owners. This value, by the very nature of standing timber, the holder neither created nor substantially enhances.[4]

In the 1940's and 1950's, merger activity in the lumber industry became intense as the economy entered into another major wave

---

[3] *The Lumber Industry*, U.S. Department of Commerce and Labor, Bureau of Corporations, Pt. I (Washington, 1913), p. 97.
[4] *Ibid.*, p. xvii.

of mergers. Of today's "Big Four" lumber producers, two were largely created as a result of this merger wave. At the close of World War II, Georgia-Pacific (then called the Georgia Hardwood Lumber Co.) was an unimportant factor in the lumber industry and did not operate in the Douglas fir region. Between 1944 and 1960 it absorbed twenty-one formerly independent firms. Today, Georgia-Pacific's timber holdings, acquired since the close of World War II, allow its management to claim "one of the largest and finest timber reserves in the United States," and give the corporation second place in regional lumber production.

United States Plywood Corporation acquired full ownership of its first plywood plant as recently as 1937, and by 1940 it still had no lumber production in the Douglas fir region. By 1960, U.S. Plywood had absorbed twenty-eight other firms and had become the third-largest lumber producer in the region. Weyerhaeuser Company, the leading firm in lumber production for the nation and the region, acquired eighteen formerly independent firms during the two decades ending in 1960. The fourth of the Big Four lumber producers, Pope and Talbot, Inc., was not a party to a merger in the period 1940–1960.

The current merger movement in the lumber industry has been concentrated in firms having timber resources and includes few, if any, acquired firms having only lumber production facilities. It has thus contributed to increased concentration in timber resource ownership, though the fears expressed in the Bureau of Corporations report of 1913 have not materialized.[5]

THE PRESENT DEGREE OF CONCENTRATION IN TIMBER RESOURCE OWNERSHIP

Considering the fears expressed above, what does the record show about the present degree of economic concentration in timber ownership and the trend of concentration over time? Table 10 shows the position of the four largest and the eight largest ownerships in the Douglas fir region. As of 1960, the Big Four held in fee ownership 13.7 percent, or nearly one-seventh, of all commercial forest land in the region. The eight largest firms, the "Big Eight," accounted for 17.9 percent of all commercial forest land in the region. Ownership concentration by the Big Four and the

---

[5] For a more detailed analysis of the merger movement in the lumber industry, including a study of the motives for merging, see W. J. Mead, *Mergers and Economic Concentration in the Douglas-Fir Lumber Industry*, U.S. Forest Service Research Paper PNW-9 (Portland, Ore., 1964).

TABLE 10

CONCENTRATION IN OWNERSHIP OF COMMERCIAL FOREST LAND IN THE
DOUGLAS FIR REGION, 1953 AND 1960

Ownership	1960			1953		
	Acres (in thousands)	Percent of all ownerships	Percent of private ownerships	Acres (in thousands)	Percent of all ownerships	Percent of private ownerships
All ownerships (1953 data)	..	..	..	25,455	100.0	..
Privately owned (1953 data)	..	..	..	13,325	52.3	100.0
Weyerhaeuser Company	2,150	8.4	16.1	..	..	..
Four largest ownerships	3,493	13.7	26.2	2,988	11.7	22.4
Eight largest ownerships	4,549	17.9	34.1	3,656	14.4	27.4

SOURCE: Data for 1960 supplied by cooperating firms, or developed from published annual reports and Federal Trade Commission records on mergers; data for 1953 developed from data supplied by Forest Service; universe data from U.S. Department of Agriculture, Forest Service, *Timber Resources for America's Future*, Forest Resources Report no. 14 (Washington, 1958), p. 548.

Big Eight may also be viewed as a share of privately owned commercial forest land. Table 10 shows that the four largest owners accounted for 26.2 percent, or a little more than one-fourth, of all privately owned commercial forest land. The eight largest owners accounted for 34.1 percent, or more than one-third, of all privately owned commercial forest land.

Finally, an examination of concentration within the "forest industries"[6] sector shows the Big Four holding approximately 48 percent, and the Big Eight holding 62 percent, of all forest industry ownership. Within the four largest ownerships there is a high degree of concentration. The largest private commercial forest land owner in the Douglas fir region owns more than half (61.6 percent) of the acreage shown for the Big Four.[7] Further, the single largest firm's holdings account for nearly half (47.3 percent) of the holdings of the eight largest in the Douglas fir region. It should be made clear that stumpage and logs are available from sources other than the forest industries category, that is, from farm and other private ownership and from public timberlands.

Concentration in timberland ownership may also be viewed in terms of ownerships in excess of 50,000 acres (see table 11). In 1953

TABLE 11

CONCENTRATION IN OWNERSHIP OF PRIVATE COMMERCIAL FOREST LAND IN THE
DOUGLAS FIR REGION, 1953

Ownership	Ownerships		Acres		
	Number	Percent	Number (in thousands)	Percent	Average size
All ownerships	67,983	100.00	13,352	100.00	196
Ownerships of 50,000 acres or more	23	0.03	5,009	37.59	217,783

SOURCE: U.S. Department of Agriculture, Forest Service, *Timber Resources for America's Future,* Forest Resources Report no. 14 (Washington, 1958), p. 553.

---

6 The "forest industries" classification is defined by the Forest Service as follows: "Property of forest owners who operate primary wood-processing plants and who apparently obtain more of their income from the sale of wood products than from any other single source, or who operate wood-processing subsidiary corporations that derive income chiefly from the sale of wood products" (*Timber Resources for America's Future,* U.S. Department of Agriculture, Forest Service, Forest Resources Report no. 14 [Washington, 1958], p. 634).

7 *Annual Report, 1958,* Weyerhaeuser Company, p. 16. Since 1958 the mergers in which Weyerhaeuser Company has acquired other firms have added no timberland within the Douglas fir region; therefore, the 1958 figure would also be approximately correct for 1960.

there were 23 such ownerships out of a total of 67,983 in the Douglas fir region. These ownerships accounted for 5,009,000 acres out of a total private ownership of 13,325,000 acres. Thus the 23 largest firms represent only 0.03 percent of the total number of timberland owners, but they owned more than 37 percent of all private commercial forest land.

Before interpreting the significance of the present degree of economic concentration in Douglas fir region timber ownership, one should have a clear understanding of the different ownership classes in the region and of the different means of measuring such ownership. Table 12 shows a breakdown of the "all ownerships" category into its several parts. In 1963 all public ownership accounted for 49.1 percent of the total acreage in the Douglas fir region, but 67.5 percent of the net volume of timber. Privately owned commercial forest land accounted for 50.9 percent of the total acreage and 32.5 percent of the net volume. These figures reveal that a higher proportion of the public ownership holds virgin old-growth timber, and a larger share of the private ownership consists of cutover lands and new, young forests.

The ownership data shown in table 12 document what is widely known: the greatest single concentration of control over timber and timberland is in public ownership. The national forests account for 71.9 percent of the public ownership. A question that automatically appears—"Is the Forest Service a monopolist?"—has been raised by Sidney Weintraub and discussed by him with reference to the consequences of concentrated control by a public agency.[8] From the point of view of economic analysis, interest in monopoly is restricted to the consequences of monopoly behavior. Behavior of a noncompetitive industry is of economic concern because, through price and output decisions, the distribution of income may be altered in favor of the monopolist compared with the pattern allowed by competition, and resource misallocation may occur. As a consequence, the allocation of resources through an economy differs from the pattern dictated by a free price mechanism. As a second consideration, monopoly is of concern to economic analysis through its effect on technological improvements and product innovations. Weintraub concludes that

Everything hinges, then, on the market behavior of the single seller; whether the consequences are exactly those of competition, or whether price is higher

8 Sidney Weintraub, "An Examination of Some Economic Aspects for Forest Service Stumpage Prices and Appraisal Policies," mimeographed report prepared for U.S. Forest Service (June, 1958), pp. 150–153.

TABLE 12

ACREAGE OF, AND NET VOLUME OF TIMBER ON, COMMERCIAL FOREST LAND
IN THE DOUGLAS FIR REGION, BY OWNERSHIP, 1963

Ownership	Number of acres (in thousands)	Percent of total	Volume of timber (in millions of board feet)	Percent of all ownership volume	Percent of private ownerships
All ownerships	26,032	100.0	667,857	100.0	..
Federal ownership or trusteeship	10,395	39.9	}		
State ownership	2,070	8.0	} 450,375	67.5	..
County or municipal ownership	324	1.2	}		
Private ownership	13,243	50.9	217,482	32.5	100.0
Forest industry	7,321	28.1	169,271	25.3	77.8
Farmer and miscellaneous	5,922	22.8	48,211	7.2	22.2

SOURCE: Pacific Northwest Forest and Range Experiment Station, *Timber Resource Statistics for the Pacific Northwest*, U.S. Forest Service Resource Bulletin PNW-9 (Portland, Ore., 1965), pp. 1, 7.

and production is lower, as under monopoly, depends on the seller's conduct. So far there has not been any evidence to suggest that the Forest Service has so manipulated its offerings as to maximize the aggregate sum of proceeds to it. The facts seem to be quite otherwise, to wit, that the volume of offerings has approached pretty close to the total that could be processed with funds available and in light of the difficulty of opening new areas because of the access road situation. . . . To make the charge of "monopoly" stick, therefore, it would have to be demonstrated that the Forest Service has consciously managed its sales offerings with a design of enlarging its aggregate sales proceeds by narrowing its stumpage offerings.[9]

Weintraub's analysis of the monopoly position of the Forest Service by no means disposes of the issue. Resolution of this interesting question would constitute a major undertaking beyond the scope of either Weintraub's report or of the present research effort. Should one be able to establish, however, that the behavior of the Forest Service is similar to that of a private monopolist the income consequences would still be of little importance. Where private monopoly profits appear, the favored few able to benefit from them would gain substantially through greater capital gains, higher dividends, and higher salaries or the bonus equivalent. The gains would be highly concentrated, except as they are distributed through public donations, tax payments, and the like. In contrast, the monopoly profit realized by monopolistic behavior of a public agency would be more widely distributed either in the form of lower taxes, or through public expenditures on schools, roads, national defense, and so on.

Although the income consequences of a Forest Service monopoly thus may be disposed of, another consequence is more troublesome. The Forest Service is often accused of a disregard for the buyer's interest, a characteristic common among monopolists. As the only significant source of timber in many geographical markets, the seller may develop a careless disinterest in the buyer's problems and needs. Indeed, one of the great merits of competition is that sellers (and buyers) are forced by impersonal market conditions to satisfy the needs and answer the complaints of buyers (and sellers). The public agency as a monopolist must develop substitute means from the field of public administration to meet these needs. Because of the significant difference in the income consequences of public and private monopoly, the principal concern in the balance of this analysis is with concentration of economic power in the private sector.

---

[9] *Ibid.*, p. 153.

THE TREND IN CONCENTRATION
IN TIMBER RESOURCE OWNERSHIP

By piecing together scanty information, it is possible to draw some conclusions concerning the trend of concentration in resource ownership. The data in table 10 show that from 1953 to 1960 merger activity in the lumber industry significantly increased concentration ratios in timberland ownership. Ownership by the Big Four increased from 2,988,000 to 3,493,000 acres, and their concentration ratios rose from 11.7 to 13.7 percent of all commercial forest land, and from 22.4 to 26.2 percent of all private commercial forest land. The increase in concentration among the eight largest ownerships was slightly greater. By expanding their ownership from 3,656,000 to 4,549,000 acres, the ratios for the Big Eight grew from 14.4 to 17.9 percent of all commercial forest land and from 27.4 to 34.1 percent of all private commercial forest land.

Table 13, giving the available data on ownership in Oregon and Washington in 1910 and 1953, shows the trend in ownership concentration between those two years. (Information for the Douglas fir region is not available because data for the 1910 base were not broken down for the region.) The 1910 data reflect the large land grants made by Congress to the railroads. The principal source of timber for Weyerhaeuser Timber Company was the Northern Pacific Railroad grant, acquired in part by Weyerhaeuser in 1900. In 1910 the railroad was still the third-largest holder of timberland in the two states.

Composition of the four largest firms changed between 1910 and 1953. Only one firm is a member of both the 1910 and the 1953 Big Four. There is a substantial decline in resource ownership concentration over the forty-four-year period. Acreage held in Oregon and Washington by the Big Four in 1953 declined from 5,941,000 to 3,714,000 acres, representing only 63 percent of the 1910 holdings. In the two states taken individually, a similar deconcentration took place. Acreage held in 1953 by the four largest in Oregon was only 52 percent of the 1910 figure; for Washington, it was 71 percent. In 1953 the Big Four ownership in Oregon and Washington accounted for 8.2 percent of all commercial forest land, both private and public, and 19 percent of private commercial forest land.

Three years after the Bureau of Corporations report containing its unattractive forecast on landownership was published, another review of land tenure was made: "The general conclusion drawn from all the data obtained is that timber buying and the consoli-

TABLE 13

Trend in Timber Resource Concentration in Oregon and Washington, 1910–1953
(In thousands of acres)

Ownership	1910			1953		
	Oregon	Washington	Total	Oregon	Washington	Total
Four largest holders	3,045	3,438	5,941	1,587a	2,454a	3,714a
Southern Pacific Railroad	2,079		2,079			
Weyerhaeuser Timber Company	393	1,533	1,926			
Northern Pacific Railroad	..	1,612	1,612			
Booth-Kelly	324	..	324			
Chicago, Milwaukee and St. Paul Railroad	..	276	276			
C. A. Smith interests	249	..	249			
Wheeler interests	129	..	129			
T. B. Walkerb interests; Missouri Lumber and Land Exchange interests	..	17	17			
Total commercial forest land				25,875	19,490	45,365
Percent of 1953 commercial forest land owned by four largest holders	11.8	17.7	13.1	6.1	12.6	8.2
Total private commercial forest land				9,768	9,806	19,574
Percent owned by four largest owners				16.2	25.0	19.0

a Four largest firms in 1953 are not entirely the same as the four largest firms in 1910.
b Milwaukee family.

Sources: For 1910 data: U.S. Department of Commerce and Labor, Bureau of Corporations, *The Lumber Industry*, Pt. III (Washington, 1914), pp. 173–176; for 1953 data: developed from data supplied by U.S. Forest Service.

dation of property was largely checked in Oregon by the year 1912. That this check in timber buying is permanent is not, however, to be inferred."[10] Further, the Capper Report published in 1920 concluded: "Since 1910 the three largest holdings in this region [Washington and Oregon] have been decreased."[11]

Between 1910 and 1953 the federal government made one major contribution to deconcentration in private ownership by revesting approximately 2.9 million acres granted in 1866 to the Oregon and California Railroad Company. The timber was not of great value at the time, and the railroad, in spite of its land grant, fell into financial difficulties; it was in receivership when the Southern Pacific Railroad Company leased it in 1887. The government was able to prove that the grantee failed to comply with the terms of the grant, and in 1916 the Supreme Court ordered title to the remaining grant lands revested in the United States.[12] These lands, now amounting to 2,637,911 acres (including 74,586 acres of reconveyed Coos Bay wagon roads), are owned by the federal government and administered by the Bureau of Land Management, Department of Interior.

Further contributing to deconcentration, the Weyerhaeuser Timber Company sold approximately 250,000 acres of its timberland, chiefly to operating companies. In its initial years, Weyerhaeuser was primarily interested in holding timber and only later became an operating company. Similarly, the Northern Pacific Railroad Company sold approximately 522,000 acres of Washington timberland to operating companies.

THE SIGNIFICANCE OF CONCENTRATED TIMBER RESOURCE OWNERSHIP

From 1910 to 1953 concentration in timber resource ownership decreased. Then, under the impact of merger activity, concentration increased over the years 1953 to 1960. What is the significance of the observed degree and trend of concentration?

First, reversal of the recent trend toward increased concentra-

---

[10] Austin Cary, "Timber Ownership and Lumber Production in Douglas-Fir Region," unpublished manuscript prepared for U.S. Department of Agriculture (1917), p. 44 (on file in School of Forestry Library, University of California, Berkeley).

[11] *Timber Depletion, Lumber Prices, Lumber Exports, and Concentration of Timber Ownership*, U.S. Department of Agriculture, Forest Service Report on Senate Resolution 311 (Washington, 1920), p. 61.

[12] For a full description of the revesting procedure see Wesley C. Ballaine, "The Revested Oregon and California Railroad Grant Lands: A Problem in Land Management," *Land Economics*, XXIX (Aug., 1953), 219–232.

tion is probably unlikely. In contrast, the high degree of concentration around 1910 was the result of large land grants to railroads; some of the grants were disposed of, and a large one was revested by the federal government. As a result, concentration declined in the early years of this century. It appears that the present large timberland owners will remain as permanent operating companies, or some of them may be merged into other even larger firms presently operating in the region. In the latter event, concentration would be expected to increase further.

Second, concentration in timber resource ownership has more serious consequences than the same degree of concentration in industrial production, which is more distant along the production process from a limited resource base. For example, the four largest firms producing motors and generators account for 48 percent of total shipments of these products. But plants may be constructed by new firms entering the business of manufacturing motors and generators which, in turn, would develop new competition for the existing firms. Additional competition cannot be established in timberland ownership with equal ease. The amount of land devoted to timber production may be increased only by shifting land from farm or other uses. To produce a merchantable timber crop requires about fifty years on the best timber-growing sites in the Douglas fir region. Thus, new supply and new competition cannot be established either with equal ease or within a comparable time period.

Third, the eight largest timberland-owning firms are also periodic bidders and buyers of federal timber. The firms having substantial timberland holdings containing large quantities of mature timber may be in a preferred bidding position. Such firms have a timber reserve to supply their mills in the event that competition forces federal stumpage prices to high levels in a given sale. The firm without reserve timber may be forced to bid relatively high prices in order to keep its processing plants operating. Again, the firm with substantial reserves is in a position to take only the more favorable sales, resulting, perhaps, from less intense bidding competition. To the extent that timber and timberland holdings are concentrated, the benefits of the reserve supply are correspondingly concentrated. It should be noted that federal agencies have the power under the Small Business Act to exclude firms having more than 500 employees from bidding under the set-aside program.

Fourth, as shown in figure 8, stumpage prices developed from bidding for national forest timber have increased sharply in recent

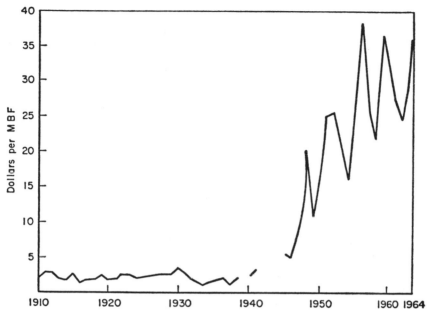

Fig. 8. Douglas fir stumpage prices, 1910–1964 (1964 data are for first six months only).

Source: U.S. Department of Agriculture, Forest Service and Commodity Stabilization Service, *The Demand and Price Situation for Forest Products* (Washington, Nov., 1964).

years. Firms holding timber over all or part of this period of rapid stumpage price increases have a substantial competitive advantage in lumber and other production.[13] In contrast, the firm currently buying federal stumpage must pay the current price, and such stumpage must be logged over a relatively short period of years. Because the cost of log input for the firm holding timber acquired before all or part of the recent price increase is much lower than for the firm currently buying federal stumpage, relatively large bookkeeping profits and cash flow may be earned by the former. The "weeding-out" function, by which a free enterprise economy eliminates the inefficient and rewards the efficient, is distorted to the extent that ownership of low-cost stumpage is concentrated.

---

[13] Firms owning timber acquired years earlier must, of course, pay annual property taxes on the land and timber held, must obtain a return on funds invested in timber resources or recognize the opportunity cost, and also must meet other charges of timber management such as protection costs. Except for imputed interest, these costs are deductible in computing income taxes on ordinary income subject to relatively high tax rates, whereas a capital gain was taxable at a rate not more than 25 percent during the period under study.

Fifth, on the other hand, the observed degree of concentration in timberland ownership is less significant owing to the availability of public timber. Further, it should be remembered that this study of timber resource concentration is restricted to the Douglas fir region, containing 37 percent of the nation's remaining sawtimber volume. Thus the observed degree of concentration implies no private monopoly control over log supplies for lumber and veneer-plywood production. Finally, the available evidence (see chapter 14, which is concerned with performance) indicates that the quality of timber resource management is positively correlated with owner-ship size classes: the larger the holding, the higher the quality of resource management.

THE STRUCTURE OF THE FEDERAL TIMBER MARKET

Relevant to the discussion of the extensive free market in timber, and the geographical limitations on and structure of a timber market, is the fact that public ownership accounts for 67.5 percent of the net volume of timber, and 44 percent of the log production, in the Douglas fir region. Of the public ownership log production, 69 percent is from lands administered by the Forest Service, and 23 percent is from Bureau of Land Management administered lands. The small remainder is from state, county, municipal, and Indian lands. The records for Forest Service and Bureau of Land Management sales are excellent. I have elected, however, to make an intensive analysis of Forest Service sales only. Conditions of sale by the two major agencies are very similar, and the relevant hypotheses can be adequately tested within the framework of Forest Service sales.

Within the Douglas fir region there are many potential and actual buyers of timber. In 1961 there were 532 active sawmills, 124 active veneer mills, and an unknown but large number of gyppo loggers. Nearly all these operators are potential bidders, yet an operator in northwest Washington would not compete for tim-ber in southwest Oregon. The geographical market for timber is very narrowly circumscribed as a result of the relatively low value of logs per unit of weight. The usual mode of transportation is by log truck. Log transportation charges can quickly equal the price of stumpage, thereby making an extended log haul economically unfeasible. For example, during the first quarter of 1962 the av-erage appraised price (the "fair market value," as estimated by the Forest Service) for timber sold in the Willamette National Forest was $20.57 per thousand board feet. At 15½ cents per mile per

thousand board feet, a 132-mile log haul would add a log transportation charge approximately equal to the estimated fair market
value of the stumpage, that is, double the stumpage cost. This additional charge, which the distant buyer must meet, normally would
effectively preclude competition against local buyers. Because of
low value per unit of weight, the market for logs is geographically
a very narrow one. As a consequence, buyers may be few in number, and the market structure may be that of an oligopsony despite
a large number of potential buyers within a lumber-producing
area such as the Douglas fir region.

Occasionally, truck transportation is combined with water
transportation when navigable waters are nearby. This situation
prevails in the Mount Hood National Forest as well as in some
others. The cost of moving logs in log rafts is substantially less than
truck transportation. For example, some logs from the Clackamas-
Sandy working circle of the Mount Hood National Forest are transported by truck approximately 50 miles to a log dump at Canby,
Oregon. By water transportation a small percent of the timber
from this working circle is transported as far away as Astoria, Oregon, an additional 136 miles northwest. The average cost per
thousand board feet per mile by this water transportation amounts
to only 4.2 cents, approximately one-fourth of the incremental
cost for the truck haul. Thus, where water transportation is available, the geographical market may be substantially increased, but
it still remains narrow compared with markets for other raw materials. As the geographical market is expanded, the potential bidders are increased in number, and a higher degree of competition
is likely to prevail.

An export market for logs has recently been revived, with Japan
being the principal country of destination. The immediate buyer
of timber continues to be one of the local operators. He may sort
logs for species valuable to the export trade and sell such species
to an exporter or directly to a Japanese importer. The revival of
the log export market has not enlarged the geographical market
consisting of the immediate buyers. Rather, it has created a more
profitable use for certain species and grades by adding a new
market. Where logs are exported, competition for federal timber
is more intense. The export possibility is limited to timber located
near a deepwater port.

Table 14, giving the volume of softwood log exports from 1961
through 1964, reveals the importance of the export market. Approximately 6 percent of the region's total log production is ex-

TABLE 14

SOFTWOOD LOG EXPORTS FROM OREGON AND WASHINGTON, 1961–1964
(IN THOUSANDS OF BOARD FEET)

Year	Total	Country of destination		
		Japan	Canada	South Korea
1961	335,675	328,116	6,775	129
1962	311,223	286,655	23,229	455
1963	709,178	638,722	51,216	17,582
1964	834,847	739,692	67,020	25,498

SOURCE: Thomas E. Hamilton, *Production, Prices, Employment and Trade in Pacific Northwest Forest Industries*, Pacific Northwest Forest and Range Experiment Station, U.S. Forest Service (Portland, Ore., 1965), p. 10.

ported. In 1964, 87 percent of the total log exports were destined for Japan, 8 percent for Canada, and the remaining 3 percent for South Korea.[14] Log exports in 1964 amounted to about 5 percent of total Oregon and Washington production.

The revival of the log export market means that secondary buyers for logs exist in an international market where low-cost water transportation is available. As a consequence, the export market has increased effective competition in certain timber markets. The initial buyers who compete in the markets for federal timber are still limited to a narrowly circumscribed area by the low-value, high-weight factor.

The record of timber sales for the year 1960 from national forests in the Douglas fir region provides a check on the foregoing analysis of the geographical limits on the log market. The data show the estimated distance from the sale location to the principal processing location used by the buyer. The data are the result of estimates made by timber sale administrators. Admittedly, it is not possible to know precisely where logs flow from a given sale. Timber buyers most frequently make two log "sorts" for the timber contained in any given sale and distribute the logs between two mills. Some buyers make more than two sorts. As a result, it is difficult or impossible to know with certainty where the logs are given their initial processing. Yet sale administrators are generally well informed about the processing facilities available in their area and about the customary log-flow pattern.

---

14 The substantial increase in log exports in 1963 and 1964 has led some economic interests in the lumber industry (both labor unions and millowners) to seek federal government restrictions on log exports from national forest timber sales. A "Save Our Logs Committee" petitioned the Secretary of Agriculture to establish export restrictions (*Western Timber Industry*, XV [Oct., 1964], pp. 1–2).

TABLE 15

WEIGHTED AVERAGE LOG HAUL AND PERCENT OF TOTAL TIMBER SALES VOLUME TRANSPORTED SELECTED DISTANCES, BY NATIONAL FOREST, DOUGLAS FIR REGION, 1960

National forest[a]	Percent of volume transported						Weighted average distance (in miles)[b]
	30 miles or less	31-40 miles	41-50 miles	51-60 miles	61-70 miles	More than 70 miles	
Gifford-Pinchot	69.9	5.9	11.0	.1	9.6	3.5	32.6
Mount Baker	1.1	30.1	17.4	12.9	32.4	6.1	56.1
Olympic	12.9	12.3	4.2	25.3	24.3	21.0	55.7
Rogue River	27.3	17.3	27.1	20.9	1.2	6.2	47.4
Siskiyou	53.5	21.5	18.8	4.9	1.3	··	30.8
Siuslaw	45.0	13.9	21.6	8.0	7.9	3.6	34.9
Snoqualmie	11.2	15.5	5.1	24.2	39.4	4.6	56.9
Umpqua	12.3	20.1	11.2	16.8	12.5	27.1	54.6
Willamette	62.3	33.2	3.7	.6	··	··	32.0
Average	36.7	20.2	12.7	10.8	11.5	8.1	42.8
Cumulative	36.7	56.9	69.6	80.4	91.9	100.0	

a No mileages recorded for Mount Hood.

b Estimated distance by sale has been weighted by volume to obtain weighted average distance.

SOURCE: Based on quarterly reports of U.S. Forest Service, "National Forest Advertised Timber Sales, Region 6," 1380 (2400) (Portland, Ore., 1960–1961).

The results of this analysis are shown in table 15. The weighted average log haul for all national forests within the Douglas fir region is 42.8 miles. But averages obscure much information. The table also shows that 36.7 percent of all volume sold was transported to mills within 30 miles of the timber location, that 69.6 percent was limited to a log haul of 50 miles or less, and that 91.9 percent was transported to primary processing mills within a 70-mile log haul. The empirical data clearly confirm the conclusions reached as a result of deductive reasoning: logs, having a relatively low value per unit of weight, have a relatively narrow market. Within a narrow market there may be, and often are, few buyers, even though the industry as a whole consists of so many independent firms that atomistic competition is approximated at the production level. Hereafter, a 75-mile radius from the location of a timber stand is regarded as the relevant timber market.

Data from the Olympic National Forest may be studied for information about the effect on the geographical market owing to the presence of water transportation to mills in the domestic market. Parts of the Olympic National Forest are restricted to land transportation, whereas others have access to the Hood Canal, Puget Sound, and Juan de Fuca Strait. Where only land transportation was available, the average log haul was 43 miles. Where combined land and water transportation was available, the average log haul was extended by 50 percent to 64 miles. The following generalization may be made: Where water transportation is available, we would expect the geographical market to be less restricted and bidding to be more competitive. Generalizing further, as a highway system is improved so as to reduce the cost of transportation for outsiders relative to insiders, the effective geographical market would be enlarged and competition would be more effective. Examples of such improvement are the building of a new road linking two relatively inaccessible drainages, and the opening of a freeway.

In narrowly circumscribed markets under transport constraints, competitors for national forest timber are likely to be limited to a few bidders. If so, the structural designation for the timber market is oligopsony. Data on 2,340 oral auction timber sales covering the four years 1959–1962 in the Douglas fir region indicate an average of only 4.2 bidders per sale.[15] Thus the data strongly

---

[15] The timber sale record is intensively analyzed in a later section concerned with performance of firms as buyers of timber. Data referred to above are shown in table 24.

indicate an oligopsonistic structure for the national forest timber markets.

SUMMARY

The present degree of concentration in resource ownership within the Douglas fir region is low relative to concentration ratios elsewhere in the American economy. The Big Four and Big Eight timberland owners in 1960 held 26.2 and 34.1 percent, respectively, of all private commercial forest land in the region. Within these concentration ratios, the largest firm held a dominant position. The largest private timberland owner holds nearly half of the Big Eight ownership and one-sixth of all private commercial forest land.

The trend of concentration in timber resource ownership passed through two phases between 1910 and 1960. It is clear that a significant degree of deconcentration took place from the early part of the twentieth century to its midpoint. This period is characterized by shifting timberland from land-grant railroads and timber-holding interests to operating companies. The period from 1953 to 1960 shows a reversal in trend of concentration ratios. It is characterized by an intensive merger movement, with operating companies attempting to gather together large blocks of timber and timberland to sustain heavy investments in utilization facilities.

Five points were discussed regarding the significance of the trend and of the present degree of concentration in timber resource ownership. First, the character of present ownership makes a reversal of recent trends unlikely. Second, any given degree of economic concentration in natural resources may be more serious than the same degree of concentration in manufacturing, as the latter is more likely to be subject to erosion through new entry and product differentiation. Third, given the very narrow geographical markets for timber, concentrated ownership of private timber carries with it concentrated advantages in bidding for federal timber. A firm with large reserves of private timber is able to pass up high-cost timber sales. A firm without such reserves may be forced to buy timber at any price up to the point where variable costs of operations are no longer covered. Fourth, where historically low-cost timber reserves are concentrated in few hands, and nontimber owners must pay currently high out-of-pocket stumpage prices, the weeding-out function of a free enterprise system is distorted. Fifth, on the other hand, the presence of large timber reserves in public ownership frees the market from an element of monopoly control of timber resources. Thus the availability of public timber reserves under auction conditions, together with the presence of timber resources in other parts of the nation, establishes that private monopoly control of resources for lumber and plywood production is not an issue. Also, effective timber management appears to be positively correlated with ownership size classes.

Timber markets are geographically circumscribed as a consequence of the relatively low value of timber per unit of weight. The record indicates that about 92 percent of national forest log production goes to primary processors within 70 miles of the timber sale. Bidders for national forest timber within each of the narrow markets are few in number, averaging 4.2 bidders per sale. As a consequence of geographically narrow markets, the appropriate structural designation for timber-buying markets is oligopsony.

In some areas, oligopsonists face a federal monopolist. In other areas, both the Forest Service and the BLM administer public lands, and a duopoly prevails. In yet other areas, there are some nonpublic sellers of timber. A public monopoly or duopoly does not raise the usual problems of the profit-maximizing noncompetitive seller. Real problems may be created for private buyers, however, when the public seller in a monopoly position acts arbitrarily. This problem is beyond the scope of this study.

CHAPTER 5

Economic Concentration in Lumber Production and Wholesale Distribution

The objectives of this chapter are to identify the structure of the lumber industry at the output level and to show the changes taking place in structure over time. Realization of these two objectives, which are important for their own sake, will assist in an analysis of the relationship between structure, conduct, and performance. Also of interest is the impact of the merger movement on structure.

The reader should be reminded that the concept of Douglas fir region lumber production as an industry is subject to serious shortcomings. By following the convention of excluding the redwood region of northwestern California, which produces a significant volume of the same species of softwood construction lumber as the Douglas fir region, an error of omission is introduced. There is obviously a high degree of substitution between Douglas fir lumber, on the one hand, and ponderosa pine or southern pine on the other. Further, imports of softwood construction lumber from Canada are of significant volume. The degree of substitution is relatively high compared, for example, with substitution of brick or aluminum for lumber as alternative building materials. As previously pointed out, there is a national market for lumber, although considerable geographical specialization follows from the importance of freight rates.

The analysis may begin with a study of the degree of concentration in the national market, followed by a similar analysis of the Douglas fir region. The regional analysis is undertaken, despite technical shortcomings in the regional industry concept, because the relationship between mergers and dropouts in the regional industry and the resulting structure must be understood; because the rapidly changing structure of the regional lumber industry is related to the problem of maintaining competition for regional federal timber; and because, in several respects, the Douglas fir sector of the lumber industry is a homogeneous and distinct part of the whole. This region contains the largest remaining concentration of old-growth timber, with its distinctive logging technology. Freight rate controversies often pit this small region, with its relatively large share of the total lumber market, against other regions. The geographically concentrated lumber industry dominates the regional economy more than it does in other important lumber-producing areas. Climatic, soil, and topographical conditions are so favorable to timber growth in this region that important segments of the industry think in terms of "perpetual" operations based on tree farming. Finally, people in the Douglas fir region consider their segment of the total lumber industry to be a separate industry.

ECONOMIC CONCENTRATION
IN THE UNITED STATES LUMBER INDUSTRY

The prime source of national data on industrial concentration is the Bureau of the Census. From this source, data are available by industries and, since 1954, by product classes. Using the newer product classification approach, table 16 shows a very low degree of economic concentration accounted for by the four, eight, and twenty largest firms in lumber production. In the "sawmill and planing-mill products" classification, the Big Four accounted for only 8 percent of the total value of 1958 shipments. Of 426 four-digit product classes studied, only five have lower concentration ratios for the four largest firms than those for the sawmill and planing-mill products class. In terms of the eight and twenty largest firms, only two product classes have lower concentration ratios than sawmill and planing-mill products. The two with lower concentration ratios are fur goods and women's suits, coats, and skirts.[1] The softwood plywood industry is only slightly less competitive in structure than lumber.

In order to establish a norm, concentration ratios in industries producing products competitive with lumber were examined. Table 16 shows that only "concrete block and brick" among the building materials industries has a more competitive structure,

---

[1] *Concentration in American Industry*, U.S. Senate, Committee of the Judiciary, 85th Cong., 1st sess. (Washington, 1957), pp. 133–165.

ECONOMIC CONCENTRATION IN THE NATIONAL LUMBER INDUSTRY AND IN PRODUCTS
COMPETING WITH LUMBER, 1958

Industry code	Class of product	Percent of value of shipments by		
		Four largest companies	Eight largest companies	Twenty largest companies
2421	Sawmill and planing-mill products	8	12	a
24211	Rough lumber and sawed ties	4	7	12
24212	Dressed lumber	12	17	25
2432	Veneer and plywood	16	23	34
24322	Softwood plywood, interior type	18	29	48
24323	Softwood plywood, exterior type	28	42	64
32751	Gypsum building materials	87	97	99
32112	Plate glass and other flat glass	a	a	100
3251	Brick and structural tile	13	20	33
32710	Concrete block and brick	3	5	10
33124	Steel productsb	64	76	89
34411	Fabricated structural iron and steel for buildings	19	23	33
3334	Primary aluminum	82	90	a

a Data not available.

b Hot rolled bars and bar shapes, plates, structural shapes and piling.

SOURCE: U.S. Senate, Committee of the Judiciary, *Concentration Ratios in Manufacturing Industry, 1958*, 87th Cong., 2d sess. (Washington, 1962), Pt. I, pp. 121–145.

but this industry sells in regional markets rather than in a national market. The average concentration ratio for the industries shown is far in excess of that prevailing in the lumber industry, ranging as high as 100 percent of all product shipment value accounted for by the "Big Twenty" in the plate-glass industry.

The industry classification is more commonly employed by the Bureau of Census as a measure of industrial concentration. Comparison over time is possible for the lumber industry for the years 1947 and 1958. Data for the lumber industry before 1947 are not comparable with 1947 or later data because the system of industrial classification was changed.

The data in table 17 indicate a clear increase in concentration ratios for the lumber industry. The four largest producers in the sawmill and planing-mill category increased their share of the market from 5 to 8 percent between 1947 and 1958, still an extremely low degree of economic concentration. Over the same period of time, an interesting deconcentration is shown for veneer and plywood plants. In 1947 plywood production was still in its early stage of growth. By 1954 knowledge of technology had spread widely,

TABLE 17

CONCENTRATION RATIOS FOR LUMBER, VENEER, AND PLYWOOD, 1947, 1954, AND 1958

Industry code and classification	Year	Number of companies	Value of shipments (in millions of dollars)	Concentration ratios (in percent of total value of shipments)		
				Four largest firms	Eight largest firms	Twenty largest firms
2421: Sawmills and planing mills	1958	15,731	3,046	8	12	18
	1954	16,394	3,247	7	11	18
	1947	19,223	2,519	5	7	11
2422: Veneer mills	1958	273	169	11	19	35
	1954	252	121	9	15	30
	1947	136	67	20	31	52
2432: Plywood plants	1958	271	724	19	28	42
	1954	219	515	17	25	42
	1947	142	272	22	34	56

SOURCE: U.S. Senate, Committee of the Judiciary, *Concentration Ratios in Manufacturing Industry, 1958*, 87th Cong., 2d sess. (Washington, 1962), Pt. I, p. 19.

and a multitude of small operations had commenced production. Production (value of shipments) had increased nearly 2 fold by 1954 and, by 1958, 2.6 fold. Entry into veneer and plywood production requires a relatively small amount of capital, products are not widely differentiated by brand names, and all producers have access to wholesalers for distribution of their product. Many operations limited to lumber in 1947 had become partially integrated by 1958 to include veneer and possibly plywood plants.

More current structural information is provided by data collected for the *Directory of the Forest Products Industry*. Reasonably accurate data on lumber production by firms in selected years between 1947 and 1963 are shown in table 18. For the United States lumber industry as a whole, the increase in concentration from 1947 to 1954 was rather modest. In the ensuing six years, however, there was a sharp increase in concentration. From 1960 to 1963 no further significant change occurred. Compared with other industries by means of concentration ratios, the lumber industry remains one of the most competitive in the United States economy, notwithstanding the accelerated merger movement of the 1950's and the consequent significant increase in concentration ratios. The ratios for the eight largest and the twenty largest lumber-producing firms are correspondingly modest, although both show significant increases over the sixteen-year period from 1947 to 1963.

ECONOMIC CONCENTRATION IN THE DOUGLAS FIR LUMBER INDUSTRY

Table 18 shows that in 1947 the Big Four producers accounted for only 15.9 percent of the region's total lumber production. By 1954 this degree of economic concentration had risen only slightly, to 16.6 percent. But in the next six years, owing to the impact of the merger movement, the concentration ratio for the Big Four increased to 23.9 percent. Since 1960 mergers of firms in the Douglas fir region have been relatively modest. Furthermore, some of the large, older mills acquired through mergers during the 1950's were closed between 1960 and 1963, with the result that concentration ratios in lumber production in the region declined substantially. The decline in concentration among the Big Four, from 23.9 percent in 1960 to 19.7 percent in 1963, can be attributed mainly to mill closures within two companies, Georgia Pacific Corporation and U.S. Plywood Corporation, both members of the Big Four in 1960. Mill closures by the former company reduced lumber production by 60 percent, and closures by the latter resulted in a 50

TABLE 18

Economic Concentration in the Lumber Industry, 1947, 1954, 1960, and 1963

Area and year	Four largest producers		Eight largest producers		Twenty largest producers		Total Production[a]
	Production[a]	Percent of total	Production[a]	Percent of total	Production[a]	Percent of total	
Douglas fir region							
1963	1,591	19.7	2,067	25.7	2,995	37.2	8,057
1960	1,936	23.9	2,379	29.4	3,292	40.6	8,100
1954	1,538	16.6	2,055	22.1	2,931	31.6	9,283
1947	1,429	15.9	1,847	20.6	2,688	30.0	8,962
United States							
1963	3,190	9.2	4,279	12.4	6,185	17.9	34,586
1960	3,021	9.2	4,104	12.5	5,872	17.9	32,880
1954	1,846	5.1	2,528	7.0	3,874	10.7	36,356
1947	1,687	4.8	2,274	6.4	3,471	9.8	35,404

a In millions of board feet.

SOURCE: Developed from annual issues of *Directory of Forest Products Industry* (Seattle: Miller Freeman Publications).

percent reduction in lumber production. Within the remaining sixteen firms in the Big Twenty group, there was no substantial change in concentration between 1960 and 1963.

The trend in concentration may also be appraised by means of the Herfindahl Index, $H = \Sigma s^2$, where s is the share of industry output accounted for by each firm in the industry. This index increased from .011 in 1947 to .026 in 1960, and then declined to .023 in 1963. Even at its peak, this degree of concentration in production is of little economic significance.

The information about the Douglas fir region in table 18 is a summary of the more detailed information in tables 19–22. The latter show the dynamic shifts in composition of the twenty largest firms. Throughout the period Weyerhaeuser has dominated the regional lumber industry. This firm, often called the "Big W," produced seven times as much lumber as its closest rival in the re-

TABLE 19

PRODUCTION BY TWENTY LARGEST LUMBER-PRODUCING FIRMS IN THE
DOUGLAS FIR REGION, 1947

Rank	Firm	Production (in millions of board feet)	Share of regional production (in percent)	Cumulative share of regional production (in percent)
1	Weyerhaeuser Timber Co.	780	8.8	8.8
2	Long-Bell Lumber Co.	291	3.2	12.0
3	Pope and Talbot, Inc.	186	2.1	14.1
4	Coos Bay Timber Co.	162	1.8	15.9
5	C. D. Johnson Lumber Corp.	123	1.4	17.3
6	Irwin and Lyons, Inc.	108	1.2	18.5
7	Inman-Poulson Timber Co.	93	1.0	19.5
8	Gardiner Lumber Co.	93	1.0	20.5
9	Santiam Lumber Co.	93	1.0	21.5
10	Shepard and Morse Lumber Co.	90	1.0	22.5
11	Willamette Valley Lumber Co.	81	0.9	23.4
12	Medford Corp.	77	0.9	24.3
13	Oregon American Lumber Corp.	72	0.8	25.1
14	Schafer Bros. Lumber Shingle Co.	72	0.8	25.9
15	St. Paul and Tacoma Lumber Co.	69	0.8	26.7
16	West Oregon Lumber Co.	64	0.7	27.4
17	Roseburg Lumber Co.	59	0.7	28.1
18	Walton Lumber Co., Inc.	57	0.6	28.7
19	Edward Hines Lumber Co.	55	0.6	29.3
20	Rosboro Lumber Co.	53	0.6	30.0

SOURCE: Developed from directories of forest industries published by *The Lumberman* and *The Timberman*, Portland, Oregon.

TABLE 20

PRODUCTION BY TWENTY LARGEST LUMBER-PRODUCING FIRMS IN THE
DOUGLAS FIR REGION, 1954

Rank	Firm	Production (in millions of board feet)	Share of regional production (in percent)	Cumulative share of regional production (in percent)
1	Weyerhaeuser Timber Co.	900	9.7	9.7
2	Long-Bell Lumber Co.	282	3.0	12.7
3	Pope and Talbot, Inc.	190	2.0	14.7
4	Coos Bay Timber Co.	165	1.8	16.5
5	Georgia-Pacific Corp.	147	1.6	18.1
6	Willamette Valley Lumber Co.	146	1.6	19.7
7	Roseburg Lumber Co.	130	1.4	21.1
8	Santiam Lumber Co.	95	1.0	22.1
9	Rainier Manufacturing Co.	89	1.0	23.1
10	Simpson Logging Co.	87	0.9	24.0
11	Irwin and Lyons, Inc.	85	0.9	24.9
12	Ross Lumber Co.	79	0.8	25.7
13	Medford Corp.	76	0.8	26.5
14	Diamond Lumber Co.	71	0.8	27.3
15	Edward Hines Lumber Co.	70	0.7	28.0
16	St. Paul and Tacoma Lumber Co.	68	0.7	28.7
17	LHL Lumber Co.	65	0.7	29.4
18	Clemens Forest Products, Inc.	63	0.7	30.1
19	Robert Dollar Co.	62	0.7	30.8
20	Booth-Kelly Lumber Co.	60	0.6	31.4

SOURCE: Developed from directories of forest industries published by *The Lumberman* and *The Timberman*, Portland, Oregon.

gion. In the national market, Weyerhaeuser's 1963 production (1,263 million board feet) was nearly twice that of the second-largest lumber producer, Georgia Pacific. Yet, when Weyerhaeuser, as the largest firm in the lumber industry, is compared with the dominant firm in other major industries, it becomes apparent that even the largest firm occupies an insignificant share of the total lumber market; Weyerhaeuser's share of the national market is only 3.7 percent.

Tables 19–22 also reveal the role of mergers in the changing composition of the Big Twenty firms. Of the firms in this group in 1947, eight were absorbed by other firms, and three firms on the 1954 list were similarly absorbed. Four firms on the 1947 list closed down as their timber was liquidated, six remained on the list through 1963, and only two dropped out of the Big Twenty group but remained as substantial producers. The findings reported in

A. D. H. Kaplan's study of the changing composition of big business would lead one to expect that more than two out of twenty firms might have dropped from the list because of reduced production.[2] A chain of mergers is identifiable. Gardiner Lumber Company and Oregon American Lumber Corporation, appearing as numbers 8 and 13, respectively, on the 1947 list, were absorbed into Long-Bell, number 2 on the 1954 list. Long-Bell was, in turn, merged into International Paper Company and became number 16 on the 1960 list.

Preoccupation with the four, eight, and twenty largest firms tends to obscure other dynamic changes that have taken place in the industrial structure of the Douglas fir lumber industry. The most significant changes occurred in the small-mill class; although a

TABLE 21

PRODUCTION BY TWENTY LARGEST LUMBER-PRODUCING FIRMS IN THE
DOUGLAS FIR REGION, 1960

Rank	Firm	Production (in millions of board feet)	Share of regional production (in percent)	Cumulative share of regional production (in percent)
1	Weyerhaeuser Co.	1,187	14.6	14.6
2	Georgia-Pacific Corp.	350	4.3	18.9
3	United States Plywood Corp.	221	2.7	21.6
4	Pope and Talbot, Inc.	178	2.2	23.8
5	Simpson Timber Co.	124	1.5	25.3
6	Willamette Valley Lumber Co.	119	1.5	26.8
7	Rainier Manufacturing Co.	106	1.3	28.1
8	Stomar Lumber Co.	93	1.2	29.3
9	Santiam Lumber Co.	91	1.1	30.4
10	Roseburg Lumber Co.	90	1.1	31.5
11	Coos Head Timber Co.	88	1.1	32.6
12	Edward Hines Lumber Co.	86	1.1	33.7
13	Olson-Lawyer Lumber, Inc.	84	1.0	34.7
14	St. Regis Paper Co.	79	1.0	35.7
15	Medford Corp.	79	1.0	36.7
16	International Paper Co.	72	0.9	37.6
17	Timber Products Co.	67	0.8	38.4
18	Steve Wilson Co.	63	0.8	39.2
19	Mountain Fir Lumber Co.	58	0.7	39.9
20	Clemens Forest Products, Inc.	57	0.7	40.6

SOURCE: Developed from directories of forest industries published by *The Lumberman* and *The Timberman*, Portland, Oregon.

---

[2] A. D. H. Kaplan, *Big Enterprise in a Competitive System* (Washington: Brookings Institution, 1954), pp. 132–155.

TABLE 22
PRODUCTION BY TWENTY LARGEST LUMBER-PRODUCING FIRMS IN THE
DOUGLAS FIR REGION, 1963

Rank	Firm	Production (in millions of board feet)	Share of regional production (in percent)	Cumulative share of regional production (in percent)
1	Weyerhaeuser Co.	1,142	14.2	14.2
2	Pope and Talbot Inc.	162	2.0	16.2
3	Simpson Timber Co.	148	1.8	18.0
4	Georgia Pacific Corp.	139	1.7	19.7
5	International Paper Co.	136	1.7	21.4
6	Willamette Valley Lumber Co.	115	1.4	22.9
7	Rainier Manufacturing Co.	113	1.4	24.3
8	Coos Head Timber Co.	112	1.4	25.7
9	U.S. Plywood Corp.	110	1.4	27.0
10	Santiam Lumber Co.	92	1.1	28.2
11	Roseburg Lumber Co.	90	1.1	29.3
12	Mountain Fir Lumber Co.	89	1.1	30.4
13	Edward Hines Lumber Co.	80	0.9	31.4
14	Olson-Lawyer Lumber Co.	73	0.9	32.3
15	Al Pierce Lumber Co.	72	0.9	33.2
16	South Coast Lumber Co.	70	0.9	34.0
17	Bohemia Lumber Co.	66	0.8	34.9
18	Cascadia Lumber Co.	63	0.8	35.6
19	Larson Lumber Co.	62	0.8	36.4
20	Diamond Lumber Co.	61	0.8	37.2

SOURCE: Developed from directories of forest industries published by *The Lumberman* and *The Timberman*, Portland, Oregon.

large number of firms left the industry, the effect on the total output or the share accounted for by the largest firms was small. Figure 9 graphically illustrates the changes that took place from 1948 to 1962, involving principally small mills in the Douglas fir region. Production in 1962 was 14 percent below the 1948 level. But the 1948 output was produced by 1,675 mills in the Douglas fir region, whereas the 1962 output was produced by only 493 mills. The disappearance of 1,182 mills over this period represents a decline of 71 percent in number of producing units. Almost the entire disappearance is accounted for by small mills—class D mills, producing less than 40,000 board feet per eight-hour shift. In 1948, 1,328 class D sawmills were in production, whereas in 1962 there were only 202; the disappearance of 1,126 mills represents an 85 percent decline.

Medium-small mills—class C mills, producing between 40,000

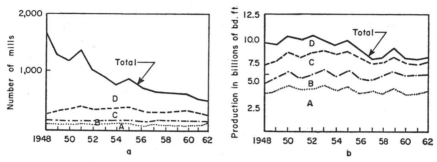

Fig. 9. Number of and production by sawmills in the Douglas fir region by size class, 1948–1962.

SOURCE: Developed from data supplied by West Coast Lumbermens Association.

and 80,000 board feet per eight-hour shift—declined modestly from 191 in 1948 to 128 in 1963, or by 33 percent. Clearly, the sharp decline in small mills is not accounted for by an expansion in output, which would reclassify them as medium-small.

Medium-large mills—class B mills, producing 80,000 to 120,000 board feet per eight-hour shift—increased by twenty-four mills from fifty-three in 1948 to seventy-seven in 1963. This 45 percent increase may be accounted for in part by the fact that some class C mills expanded output and shifted into class B.

Large mills—class A mills, producing 120,000 board feet or more per eight-hour shift—declined by 17 percent, from 103 mills in 1948 to 86 in 1960. As the medium-small, medium-large, and large mills declined in total number, it is likely that most small mills ceased production entirely instead of shifting to a larger class. The strong decline in number of active sawmills is not accounted for by merger activity. The data shown are not influenced by merger activity, as they refer to plants rather than to firms. There is a minor exception to this generalization: if a mill is closed down because of a merger, its timber may be used to supply existing plants of the acquiring firm.[3]

The exceedingly high dropout rate among small firms, in conjunction with the merger movement of the 1950's, has helped to raise concentration ratios in lumber production. The two forces in combination have not created a situation either in the national lumber industry or in the Douglas fir segment of it which repre-

---

[3] In chapter 1, concerned with economies of scale, the inability of small and very large firms to survive in competitive markets was accepted as evidence of inefficiency.

sents a significant departure from a highly competitive structure. Before drawing final conclusions concerning the competitive structure of the lumber industry at the output level, however, we must briefly examine the structure of wholesale lumber distribution. It is conceivable that a competitive structure at the production level might be thwarted by economic concentration in wholesale lumber distribution.

ECONOMIC CONCENTRATION
IN WHOLESALE LUMBER DISTRIBUTION

Knowledge of the structure of the wholesale lumber distributing function is important for at least two reasons. First, if this function is served by a few enterprisers (an oligopoly) with barriers to entry into the business, it would be possible for the few to exploit the many lumber producers. Second, even though a high degree of competition prevails at the production level, oligopoly at the wholesale level can produce oligopolistic effects for consumers of lumber. A collusive oligopoly at the wholesale level would be able to establish noncompetitive wholesaler markups and pass the cost on to consumers and/or back to producers.

Figure 10 shows the multitude of possible routes that lumber may take between its production and final consumption. About 85 percent of all the Douglas fir region lumber production moves through independent wholesalers. These firms take title to the lumber and extend normal trade credits. The so-called Western wholesalers maintain close contact with supplying mills, buying from them and, in turn, selling to Eastern wholesalers who have relatively close contacts with distribution yards, retailers, and large consumers. The Western wholesaler also may sell directly to the same level of customers to which the Eastern wholesaler attempts to sell; or the Western wholesaler may utilize the services of a commission man who, in turn, is a step closer to the ultimate consumer.

About 7 percent of total Douglas fir region lumber production is sold directly to distribution yards where lumber inventories are maintained, or is sold directly to retailers. An estimated 5 percent of regional production is sold through commission men who do not take title to lumber and generally do not extend credit, but rather operate on a commission that seems to vary between 1 and 2 dollars per thousand board feet. The remaining approximately 3 percent of production is sold directly to consumers, including contractors and industrial users.

The wholesaling function is a highly fluid business. Two well-informed observers have estimated widely differing numbers of

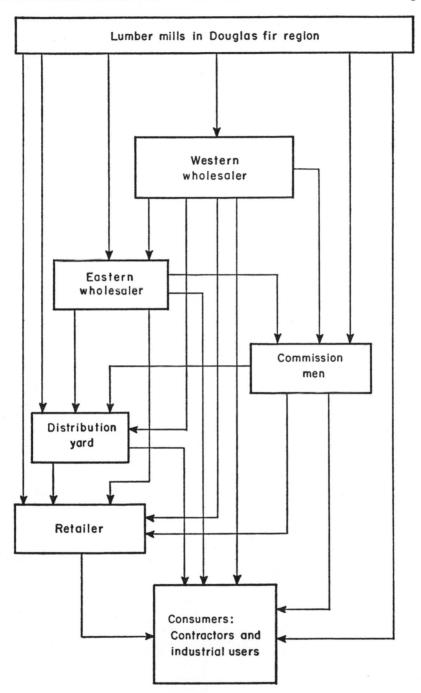

Fig. 10. Organization of lumber distribution.

wholesalers and commission men actively engaged in lumber distribution. One estimated there are about 1,500 Western and Eastern wholesalers operating in the United States and that about 800 commission men are actively in business; the other estimated there are 5,000 to 6,000 wholesalers and 300 to 400 commission men. One source of the disparity in estimates is that there are no precise definitions of wholesalers, commission men, and retailers. Wholesalers also commonly perform a commission service. Retailers may attempt to operate as wholesalers, and wholesalers may do a retail business. Regardless of which estimate approximates the true universe, the industry is clearly not made up of a few operators with rigid barriers to entry. One wholesaler complained that "all it takes to enter this business is a telephone, a ditto machine, and $10,000 to $20,000 of working capital." Anyone can get on mailing lists to receive offerings from mills and can, in turn, send out price lists to potential buyers. Entry is free and easy to anyone, including a lumber producer who may feel that he can perform the wholesaling function at a cost saving.

SUMMARY

The United States lumber industry and the Douglas fir segment of it have highly competitive structures at both production and wholesale distribution levels. The merger movement of the 1950's, in conjunction with an uncommonly high dropout rate among smaller firms, resulted in a substantial increase in concentration ratios between 1947 and 1960. In the Douglas fir region, however, there was a slight decline in concentration between 1960 and 1963, the result of closure of some large sawmills previously acquired by mergers among the largest firms. The observed structural features suggest competitive conduct in lumber markets and an attractive performance record in the industry. The impressive decline in the number of sawmills unless offset by an increase in the number of veneer mills, suggests increasing difficulty in maintaining competitive conditions in the federal timber markets of the Douglas fir region.

CHAPTER 6

Conditions of Entry
into the Lumber Industry

The classical economic theory of competition assumes free entry into competitive industries. Given free entry, the temporary market conditions that produced attractive rates of return would, in turn, induce firms already in the industry to expand production and would induce others to enter the industry with new production. Under these conditions, long-run profits could never exceed the competitive rate of return required to keep capital fully employed.

An analysis of the conditions of entry is concerned with "potential competition" from sources other than existing producers. The degree to which there is freedom of entry may be measured by the degree to which the actual rate of return in the long run exceeds the competitive rate of return. The most comprehensive piece of research concerned with conditions of entry, Joe Bain's *Barriers to New Competition*,[1] analyzes (1) the circumstances giving rise to absolute cost advantages for established firms; (2) the circumstances giving rise to product differentiation advantages for established firms; and (3) the circumstances discouraging entry by reason of significant economies of large-scale production and distribution. This framework of analysis is employed here in examining the conditions of entry into the Douglas fir lumber industry.

Absolute Cost Advantages

The circumstances giving rise to absolute cost advantages for established firms may consist of the following: (1) Control of production techniques by established firms, including patents, secrecy, and discriminatory royalty charges for the use of patented pro-

---

[1] Joe S. Bain, *Barriers to New Competition* (Cambridge: Harvard University Press, 1956).

cesses. (2) Imperfections in the market for factors of production, allowing lower supply prices to established firms. (3) Significant limitation of supplies of productive factors relative to the demands of an efficient entrant into the industry. (4) High absolute capital requirements for entry into the industry, perhaps also involving relatively unfavorable money-market conditions.

Control of production techniques by established firms.—The lumber industry is an "old industry" characterized by relatively few revolutionary changes in production methods. One manager describes the industry as being like a department store window: anybody can walk by and look in. If their curiosity persists, observers may venture inside the plant and freely examine the contents of the showcase. New machinery frequently comes from the machine shop of the millwright and is rarely patented. Successful innovations are normally reproduced by other millwrights and may be formalized in mass production by an equipment manufacturer. With few patents and little secrecy, subjection of machinery or process use to royalty charges is rarely found in the lumber industry. Control of production techniques is not a factor limiting entry into the lumber industry.

Imperfections in the market for factors of production.—There are substantial imperfections in the market for only one factor of production required by lumber mills. As has been pointed out, timber resources are increasingly concentrated in secure ownerships. Large stands seldom become available to the market, particularly since the mergers consummated in the 1950's. There are no "undiscovered" timber stands in the United States. Market imperfection in industries using natural resources is a frequent barrier to entry in such industries. Effective entry into integrated steel production, for example, would be possible "only if the entrant could secure or have assured to him an adequate supply of iron ore"[2] Similarly, entry into copper production is limited by resource availability. Although timber resources are becoming increasingly concentrated, neither present conditions nor those in the foreseeable future approach the degree of concentration at present existing in either steel or copper. As of January 1, 1963, 49.1 percent of all commercial forest lands in the Douglas fir region were in public ownership. Excepting the Shelton Cooperative Sustained Yield Unit in the Shelton working circle of the Olympic National Forest, all federal timber is sold to the highest qualified bidder. In

---

2 *Ibid.*, p. 153.

the Shelton exception, timber controlled by the Forest Service is joined with timber owned by Simpson Timber Company and dedicated, under a 100-year agreement, to supplying the integrated processing facilities of Simpson Timber Company. In the United States there are, in addition, five federal sustained-yield units in which bidding for federal timber is limited to firms qualified by inclusion within geographical boundaries of a given community. One such restricted bidding unit exists in the Douglas fir region near Grays Harbor, Washington. Further, bidding is somewhat restricted when public timber is offered as set-aside sales. Bidding for these offerings is limited to firms having fewer than 500 employees. All cooperative sustained-yield units, federal sustained-yield units, and set-aside sales combined account for only a minor share of the federal timber supply. The presence of large reserves of public timber managed on a conservative basis will presumably always offer a potential entrant access to a log supply.

Although the source of logs seems assured for a potential entrant, cost factors are less favorable. In connection with the analysis of scale economies, I have already shown that firms owning large reserves of old-growth timber have a very substantial absolute advantage in raw-material cost. The original cost of timber to the Weyerhaeuser Company in 1900 was estimated at 10 cents per thousand board feet, whereas the 1959–1962 average out-of-pocket cost of timber purchased from the national forests of the Douglas fir region was about 24 dollars per thousand board feet.

Absolute cost advantages for timber resources are also realized by existing firms that acquired their timber more recently. As pointed out earlier, Georgia Pacific Corporation holds timber valued in its accounting record at 10 dollars per thousand feet "without assigning any value to either the land or the young growth." Pope and Talbot owns a smaller amount of timber than either Georgia Pacific or Weyerhaeuser, but at cost conditions approaching those of Weyerhaeuser Company. Pope and Talbot management refers to its low-cost timber as its "gold nuggets." These gold nuggets may be harvested in varying amounts over time so long as they last, allowing the company to show an operating profit higher than would be possible if open-market logs were the only source.

Accounting convention does not normally permit revision upward of capital assets to reflect rising economic values. If realistic present values were capitalized, the gain in economic value would be shown as a capital gain rather than as an operating profit. The

absolute cost advantage presently appearing in profit and loss statements would either disappear or be substantially reduced. One
important competitive fact would remain, however. For the entrant, the cost of timber is an out-of-pocket cost (a cash cost),
whereas the established firm using its own timber incurs only an
accounting cost plus certain out-of-pocket costs of holding timber
assets.

Low-cost timber further allows its owner certain bidding advantages vis-à-vis other firms that must obtain all their timber at current market values. A firm without privately owned timber is
vulnerable by reason of its not having a timber reserve to supply
its mills in event of failure to obtain a given federal timber sale.
Further, timber sales acquired at current high market prices may
be offset by low-cost privately owned timber where the existing
firms have low-cost ownership. In contrast, the firm without timber
resources of its own has no similarly offsetting low-cost timber to
"sweeten" the accounting statement of profit and loss. Thus, while
it is true that potential entrants may bid and perhaps buy public
timber for a current cash cost, there is a substantial absolute cost
disadvantage in current cost auction market timber.[3]

In an area where the demand for timber is approximately equal
to the supply from all sources (where there is excess capacity), an
outsider attempting to secure a share of the fixed supply may encounter serious problems. In the South Santiam working circle of
the Willamette National Forest, one outsider has been attempting
to obtain federal timber since 1954. During a period extending
through 1962, he succeeded in obtaining only three sales, two of
which were sealed-bid sales. He claims to have lost more than a
quarter of a million dollars in his attempt to gain entry into the
working circle. An attitude commonly encountered in interview-
ing established buyers within a specific area is that, given an existing excess milling capacity, the established firms prohibit entry
by not allowing outsiders to successfully bid for timber or, alternatively, by making entry very expensive through forcing them to
pay a high auction price. As demonstrated earlier, a single firm
with a substantial quantity of its own low-cost timber can afford
to sustain a few high-cost auction purchases without substantially

---

[3] The opportunity cost of timber owned in fee and utilized in one's own mill is
indicated by the value of the next-best alternative use of such resources. This value
would be approximated by current bid prices for federal stumpage and adjusted for
such factors as road construction, transportation, quality differentials, etc. Opportunity costs should be used for appraising efficiency and making certain management
decisions. But, in considering short-term survivability, cash flows are more relevant.

affecting the profit and loss statement. Whereas any firm may bid
for federal timber, it does not follow that such timber may be obtained at prices that will afford entry and profitable operations to
the outsider. Absolute cost advantages may therefore accrue to established firms, especially to those well endowed with low-cost
timber within their own ownership.

Significant factor supply limitations.—A limited timber supply
relative to milling capacity of an optimum-size entrant further
limits entry into the industry. As noted earlier (see chap. 1), optimum plant efficiency requires production within the range of
60,000 to 140,000 board feet per eight-hour day, or up to 280,000
feet on a two-shift basis. On an annual output basis, the optimum
range varies from 20 to 60 million feet. As a maximum, this is
only 0.74 percent of total lumber production from the Douglas fir
region and is hence an insignificant increase in the total demand
for sawlogs. The low-value, high-weight factor, however, severely
restricts the geographical market for timber (see chap. 4). The impact of entry by an optimum-size firm must be gauged against
timber available within a manufacturing area substantially smaller
than the Douglas-fir region. The entry of an optimum firm de-
manding 60 million feet per year from the Oakridge working circle
of the Willamette National Forest would increase the quantity of
timber demanded in this major area by 34 percent of its annual
allowable cut. But the supply of timber is relatively inelastic (see
chap. 3). Although the total log supply is large relative to the needs
of an optimum-size mill, such additional competition would substantially increase the demand for limited timber within its prac-
tical operating area. As a consequence of a substantial increase in
demand and an inelastic supply function, the price of log input
would increase significantly unless comparable existing capacity
disappears from the market. Thus, given the narrow geographical
market and optimum firm size, new entry may be impeded because
of its significant impact on the factor market.

Capital requirements for entry.—A high capital requirement to
establish a new plant may constitute a barrier to entry, particularly
if interest costs or equity capital costs for new financing are high
relative to the cost of capital for existing firms. Conversely, very
low capital requirements render entry into such an industry accessible to a correspondingly large number of potential entrants. Two
points must be considered: first, the cost of entering production
with the optimum-size plant, and, second, minimum capital cost
of entry regardless of efficiency.

Estimates of capital costs were obtained in interviews with four different classes of people: (1) practicing lumber-mill design engineers, (2) individuals currently studying the economic feasibility of constructing a new lumber mill, (3) individuals who had recently constructed new production facilities, and (4) used-equipment dealers.

One estimate indicated that a mill designed to produce 60,000 to 75,000 board-feet per eight-hour shift with an 8-foot band headrig followed by a modern high-speed cant gang saw and including a barker and chipping equipment, kiln drying facilities, and a planing mill could be constructed for between $850,000 and $1 million. Another estimate, based on similar equipment and facilities but designed to produce approximately 100,000 feet per eight-hour shift, was that slightly more than $800,000 capital would be required. An additional $150,000 should be added for working capital requirements. Thus, by these two estimates, the total capital requirement for entry with the most efficient mill size would vary between $950,000 and $1,150,000. Kiln drying facilities may be eliminated from the above complex. A lumber and planing facility producing green lumber at a rate of approximately 100,000 feet per day could be constructed for approximately $700,000. Working capital needed would bring this estimate to $850,000.

These estimates, based on an assumed most efficient mill size range, indicate relatively low capital costs and correspondingly easy entry. Bain classifies mills requiring less than $2 million capital for entry as "so small as to provide little added restraint on entry."[4] To illustrate an industry where capital costs become a severe barrier to entry, Bain's study of steel and automobiles may be drawn upon. Bain estimates that between $265 million and $665 million is required to enter steel production with the minimum optimal-scale plant, and that for entry into the automobile industry, capital costs run between $250 million and $500 million. Neither estimate includes the high cost of developing a distribution system.

The foregoing statement of entry cost for an optimum-size plant is relevant to a discussion of long-run sustainable entry into the lumber industry. Another question remains, however. The lumber industry is characterized by rapid price changes and severe economic fluctuations which roughly follow a three-year cyclical pattern. When economic conditions in the industry improve so that profit margins are higher, new firms enter the industry at a rapid

---

[4] *Op. cit.*, p. 160.

rate. The new entrant is usually at a suboptimal level of efficiency, and can operate profitably only under the temporarily favorable profit-margin conditions that invited entry. It is necessary, therefore, to further analyze the cost of entry, not for the optimum-size plant, but rather for one that enjoys only short-run profitability. Such an entrant nevertheless serves to increase lumber output under inviting cost-price conditions. For this purpose, used-equipment dealers were asked to estimate the cost of entering the lumber industry with small-scale (suboptimal) output and minimum capital cost. According to their estimates, a band headrig mill producing rough, green lumber could be established for approximately $70,000. This estimate, of course, does not include a barker or a chipper. Used-equipment dealers commonly encourage entry by credit sales of sawmill machinery. One dealer indicated that a one-third down payment is normally required with the balance payable within three years. Thus, about $25,000 equity would allow entry. Nominally, interest requirements are only 6 and 6.5 percent, but a further hidden interest charge is included in the purchase price. A cash buyer is normally given a 10 percent dealer discount not available to the credit buyer. Total interest charges are therefore approximately 10 percent for minimum new entry on credit.

There is a difference in interest cost for large well-established firms, on the one hand, and new entrants on the other. Large firms operating in the lumber industry are able to obtain capital funds on long-term conditions at the prime rate, or up to about three-quarters of a point above the prime rate. Working capital loans from banks are available on the basis of either logs or lumber in inventory or lumber in transit. The new entrant, however, is not likely to qualify under the security conditions banks require. The method most commonly chosen by small mills to finance working capital needs is early sale of their production to a transit wholesaler. By this method, lumber is loaded directly from the green chain into railroad cars and is then sold to a wholesaler who transports it to the Mid-Western and Eastern lumber markets. Thus, lumber is moved toward a market without a prior buyer. A buyer is found while the lumber is at some intermediate point between point of origin and final destination.

Wholesale lumber firms frequently enter into longer-term financing arrangements with lumber mills. West Coast wholesalers have been called "the bankers of the lumber industry." Loans are made from wholesaler to producer in order to finance working capital needs with liquidation of the loan usually established on the basis of lumber production. Again, it is not possible to calculate the true interest charge on such loans, as the wholesaler obtains a prior claim on the mill's lumber production; such production is a step removed from the usual market mechanism by which prices are established. One arrangement in lieu of formal interest charges requires payment of 1 dollar per thousand feet of lumber production as compensation for use of capital supplied by a wholesaler. For the lumber company producing 10 million feet of lumber per year (about 45,000 feet per day) and borrowing $50,000, the effective annual interest charge amounts to 20 percent. This interest payment, however, may save the producer some sales costs if an exclusive sales contract is part of the financing agreement.

The executive of one wholesale firm that frequently supplies working capital estimated that net interest charges varied between 15 and 25 percent. The high degree of risk attending such a loan was also pointed out. The process of mixing the wholesale function with the financial function frequently turns wholesalers into involuntary millowners.

The foregoing analysis indicates that the magnitude of capital requirements does not present a meaningful barrier to entry into lumber production. Not only are the capital requirements low, but there are also several means by which a new firm may finance both its equipment needs and its working capital requirements, although the terms are higher by an unknown degree compared with financing charges incurred by well-established lumber producers.

With capital requirements for entry at a relatively low level, one would expect that favorable demand conditions in lumber markets would produce significant entry. The record from 1925 through 1961 confirms this expectation. Figure 11 shows a close correlation between the number of sawmills and lumber prices. As lumber prices increased from 21 dollars per thousand board feet in 1926 to 77 dollars per thousand in 1948, the number of operating sawmills increased from 631 to 1,675. The sharp increase in lumber prices starting in 1932 terminated in 1948. From that point forward, lumber prices have varied up and down with construction cycles. Correspondingly, the number of operating mills expanded and contracted, but with a persistent pressure for exit. Under force of relatively high lumber prices, the price of stumpage, as an item in derived demand, moved upward relative to lumber prices. Thus, high lumber prices have produced quasi-economic rent for timber owners, including the federal government. Firms producing lum-

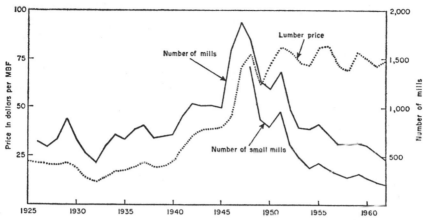

Fig. 11. Relationship between lumber prices and number of mills.
Source: West Coast Lumbermens Association.

ber from their own timber resources enjoy sizable capital gains. Nontimber-owning lumber mills have been forced to compete in the federal auction markets for timber, with the result that higher stumpage costs have reduced profits to low levels and brought about losses for the least efficient nontimber-owning mills. Therefore, even though lumber prices have followed a level trend since 1950, a large number of mills have made their exit from the industry. When lumber prices decline, the exit rate is accelerated. When lumber prices improve, some mills that have recently ceased production reenter the industry.

Beginning with 1948, data are available on mill size classes. Entry and exit of small mills (those producing less than 40,000 board feet per eight-hour shift) provide much of the necessary adaptation to changing lumber demand. Small mills apparently produce at a profit only when lumber enjoys a favorable market and before the cost of stumpage "catches up" with lumber prices. Given an attractive cost-price relationship, this class of mill provides an increase in lumber production (subject to a log supply constraint) to meet, at least in part, a higher demand for lumber, thereby preventing a potentially greater rise in lumber prices.

Profit in lumber manufacturing both on a per-dollar-of-sales basis and on a stockholder-equity basis reflects the easy entry conditions prevailing in the lumber industry. The profit rate tends toward that necessary minimum alluded to in classical economic theory. The relative ease of entering the lumber industry produces

a rate of return significantly lower than that found in other manufacturing industries.[5] After the great depression and World War
II, the demand for lumber expanded rapidly to a postwar high in
the 1950's. Free entry was not able to prevent substantial relative
price increases in lumber. From 1939 to 1948, the All Commodities
Wholesale Price Index doubled, but lumber prices increased three
and one-half times.

PRODUCT DIFFERENTIATION ADVANTAGES

Bain holds that "product differentiation is of at least the same
general order of importance as an impediment to entry as are economies of large-scale production and distribution."[6] Product differentiation refers to real or imaginary differences between products
within the same industry classification. Such product differences
may be based upon physical qualities of the product, or may be attained through branding or packaging or by means of various
services that the seller performs for the buyer. The automobile
industry may be cited as a classic example of important product
differentiation advantages for established firms. As most of the
buyers are not professional buyers, advertising to create brand allegiances among buyers is extensive and expensive. In addition,
products develop reputations based upon performance. Allegiances
to established dealer service organizations also hold a customer
through a series of automobile purchases. A new entrant into the
automobile industry must overcome the foregoing advantages of
existing firms while suffering the disadvantage of inadequate service organizations throughout a national market in the initial stage
of entry and lower trade-in value of the entrant's[7] used products.

Lumber should be classified, with copper and cement, as an industry in which product differentiation is a negligible or slight
barrier to entry. Advertising outlay by the lumber industry has
historically been slight. In promoting lumber in general, the National Lumber Manufacturers Association, through its National
Wood Promotion Program, spent $1,250,000 in 1959. This amount
is only 0.03 percent of the $3.5 billion average annual lumber ship-
ments. These expenditures merely attempt to differentiate and
promote wood versus other building materials. The seventeen regional and species associations in 1958 spent approximately $1
million in trade and consumer magazine advertising in an effort

---

5 The profitability record is documented in chapter 14, where the record of performance is analyzed and appraised.

6 *Op cit.*, p. 142.

7 *Ibid.*, pp. 114–143.

to promote one species of lumber as opposed to another or as opposed to other building materials. Finally, the National Lumber Manufacturers Association estimates that various manufacturers of lumber and wood products spent approximately $8 million in 1958 in an attempt to establish brand preferences for their own lumber and for other purposes. But an $8 million advertising budget is still only 0.2 percent of the value of all lumber shipments in the United States.

The practice of end- and edge-branding lumber has grown in recent years, and most lumber now bears a brand. There is no suggestion that end-branding allows the seller to obtain a premium for his lumber; rather, the practice appears to make the sales task somewhat easier. Recently, lumber packaging has been expanded, allowing clearer brand identification than was previously possible. Packaging has definite advantages, the most important of which are (1) weather protection of lumber in transit from producer to final user; (2) lower rail shipping costs, as flatcars may be used instead of the more limited boxcars; (3) lower handling costs, as power equipment may be used to handle large packages, but cannot be used for individual boards of nonpackaged lumber.

The mass of nonprofessional lumber buyers show no apparent awareness of a brand preference. Professional buyers who represent residential construction firms and industrial concerns become aware of quality differences within official lumber grades. Such brand preferences and aversions are transmitted to wholesalers who may then exercise choice among suppliers by brand. Wholesalers differ, however, as to whether and to what degree brand preference manifests itself in premiums for preferred brands. In isolated instances, a manufacturer may be able to obtain a modest premium by virtue of manufacturing perfection and packaging techniques.

But premium prices are not based on advertising campaigns. Rather, they are based on real product differences obtainable at additional processing cost to the manufacturer. These product differences are of little or no significance as barriers to entry. Therefore, product differentiation advantages possessed by existing firms appear to be at a minimum as entry barriers in the lumber industry.

Advantages of Economies in Large-Scale Production and Distribution

The hypothesis that economies of scale exist asserts that, at increasingly higher levels of output for the firm, average cost of production declines up to a relatively large plant size. The firm may consist of one plant or multiple plants; correspondingly, a declining average cost per unit of output may appear because a single plant's output is expanded or because economies are associated with the grouping of several plants under one coordinated management. The presence of substantial scale economies becomes an issue in the study of barriers to entry, as their occurrence may necessitate large-scale operations for new entry which, in turn, may have a significant impact on market price. This is particularly true in such industries as lumber where the demand function appears to be inelastic.

The analysis of scale economies (see chap. 1) reveals that plant scale economies are of no significance. The optimal plant size is very small compared with the large market for lumber. There is no convincing evidence to indicate scale economies beyond a single-plant firm, or to suggest that large firms possess any degree of market power in the final product market for lumber. In sum, no economies of any kind arise from large-scale production and distribution and, hence, no entry barriers arise from this source.

SUMMARY

Barriers to entry have been examined from three points of view. First, the absolute cost advantages possessed by existing firms raise no barriers to entry owing to production techniques or to high capital costs. The availability of large quantities of federal timber, a unique raw-material position, allows relatively free entry. But the geographical area of effective competition for federal timber is relatively small, and, because the supply curve for timber is inelastic, a new entrant with an optimum-size mill will cause a significant increase in timber (stumpage) prices. This factor becomes the only potential barrier to entry of any importance.

Second, product differentiation barriers to entry are of no importance. End- and edge-branding of lumber is increasingly common and facilitates sale, but the general public seems to consider lumber as a homogeneous product. Packaging and labeling of lumber has recently been expanded, and this procedure leads to some differentiation and small premium prices. But one must conclude that product differentiation is not so important in the lumber industry as it is in other industries.

Third, real economies of scale are of relatively no importance as barriers to entry. The optimum plant size is small, both absolutely and relatively, and large firms possess no known market power in lumber sales. Similarly, there are no advertising economies of scale.

Overall, the conclusion is inescapable that barriers to entry into the lumber industry are minimal, relative to other important segments of the American industrial economy. The result is a low rate of return, both on invested capital and on sales. With relatively free entry, lumber-mill profits in the long run logically and empirically conform to the necessary minimum indicated by classical economic theory. When demand conditions improve significantly, lumber prices increase and milling profits temperarily improve, thereby inviting entry into the industry. Small mills enter in response to the invitation, and the favorable operating profit position is quickly eroded away. The inelastic supply of timber produces higher stumpage prices by virtue of the long reproduction cycle. A market improvement for lumber produces only short-lived profit in lumber milling, and a profit shift to the timber owner where the more durable profit becomes quasi-economic rent taxable as a capital gain.

PART III

*Market Conduct
and Performance
of Lumber Sellers
and Timber Buyers*

Having identified structure at both the input and output levels, we must now analyze market conduct (behavior) and performance in order to clarify the structure-conduct-performance relationship. To what extent are conduct and performance predictable from the known competitive structure of the lumber industry at the output level, and from the known oligopsonistic structure at the input level?

Chapter 7 gives a brief account of the conduct of competitors with respect to output and price determination in the lumber market. In chapter 8, timber sale procedures that are relevant to and influence the conduct of competition or provide necessary background information for a full understanding of the analysis are explained. As the federal government is the seller of most timber entering the free market, and as the Forest Service is the federal agency responsible for most government timber sales, the sales procedures followed by the Forest Service receive the most attention.

Chapter 9 contains a detailed analysis of the strategy alternatives open to potential timber buyers. The many possible choices are indicated, as well as the points in the bidding process where decisions must be made. Chapter 10 sets forth the theoretical background necessary for an examination of price determination in the national forest timber market, and also analyzes price determination under differing market conditions.

Chapters 11 and 12 present a detailed analysis of the results of bidding for national forest timber in the Douglas fir region. In the former, the record of sales based on 2,585 individual timber sales in the four-year period 1959–1962 is examined. The analysis in chapter 12 is based on forty-three separate geographical markets, called working circles. Several hypotheses are tested in an effort to account for the observed wide variation in degree of competition among individual timber sales and geographical markets. Evidence of market power exercised by large firms is examined. In chapter 13 an explanation is presented to account for large-firm market power. Chapter 14 evaluates performance in timber resource ownership and in lumber production against the concept of "workable competition." Finally, conclusions are drawn concerning the relationship between structure, conduct, and performance in the lumber industry.

CHAPTER 7

Conduct of Sellers in the Lumber Industry

The analysis in this chapter consists of two parts. First, because the relationship between structure and behavior is of interest, the expected behavior based on known structural conditions is set forth. Second, the structural forecast is tested against empirical data.

Behavioral Forecast from Structure

A firm in a competitive industry does not affect price by its control over output. Rather, price is taken as a datum, and the firm consciously selects its output, presumably to maximize profit. A firm in a noncompetitive industry is in a position to influence prices, and may consciously select a price and then produce whatever output buyers decide to take at the chosen price.

Knowledge of the structure of the lumber industry makes possible a clear forecast of price-output behavior. Since the largest firm in the industry produces only 3.7 percent of the national lumber output, and since the Big Four and the Big Eight, which might conceivably join together to control price through control of output, account for only 9.2 and 12.4 percent, respectively, of the national lumber market, producer influence over price is expected to be nil; that is, the demand curve should be horizontal. There should be no evidence that sellers individually or collectively curtail output in order to maintain price. The homogeneous product and the competitive structure indicate an absence of product modification of the "forced obsolescence" variety. We would expect minimal advertising of the market share variety. Further, there should be no evidence of predatory acts and exclusionary tactics at the output level.[1]

---

[1] The line between conduct (policies followed by firms with respect to such variables as price, output, selling cost, and collusion) and performance (the net results

EMPIRICAL TESTS OF BEHAVIORAL FORECASTS

The relevant market for the purpose of reasoning about price determination and other aspects of conduct is the national market rather than a regional or species market. If the producers in any region attempt to restrict output and shipments to a subnational consumer market that they dominate, thereby causing an initial price increase within that market, there is sufficient shifting possible from adjacent markets where sellers will be motivated by the initially attractive price. Consequently, any regional price increase will be temporary. Similarly, there is sufficient substitutability between species so that any attempt by the producers of a given species to restrict its output in order to gain a higher price will quickly bring forth a shift in demand away from the high-price item and in favor of the relatively low-price item.

Price determination at the producer and wholesale levels.—Price determination at the producer and wholesale levels follows a fairly standard procedure. First, both lumber producers and wholesalers send prospective buyers an offering list, usually on a weekly basis. This list identifies the species, grade, quantity, and price of lumber available. From this point on, most lumber is sold over the telephone, although some large firms maintain a sizable number of salesmen to call on customers.[2] The larger producers maintain sales departments and sell to wholesalers, retailers, and large industrial buyers at "wholesale" prices. Some producers even have retail yards. Except in the latter instance, there are no firm prices, but only negotiated ones. Smaller producers without sales departments also have a variety of sales arrangements. Some use a wholesale lumber company as their sales agent. Others sell to a variety of wholesalers or commission men. Again, prices differ from day to day and are negotiated, except when commission selling is employed.

Relationships between wholesalers and their usual customers differ with the personalities concerned. One wholesaler analyzed his telephone selling this way: When a customer inquires about a given carload offer contained on the wholesaler's list and finds it

---

of conduct policies) is not always clear in the traditional division of industrial organization analysis. Following conventional practice, I am reserving study of the rate of return on investments in lumber production for a later discussion concerned with performance. These data, however, might also be treated as evidence of behavior.

[2] A similar situation exists in the textile industry, where the condition of little control over prices is "aggravated by the fact that most textile sales are made over the telephone" (Jules Backman and M. R. Gainsbrugh, *Economics of the Cotton Textile Industry* [New York: National Industrial Conference Board, 1946], p. 125).

still available, a price must be agreed upon. The starting point is the published offering price. This price becomes the agreed upon price in approximately 50 percent of the sales consummated. In the other 50 percent, bargaining produces a lower price. The prospective buyer usually makes an offer that varies between 50 cents and 2 dollars per thousand board feet below the listed price. Approximately 25 percent of such offers are accepted. The other 75 percent are split between the price offered by the prospective buyer and the price listed by the wholesaler. Thus a large amount of lumber buying is transacted at the wholesale level under individual bargaining conditions. The wholesale price index for any species and grade of lumber would be expected to change daily, or, indeed, as often as information is collected and identified by time periods. The agreed price moves up when mill inventories are low and moves down when inventories are plentiful. Anticipated events cause an increase or decrease in the flow of orders and corresponding changes in prices. The price received by the producer varies with the market and deviates from the wholesaler's selling price by a competitive margin. There is no evidence in the method of price determination to indicate that producers select their price and let the market determine output. Rather, price is market determined by the interaction of supply and demand.

The firm demand curve.—In the course of about 140 interviews, fifteen lumber-mill operators or their sales managers were asked what effect a change in their level of production would have on price. The range of alternative levels of output was limited to the probable change that might occur in each operation. Mills on a single eight-hour shift were asked about the price effect of a 100 percent increase in output and a 20 percent reduction. The latter might occur as a result of reducing operations to a four-day week. Firms operating on a two-shift basis were asked about a 20 percent increase in output and a 50 percent decline. The question was always thoroughly discussed to avoid confusion in either the answer or the question. Replies were uniform and consistent with expectations: Any probable change in output by the individual plant would have no significant effect on the average price received for the standard lumber items. The individual firm demand curve is therefore assumed to have infinite elasticity, and the price is a datum to decision makers in the lumber industry. It is questionable that even the largest firm in the industry has any influence over price through any probable change in its output. Even the improbable event of complete cessation of production by the Weyerhaeuser Company would produce only temporary higher prices and profits, given the free entry condition.

As noted earlier (chap. 1), entry by an optimal firm would tend to reduce price by 0.06 percent, well within the range of price uncertainty discussed below. Thus, the price effect of new single-plant entry is unimportant. It is apparent from interviews that the demand curve has width. At any point in time there is uncertainty, within 2 or 3 percentage points, about the exact market price for any given lumber item. The uncertainty follows from the facts that prices fluctuate daily and that every sale is transacted on an individual basis, with the seller trying to obtain the highest and the buyer the lowest possible price. Even the largest firm may be uncertain of the market price, especially when prices are in a clear upward or downward trend. For example, a Weyerhaeuser report carried the following notation: "Even as this report is being written [mid-February, 1947] there is no clearly defined price."[3] Again in December, 1948, the general manager used the following words to describe the lumber market: "We tried to find the market on Coast species."[4] Producers believe they face a horizontal demand curve, although the demand curve has width as a result of uncertainty about the momentary price.

Miscellaneous noncompetitive practices.—The interview approach was used to obtain current evidence of miscellaneous manifestations of noncompetitive market behavior in the lumber market. No evidence was found of predatory or exclusionary acts, nor of any form of basing point pricing. Advertising of the type designed to maintain a firm's market share was not apparent. Promotional advertising of lumber is almost entirely limited to association-sponsored activity. Product modification of the forced obsolescence variety is nonexistent. These behavioral findings correspond with what one would expect to find in an industry with a highly competitive structure.

In 1940 the principal trade association of Douglas fir region lumber producers, the West Coast Lumbermens Association, was indicted by a federal grand jury for miscellaneous acts allegedly committed during the post-NRA years 1935–1939.[5] Although the

---

[3] General Manager's Report from the Weyerhaeuser Sales Company to the parent company for year ending December 31, 1946, quoted by permission. The Sales Company sells to both wholesalers and retailers.

[4] *Ibid.*, for year ending December 31, 1948, quoted by permission.

[5] *United States of America v. West Coast Lumbermens Association, et al.*, U.S. District Court for the Southern District of California, Central Division, September Term, 1940.

indictment included the charge that the WCLA attempted to orga-
nize a reduction in lumber production in order to yield a higher
and noncompetitive price, the principal allegation appears to be
that the association was guilty of exclusionary practice on lumber
grading. The indictment alleges that the grade-marking and inspection service provided by the WCLA to members and nonmembers alike was available to nonmembers at discriminatory higher
fees. Inspection and grade stamping were necessary for most uses
of lumber, and helpful for others. The case was never tried. Instead, on April 16, 1941, a consent decree was entered wherein the
defendants agreed, without admission of guilt, to abstain from
specified acts.

The record of price flexibility: lumber versus steel.—An examination of any price series for specific lumber items confirms that
the price of lumber, except in periods of tight price controls, varies
about as often as the time dimension permits. The data on price
behavior of Douglas fir two-by-fours, random length, construction,
dried, for the eight years 1953 to 1960, shown in figure 12, indicate
that lumber prices vary under the impact of business cycles: lumber prices changed eighty-nine times out of ninety-two possibilities.
Knowing the process of price determination, I suspect that a faulty
method of data collection or classification accounts for the three
occasions when reported prices are unchanged.

The United States lumber industry has a highly competitive
structure, and prices are market determined. The steel industry,
in contrast, is a classic example of an oligopoly. The four largest
producers of structural steel shapes in 1954 accounted for 92 percent of the total value of shipments, and the eight largest producers
accounted for 97 percent.[6] With only a few producers, implicit or
explicit control over output in order to produce desired price effects becomes possible. The contrast in price and output behavior
between lumber and steel products is striking. Figure 13 shows the
price and output record for structural steel shapes in the period
1953–1960, including three recessions. The cyclical price variations
expected of a durable producer good have been avoided, apparently through producer control, either implicit or explicit, over
output. During the 1953–54 recession, steel production was reduced
from 100 to 63 percent of capacity. During this period of weak
demand, steel prices were increased as a result of output control.

---

[6] *Concentration in American Industry*, U.S. Senate, Subcommittee on Antitrust and
Monopoly, 85th Cong., 1st sess. (Washington, 1957), p. 83.

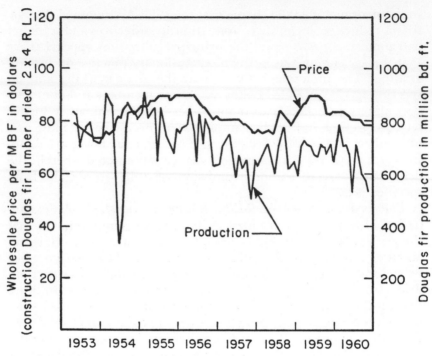

Fig. 12. Fluctuations in price and output, lumber, 1953–1960.
SOURCE: U.S. Department of Commerce, *Business Statistics*, 1957, 1961 editions.

During the ensuing prosperity in 1955 and 1956, steel production returned to full capacity, and reported prices continued their upward movement. Then the recession of 1957–58 followed, during which production was again curtailed, this time to about 50 percent of capacity. Again, prices did not weaken but were increased, facilitated by curtailed output. In the 1960–61 recession, production was reduced to a point below 50 percent of capacity. In this instance, prices remained steady; the approaching presidential election of 1960 and strong political influence in the preceding steel strike may have exerted a restraining influence.

Stigler, drawing on evidence supplied by others, has pointed out that quoted prices differ from transaction prices: When quoted prices are rigid, prices actually paid by buyers show wider and more frequent price variations.[7] Prices actually paid for structural steel

---

[7] George J. Stigler, "Administered Prices and Oligopolistic Inflation," *Journal of Business*, XXXV (Jan., 1962), 5–8.

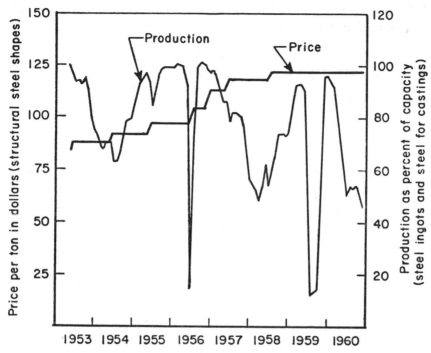

Fig. 13. Fluctuations in price and output, steel, 1953–1960.
SOURCE: U.S. Department of Commerce, *Business Statistics*, 1957, 1961 editions.

shapes are not available. It is highly doubtful that more accurate price reporting would substantially alter the record of price behavior in view of the coordinated control of output shown in the record.

The record of oligopoly price behavior in the steel industry may be compared with competitive price behavior in the lumber industry. The same recessions brought about modest curtailments in lumber production. But data presented in chapter 6 indicate that output curtailments resulted from firms leaving the industry (presumably through bankruptcy) rather than from judicious reductions in output by continuously operating firms. Because the reductions in output were modest, the price variable performed its expected adjustment function. In all three recessions, lumber prices declined under the impact of reduced demand. The price-output data thus show the kind of periodic and cyclical fluctuations that structural conditions would lead one to expect and that are in sharp contrast with the behavior of steel prices, which reflect an oligopol-

istic structure. Conduct in lumber appears to follow directly from
a competitive structure.

SUMMARY

This brief examination of competitor conduct in the lumber industry generally confirms theoretical expectations based on knowledge
of a competitive structure. Lumber prices are market determined.
The individual firm demand curve is horizontal. There is, however, some uncertainty from moment to moment about the exact
market price; hence, the demand curve has width. No evidence has
been found of predatory or exclusionary acts in the lumber market.
Advertising for product promotion by individaul firms is minimal.
There is no forced obsolescence. Even in a competitive structure,
however, association activity may introduce some elements of noncompetitive behavior. The relationship between structure, conduct, and final performance is taken up at a later point.

CHAPTER 8

Timber Sale Procedures

As the bulk of the remaining sawtimber volume in the Douglas fir subregion is owned by the federal government, which excludes itself from the business of manufacturing lumber, a brief examination of the procedure employed to sell stumpage is a prerequisite to understanding the timber market. Sales methods have implications for competitive conditions. The method chosen may aid and stimulate many small competing firms or, conversely, may facilitate the development of large firms. This examination of sales procedures is primarily descriptive and involves six points: (1) appraisal methods, (2) the offer to sell, (3) requirements to qualify as a bidder, (4) sale type, (5) set-aside sales, and (6) the auction.

APPRAISAL METHODS

The objective of timber appraisal is to estimate its "fair market value," defined as "the price acceptable to a willing buyer and seller, both with knowledge of the relevant facts and not under pressure or compulsion to deal."[1] The timber alone is appraised and sold. The land is retained by the government. Timber appraisals are based on the proposition that "timber is worth the selling value of the products manufactured from it, minus cost of production and margin for profit and risk to the purchaser."[2] This approach is consistent with the derived demand status of timber as a resource. The value thus estimated is termed the "appraised price." The function of this price is to protect the seller against inadequate competition and collusion: "The effective market is so 'thin' . . . that competitive bidding under no restrictions would produce a low price. There is always the danger of collusion among potential buyers."[3]

---

1 "Forest Service Handbook," U.S. Forest Service, sec. 2423.12.
2 *Ibid.*, sec. 2423.21.
3 Marion Clawson and Burnell Held, *The Federal Lands* (Baltimore: Johns Hopkins Press, 1957), p. 203.

a

In the context of a free enterprise system, the best approach to estimating fair market value is to begin with market-determined prices. The private free market in stumpage, however, is not extensive enough to serve as a reliable guide. Furthermore, private stumpage sales that do occur take place under widely differing conditions. Prices differ by the size of the sale, timber species, grade, quality, accessibility, age, scaling method, tax liability, and the like. In the absence of a broad private free market for stumpage, the next most reliable free market that might be tapped is the log market. As shown earlier (p. 66), estimated sales of privately owned stumpage in the Douglas fir region account for only about 2 percent of regional log production. To a lesser degree, the log market is similarly too small to be reliable. Logs are traded with differentiation by species, grade, and location. Several decades earlier a broad free log market did exist. With the continuous trend toward firm integration and the accelerated merger movement in the 1950's, the volume of logs traded in the open market has steadily declined. No exact measure of the volume of logs traded in the open market exists, but a reasonably reliable index indicates the trend in volume traded over time. Figure 14 shows an index of the volume of Douglas fir log sales in the Columbia River, Grays Harbor, and Puget Sound areas as reported to the Pacific Northwest Loggers Association. Over the fifteen years from 1947 through 1961 total volume of Douglas fir log sales declined nearly 82 percent.[4] During this same period total log production dipped only 9 percent.

This trend supports the opinion widely held in the industry that free-market log sales account for a small and declining share of present log production. In view of the trend and the present position of open-market log sales, one is forced to search elsewhere for a free market–based appraisal system. The Forest Service finds these free-market prices in lumber, plywood, and other minor forest products.

---

[4] The volume of log sales consummated, as reported by the Pacific Northwest Loggers Association, must be interpreted with caution as an index of trend in total free log market sales. Data reported by the association include only volumes from cooperating mills. Generally speaking, small loggers do not report their sales to the association, and only sales in the three towable water areas mentioned are reported. All sales consummated elsewhere in the subregion are excluded from the report. This shortcoming is not a serious one provided the nonreported share is constant over the fifteen-year period. There has been some shift inland, however, owing to the early logging of timber most convenient to water transportation. This factor would lead to an overstatement of the free log market decline.

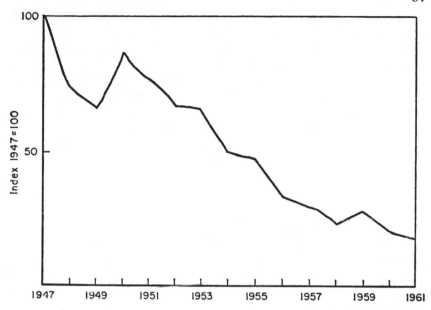

Fig. 14. Index of Douglas fir log sales consummated in the Columbia River, Grays Harbor, and Puget Sound areas, 1947–1961.

SOURCE: Computed from data supplied by the Pacific Northwest Loggers Association. Data are incomplete because not all firms report to the association.

Appraisal begins with free-market prices. Product yields from estimated log production must then be calculated in order to obtain an estimate of final product value. Lumber-milling and logging costs for "operators of average efficiency," together with any road-construction costs, are subtracted from the final product value to obtain what the Forest Service calls "the conversion return." A profit margin is then subtracted from the conversion return to arrive at the value of stumpage or the appraised value of the timber. When the total appraised value is divided by the estimated volume contained in the sale, the appraised price per thousand board feet is obtained. The appraised price is expected to be responsive to "actual prices being paid for stumpage thus giving the United States a fair return for its stumpage."[5]

A successful bidder for federal timber buys not only timber but a road-construction job as well. In the 1959–1962 period, 70.2 percent of all national forest timber sales required road construction

---

[5] "Forest Service Handbook," sec. 2423.13.

by the buyer as one of the conditions of the sale. The average road-construction obligation was appraised by the Forest Service at $58,625. The average appraised value of all national forest timber sales in the four-year period ending in 1962 was $81,600. This appraised value reflects deductions for all logging and milling costs and is further reduced by the estimated road-construction cost. Thus, the residual value of the timber is appraised at 1.4 times the road-construction cost.[6]

The appraised price of timber is of great significance in the federal timber sale process, since it becomes the minimum price the Forest Service will accept for any given timber sale. When competition for federal timber is not present, the appraised price becomes the sale price. If significant competition exists, free-market bidding causes the sale price to exceed the appraised price. Further, the appraised price is of added significance for this study, as it is assumed to be a constant percentage of market value. The ratios of bid prices to appraised prices are then assumed to offer one measure of the degree of competition prevailing among several geographical markets.

THE OFFER TO SELL

After a proposed sale of national forest stumpage has been appraised, the next step is to advertise the offer at least thirty days before the actual sale. In addition to notification of the appraised price, the offer to sell contains other necessary information describing the proposed sale. Except for the relatively small amount of timber sold (1) under a cooperative sustained-yield unit, (2) under one of the federal sustained-yield units, or (3) under the small-business set-aside sales, any qualified person may bid for Forest Service timber.

REQUIREMENTS TO QUALIFY AS A BIDDER

In order to become qualified, a bidder must submit a sealed bid at not less than the appraised price, and his bid must be accompanied by a minimum deposit fixed by the Forest Service. Only qualified bidders are permitted to participate in a timber auction. The minimum deposit is set to approximate the value of a one-month cut from the proposed sale. The maximum deposit that may be required is $100,000. Amounts actually required appear to average

---

[6] Data are developed from "National Forest Advertised Timber Sales, Region 6," U.S. Forest Service, 1380 (2400) (Portland, Ore.).

about 5 percent of the appraised value. In addition, the Forest Service may require evidence of financial ability to meet the requirements of logging the proposed sale.

SALE TYPE

Timber may be offered for sale by either the sealed-bid or oral auction procedure. Under the first method, sealed bids equal to or higher than the appraised price must be submitted before the sale; sealed bids are final. Equal sealed bids may be rejected or may be resolved by dividing the timber between the tie bidders or drawing lots. Under the second method, sealed bids are again required, but only as one step in the process of qualifying to cast oral auction bids. When two or more bidders have submitted identical sealed bids at the appraised price, oral auction bidding normally follows, with the sale being awarded to the highest qualified bidder. When unequal sealed bids are submitted, oral auction bidding may follow. In the event that only one sealed bid has been submitted, the sale is normally awarded to that bidder, even though it is classified as an oral auction sale. Forest Service regulations permit the sale administrator to select the sale type that "will result as far as possible in equitable competitive conditions among all classes of bidders." Sale administrators are encouraged to follow the prevailing practice of the region, though departures are permitted "to foster community stability or to facilitate National Forest administration."[7] No mention is made in the Forest Service handbook of deliberate use of the sealed-bid sale to foster competitive conditions. In 1956 and again in 1965, federal government reports strongly urged use of sealed-bid sales where collusion was suspected.[8] Following the Comptroller General's recommendation, the Bureau of Land Management announced in 1965 that it would, on an experimental basis, use sealed bids on 10 percent of its sales. The Forest Service has been particularly reluctant to expand sealed-bid selling in the Douglas fir region for any reason. The principal argument advanced in support of its position is that many mills in the Northwest are dependent upon national forest timber, and that the

---

[7] "Forest Service Handbook," sec. 2431.55.
[8] "Federal Timber Sales Policies," U.S. House of Representatives, Thirty-First Intermediate Report of Committee on Government Operations, 84th Cong., 2d sess., House Report no. 2960 (Washington, 1956), p. 26; "Report to the Congress of the United States, Questionable Aspects of Oral Auction Bidding for Federal Timber Sold at Certain Locations in the Pacific Northwest," Comptroller General of the United States (Washington, Feb., 1965), p. 20.

sealed-bid method offers no "second chance" to bid and protect one's position. Further, when the sealed bid method is used, potential buyers in the area strongly object, charging "they are the victims of unfair discrimination."[9]

SET-ASIDE SALES

By act of Congress in 1958, the federal timber-selling agencies were given power to restrict competitive bidding for federal timber. Section 15 of the Small Business Act of 1958 allows the selling agency to offer set-aside sales in which bidding is restricted to firms having not more than 500 employees.[10] Buyers are further restricted to firms that will not sell more than 30 percent of such timber to a concern that does not qualify as small business.

Qualified small firms may request the Small Business Administration to arrange with the selling agency to set aside specific scheduled timber tracts. When both the SBA and the selling agency are satisfied that the specific tract meets the requirements as set forth in the act, bidding is restricted as indicated above.

Only minor use has been made of set-aside sales. In the two years 1963–1964, there were sixty-one such sales by the Forest Service in the Douglas fir region involving a total of 242 million board feet, or only 3.2 percent of total Forest Service sales. After investigating the attitude of operators toward the program, Franklin Ho concluded: "There is an apparent apathy toward the program in Oregon. The Federal timber sales agencies, moreover, are inclined to regard the program as unwise and unnecessary. . . . People in the lumber industry, in general, have shown little enthusiasm for it. . . . Smaller companies for whose benefit this program was initiated are more apathetic toward it than larger companies."[11]

THE AUCTION

All persons qualified to bid in a national forest timber sale may submit bids. The sale begins when the sale administrator asks for further qualifying sealed bids; he then declares the period of qualification closed. The appraised prices by species, together with sealed-bid prices, are posted. Oral bidding takes place by species. For example, a sale including 2 million feet of Douglas fir ap-

---

[9] Letter from Orville L. Freeman, secretary of agriculture, to Congressman William L. Dawson, chairman, Committee on Government Operations, House of Representatives (June 10, 1965).

[10] 72 *U.S. Stat. at L.*, 384.

[11] Franklin Y. H. Ho, *Small Lumber Companies in Western Oregon* (Portland: University of Portland, 1963), p. 69.

praised at 20 dollars per thousand board feet and 1 million feet of hemlock appraised at 10 dollars per thousand board feet, where sealed bids were submitted at appraised price, may receive its first oral bid at $21.05 on the Douglas fir or $10.05 on the hemlock. Subsequent bids may specifiy either species. When the oral auction has been completed, the sale is awarded to the highest qualified bidder.

CHAPTER 9

Bidding Strategy in the Market for Federal Timber

In order to gain insight into the complex relationships among bidders and potential bidders, it is helpful to understand their objectives and strategies as they prepare to bid in the auction market for national forest timber. Bidding strategy is the art of employing one's bargaining power in choosing among alternative courses of action in a manner designed to attain the bidder's objectives. Such objectives usually include obtaining a sufficient quantity of a desired type of timber at the lowest possible cost at a point in time when needed, and avoiding an unfavorable change in the status quo with reference to one's competitors.

The economic situation calling for a bidding strategy has arisen in recent years as private timber sources have been progressively depleted and public timber has been drawn upon as a necessary substitute. As this shift progressed, institutional patterns, procedures, and understandings developed among the growing number of mills resorting to federal timber supplies. These patterns of conduct were based upon friendships, interlocking business relationships, the hard necessity of obtaining timber for existing milling capacity, and the realization (without knowledge of technical terminology) that the supply of federal timber is inelastic with respect to price. Standard patterns of conduct are discernible; a customary set of required decisions is identifiable.

Theory that would normally guide analysis of bidding strategy leaves much to be desired. Game theory is suggestive at best. Bidding in the market for federal timber is neither a zero sum nor a two-person game. As indicated above, several objectives are sought in bidding, and minimizing cost in order to maximize profit is important. Collusion among bidders, if effective, reduces the cost of timber toward a minimum given by the appraised price. Further,

[142]

within the Douglas fir region, in no instances is bidding limited to two predictable bidders in successive sales.

Recent developments in bargaining theory offer fruitful insights and interpretations.[1] The setting for bargaining involves two or more potential buyers. Such bargaining may be explicit before the sealed bids are opened. There is only minimal opportunity for communication (implicit bargaining) during the bidding process.

FUNDAMENTAL BIDDING DECISIONS

Interviews were conducted with approximately 140 individuals actively engaged in the purchase or sale of public timber. Interviewees were purchasers of all forms of public timber. Sellers interviewed included representatives of the Forest Service and the Bureau of Land Management. The pattern of conduct emerging from these interviews is outlined in figure 15. The multitude of decisions and alternatives discussed here are not intended to suggest that all bidders are consciously aware of their complex problems. Many of the decisions outlined are made explicitly and only after careful study. There appear to be seven fundamental decisions to be made as a potential bidder proceeds from the prospectus through the bidding process:

1. Is the timber suitable to the needs of the potential buyer and therefore desired for purchase?

2. If the timber is desired by the potential buyer, how much is wanted?

3. Is it desirable to enter into an agreement or understanding with other potential bidders?

4. If the timber is desired and the logs are to be distributed among several users, which users or representatives of such users should engage in bidding?

5. Should the potential bidder qualify to bid?

6. If qualified, should the potential bidder engage in oral bidding?

7. If the potential bidder is likely to engage in bidding, how high should he bid?

Uncertainty is present in these decisions wherever one's action is

---

[1] See particularly T. C. Schelling, "An Essay on Bargaining," *American Economic Review*, XLVI (June, 1956), 281–306; "Bargaining, Communication, and Limited War," *Journal of Conflict Resolution*, I (March, 1957), 19–36; and "The Strategy of Conflict: Prospectus for a Reorientation of Game Theory," *Journal of Conflict Resolution*, II (Sept., 1958), 203–264.

dependent on the action of others. Agreements may not be honored and often cannot be legally enforced. The action of others can be forecast only in a probability sense.

A MODEL OF BIDDER DECISION MAKING

The flow-charting device employed in computer programming is used to identify the complex decision-making structure faced by bidders in the auction markets for federal timber (see fig. 15). There are certain mechanical problems in connection with the model which should be clearly understood. The model has been constructed on the assumption that the alternatives and the decisions identified are those faced by a lumber-mill operator and potential buyer, whom we may call bidder A. Therefore, bidder A may be thought of as the central character. Bidder B is identified as another mill (lumber and/or veneer) operator who is also a potential buyer of public timber. Bidder C is identified as a contract logger (commonly called a gyppo logger) who may independently buy the timber and resell logs to sawmill, veneer-mill, and pulp-mill users. All decisions are definite and unambiguous; there are no "maybe's." The decisions diagrammed should be thought of as a decision-making process in time. Alternatives shown at a given point in the logical process, however, may reappear for new decisions at several additional points not repeated in the diagram.

The reader should be reminded of the obvious fact that reality is infinitely complicated. One may endlessly identify forces with varying relevancy which affect any decision, whether it be to cross a busy downtown intersection or to bid for federal timber. Progress in knowledge of the nature of a given decision-making setting requires abstraction. The most important forces and considerations must be emphasized at the expense of omitting the least important. Figure 15 identifies the most significant decisions to be made by a potential buyer and the relationships among the several choices.

The process of considering a federal timber sale logically begins with examination of the written prospectus available to all potential buyers and, with various degrees of diligence, of both the timber quality and the road-construction problem. For most potential buyers of federal timber, and for nearly all large operators, the cost of cruising and estimating the value of a federal timber sale is a fixed rather than an incremental cost. Large operators customarily employ a full-time timber buyer and staff to cruise and evaluate a sale. Some of the smaller potential bidders incur an in-

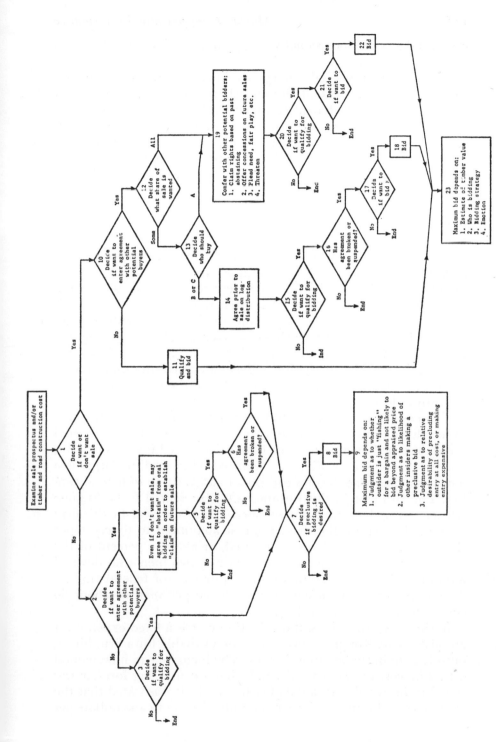

Fig. 15. Decision-making process in bidding on federal timber sales.

cremental cost by occasionally employing outside consultants to
evaluate a given sale.

The larger timber sales normally involve a road-construction
requirement. The federal timber seller estimates, but does not
guarantee, the cost of road construction. All such costs must be
borne by the buyer, and the appraised value of federal timber is
reduced by the estimated road-construction cost. Timber-purchase
contracts are not normally subject to renegotiation in the event
that road-construction costs substantially exceed estimated costs.
The successful buyer of federal timber where road construction is
involved buys not only timber, but a construction job as well. The
road-construction situation must therefore be carefully surveyed
and appraised. Again, the larger firms often maintain on their pay-
roll one or more full-time construction engineers. Other operators
may hire professional road-appraisal services. Small operators frequently request appraisals from independent contractors whom
they normally employ for road construction.

Other interested bidders enter the auction arena with only superficial impressions of the value of a given sale. Some interviewees
reported that small operators occasionally assume that, if a large
firm is interested in purchasing a given sale, such interest follows a
careful examination of the sale and leads to the conclusion that it
is worth at least as much as its appraised value.

The cost of preparing to bid on a national forest timber sale
differs depending on the volume, on whether valuation personnel
are maintained on a permanent basis or are hired for the occasion,
and on the degree of diligence required. One medium-large firm
employs a man who devotes full time to acquisition of federal timber. The full cost in this instance was represented to be $14,000
per year. As federal timber purchased in a recent year by this firm
amounted to 22 million feet, the cost amounted to 65 cents per
thousand board feet of logs purchased, or about 3 percent of the
stumpage value. Another mill maintained two men who devoted
most of their time to evaluation and purchase of federal timber.
The total cost in this instance was $18,000 per year, or about 60
cents per thousand board feet.

In these two situations, the valuation cost is a fixed expense for
any given sale. Rough estimates are also available for a firm hiring
outside help in timber appraisal, thereby incurring an incremental
cost. The cost to one firm of employing a consulting forester was
found to be 100 dollars a day. On this basis, it was stated that the
average cost of cruising timber amounted to 300 to 400 dollars per

sale. In this instance, road-construction costs were estimated by road contractors normally utilized by the firm. No incremental costs were incurred for road-cost appraisal other than those embodied in a subsequent road-construction contract. If the cruise cost amounted to 400 dollars on a 4 million board feet sale, the cost per thousand feet would amount to 10 cents. Success ratios vary among firms and working circles. The latter firm achieved a 40 percent success ratio, apparently above average for timber sales in the Douglas fir region. For the region as a whole, the average success ratio based on 1959–1962 oral auction sales was 19 percent. This calculation is based on the fact that the average number of bidders per sale was 5.28. The reciprocal of the average number of bidders gives the average success ratio.

The fact that considerable cost is involved in preparing to bid on a given sale requires that a firm minimize its "shopping around" and attempt instead to maximize its success ratio, particularly when evaluation costs are incremental rather than fixed. One would expect that the prospective buyer would be highly selective, that he would incur evaluation costs only when there is a good probability of his becoming a bidder, and further that his efforts as a bidder would be serious. A decision to "get on the board" (become a qualified bidder) usually indicates a serious intent to bid and purchase; abstaining from bidding would follow from valid economic reasoning.

The decision that the sale is or is not wanted may be made at any time during the preliminary or complete examination of the prospectus, the timber, and the road-construction cost. In figure 15 (point 1) the decision is shown as a clear-cut yes or no. If examination indicates that the timber in question is not suitable to the needs of bidder A, he may still consider bargaining and entering into an agreement (point 2) with other potential buyers. The opportunity to enter into an agreement may come repeatedly and at several points in time beween the announcement of a sale and its point of auction. Bidder A may reject the opportunity to enter into an agreement for one of several reasons: (1) an acknowledged lack of interest in the timber, (2) no obvious gain resulting from an agreement, (3) uncertainty that any agreement would be followed, or (4) fear of antitrust involvement. If the possibility of an agreement is rejected, then bidder A must still decide whether or not to qualify for bidding (point 3). If he decides against qualification, no further decisions need be made and his interest in the timber is concluded. He may decide, however, to qualify for bidding even after his decision that the timber in question is not desirable. An affirmative decision to qualify might be made (1) out of indifference to the sale but willingness to take it at appraised price if no other bidders appear, (2) in order to demonstrate in subsequent bargaining with other insiders that he has a low success ratio and ought not to be challenged in a specific desired sale, (3) in order to plead at a later point with the successful bidder that "I didn't bid against you on the last sale, now let me have the next sale," or (4) in order to offer an opportunity at the auction to cast a preclusive bid, that is, a bid designed to prevent entry into "his area" by an outsider. The reasoning at this juncture (point 7) is discussed later.

Returning now to point 2 in the diagram, bidder A may decide to enter into an agreement with other potential purchasers even though he has previously decided that the timber is not suitable to his needs. He may agree to abstain from oral bidding, thus allowing other competitors to take the sale. Such an agreement would be to bidder A's bargaining advantage in that it would allow him at a later point to claim priority for a sale on the basis that he had abstained from the previous sale. Agreeing to abstain from bidding may establish a claim on a future sale as part of bidding strategy, even though the previous sale was not wanted. After deciding to enter into an agreement, bidder A must then decide whether or not to qualify for bidding, a decision indicated at point 5. A negative decision again ends his interest in the sale. An affirmative decision allows him to make an oral bid after the opening of sealed bids at the auction. If the agreement has been maintained, the interest of buyer A comes to an end. On the other hand, if the agreement has been broken and an outsider appears to be winning the sale, then bidder A, being qualified, is in the position at point 7 to decide whether or not he wishes to engage in preclusive bidding. If he does not, his interest in the sale ends.

A preclusive bid is one designed to prevent an outsider from acquiring timber and "insider" status within a semiclosed area. The following phrases are heard frequently: "He tried to buy timber outside his area," and "This is my area." Buying patterns become established. Mills located within easy access to a given working circle or ranger district become established as inside mills and jealously treat all others as outsiders. Considerable pressure is exerted to maintain a code of conduct based upon spheres of influence. Small firms with limited resources find entry difficult in an area where they do not traditionally operate. One bidder, whom I shall identify as bidder X, wanted to bid on a national forest sale outside his usual operating area. Bidder X was primarily a gyppo logger, but he also needed logs to supply his own small veneer plant. Bidder X approached the principal buyer, whom I shall identify as bidder Y, and informed him of his interest in a given timber sale. The argument presented by bidder X in support of his position was that the quality and the species of the timber sale in question were ideally suited to his veneer-plant needs and that he would willingly sell other logs in the sale to bidder Y. Bidder X reported that the conversation ended by bidder Y saying in essence, "You come in here and try to buy timber in my area and I'll force you out." Bidder X, disregarding the threat, proceeded to bid for and buy the sale.

The insider attempting to protect "his area" against new competition has several economic weapons at his command. The first is the preclusive bid. In calculating his maximum bid (point 9, fig. 15), the insider must reach a judgment as to the relative desirability of preclusive bidding to make entry by an outsider impossible at any cost, or at least to make entry expensive. The first approach would absolutely deny the sale to an outsider, but possibly at a very high cost to the insider. The insider would, by this approach, be required to purchase the timber at a price beyond the willingness of the outsider to bid. The second approach would allow purchase, but at onerous terms designed to make the sale unprofitable to the outsider. In the words of one operator, "To beat competition we must let them have a few expensive ones, too."

Other weapons may be used to make the practice of "jumping" areas unprofitable. One such device is for the insider to approach other insiders and advise them against purchasing logs from the outsider. The value of this weapon depends on the number of mills in the area, the degree of cooperation extended, and the milling facilities available to the outside buyer.

Yet another approach is harassment. One technique allows the insider to insist that the seller agency enforce the letter of the law in road building and logging. Governing laws and regulations are written for sales in general rather than for a particular sale. They must be interpreted with some degree of judgment. An administering ranger, when pressed, is likely to feel obliged to enforce regulations according to the letter of the law in order to protect his own position. Hence, harassment of this kind may become an effective weapon.

The maximum preclusive bid also depends on other factors. Judgment must be exercised as to whether the outsider is just "fishing" for a bargain and is not likely to bid beyond the appraised price established for the sale. The qualifying bidders may include some outsiders who bid at appraised price hoping to pick up a sale having no other qualified bidders. Such a person may not even bother to show up for the sale, or, if present, may not make an oral bid beyond his sealed bid, normally at appraised price. Finally, bidder A, stalling for time, may withhold a preclusive bid, hoping that another insider will take up the burden of the preclusive bid.

The above concludes discussion of the principal alternatives facing a prospective bidder who decides at point 1 that the sale in question does not particularly suit his needs. We shift now to an analysis of the alternatives following an affirmative decision on the desirability of the sale. Point 10 in figure 15 again requires a decision as to whether or not to enter into an agreement with other potential bidders. If a negative decision is reached, bidder A must decide whether to qualify and, if to qualify, whether to bid. He may decide against qualifying and bidding if he concludes that the buyer is predetermined because the timber is located in an established firm's sphere of influence, that the established firm has indicated its intention to take the sale, and, finally, that bidding would be a futile and antagonistic effort. Alternatively, he may conclude that he is unable to qualify financially as a bidder and/or a buyer. As indicated earlier, qualification for bidding requires a cash deposit averaging about 5 percent of the value of the sale. Furthermore, financial responsibility must be demonstrated to the satisfaction of the seller.

Alternatively, after reaching an affirmative decision to enter into an agreement with other potential bidders, bidder A must decide, by species and grade, how much of the sale is desired. If some, but not all, of the timber is desired, the agreement normally specifies the *de jure* buyer. This could be bidder A or another operator, bidder B, who desires part of the logs; or it could be a gyppo logger, bidder C, who has no milling facilities but instead buys timber and sells logs to other users including bidder A, as indicated at point 14.

If the timber is to be divided among several users, a log distribution agreement, wherein certain log classes are channeled to given buyers, is normally reached prior to the sale. Buyers B and C thereby hope to eliminate bidding against them by buyers who need a small portion of the production. Gyppo loggers are frequently quoted as saying, in effect, "If you don't run me up on this sale, I'll sell you the logs." Or a lumberman may say to a veneer-mill operator, "Let me have it and I'll give you the peelable culls, number three sawlogs, peelers, and I'll keep the other sawlogs."

Given an agreement allowing B or C to make the purchase and another agreement covering log distribution, buyer A must again decide whether he wishes to qualify for bidding. A negative decision precludes a later opportunity to make an oral bid; an affirmative decision allows an opportunity for oral bidding. Such an opportunity may be desired if a previous agreement has been broken or if preselected bidder B or C withdraws after heated bidding. An agreement normally states that a given buyer, perhaps bidder B, will engage in bidding and will not be opposed by other parties to the agreement. If bidder B should cease bidding, however, leaving a contender from outside the agreement as high bidder, individual parties to the agreement would normally be free to enter bidding if they so desired.

If an agreement has been ended by bidder B or C withdrawing from bidding, then (point 17) bidder A must decide whether or not he wishes to enter bidding to obtain the desired timber. If the decision is negative, his activity for the sale ends. An affirmative decision would lead to bidding, with the only other question being how high he wishes to go. This point is discussed below.

Returning to point 12 in figure 15, we must now analyze the course of events following bidder A's decision to bid for all logs from a given sale. One interviewee stated, "In one area buyers meet before the sale and agree on who is to get the timber. Anybody who breaks the agreement will get no timber, others will bid him out even at a loss." An agreement may result from a meeting of the several interested bidders. Alternatively, bidder A may contact each of the other potential bidders separately. The basis for claiming a given sale may rest upon several points. First, bidder A may claim rights to a given sale based on his past abstention from bidding, allowing others to take the sales. As pointed out earlier, abstaining from bidding may take place even when bidder A does not want the timber under any circumstances. Alternatively, there may be a real sacrifice involved in hopes of obtaining future bargaining benefits. Second, bidder A may offer concessions on future sales. The pertinent phrase often heard in interviews is, "Let me have this one and I'll let you have the next one." In making such an offer, bidder A obligates himself to abstain from bidding on specified future sales for the requested consideration, which, in turn, may prove to be an empty reward. If an agreement is negotiated and other bidders honor it, bidder A may still lose the timber to a bidder not a party to the agreement. Bidder A ends up with an obligation, but no timber. Further, he may have obligated himself to other parties who, in turn, had no real interest in the timber.

Third, bidder A may plead a need for timber to satisfy his milling capacity. He may plead fair play, pointing out that others have obtained recent sales and have backlogs of purchased timber in contrast with his own lack of timber under contract. One interviewee reported, "Other mills continuously plead with us to stay out of this one and I'll stay out of the next one. I've got to have logs." Fourth, when all other approaches have been exhausted, bidder A may resort to threats.[2] One large producer is reported to have told a gyppo logger, "If you bid against us, you will never get another [logging] contract with us." The gyppo logger in question did not heed the threat. Up to the time of interview, the gyppo logger had not received another contract from the producer issuing the threat.

Bidder A may also threaten to retaliate against bidder B by bidding against him in subsequent sales he may hope to obtain. This threat may result in a mutually ruinous stalemate, a result the threatener has no desire to bring about. There is much for bidder A to gain by making such a threat, and only credibility of his future threats to be gained from carrying it out.[3]

When bidder A has exhausted the opportunities indicated above, he must decide whether or not to qualify for bidding. If the answer is negative, his chances of obtaining the sale come to an end. This decision would follow from the conclusion that the probability of his getting the sale is not sufficiently good to justify the trouble and expense of qualifying. Should he decide to qualify, he must then further decide whether or not to bid. He has previously decided that the timber is wanted and that an agreement is desirable, but he may not have been successful in drawing concessions from all others. If competition for the sale is keen, qualified bidders may number a half-dozen, but they seldom exceed ten. Bidding starts at the appraised price. Bidder A may remain quiet while bidding takes place between two or more other qualified bidders. If bidding proceeds to a point beyond the highest value that bidder A is willing to offer, he does not, unless overruled by emotion or preclusive bidding, become an active bidder.

Alternatively, if bidding between two or more other qualified bidders stops short of the maximum value bidder A would offer, he may enter competitive oral bidding. The maximum bid that

---

2 The term "threat" in the bargaining theory context has been defined as "no more than a communication of one's own incentives, designed to impress on the other the automatic consequences of his act" (Schelling, "An Essay on Bargaining," p. 292).

3 For an analysis of threats, see Schelling, "The Strategy of Conflict," pp. 223–228.

bidder A would make (point 23) depends upon several factors. First, an interested bidder normally enters the auction process with at least two values calculated prior to the auction. One of these values reflects his estimate of the buying price which will yield him all his costs plus a "fair profit." Whether or not he goes beyond this value depends on the emotion of the moment, how badly he is pressed for logs, and who his bidding opposition is. A second value reflects a rational maximum bid normally calculated to cover variable costs only. As bidder A approaches this second value, he is progressively bidding away gross income that would cover his depreciation and yield him a profit. This bid is a rational one for an operator whose alternative is to cease operations either temporarily or permanently.

Second, the maximum bid depends upon the identity of the bidding opposition. The previous high bidder may be a personal or business friend, an enemy in the competion for timber, or simply a competitor trying to buy timber within the framework of the free-price system. A statement made by one interviewee—"It's routine not to bid against friends"—is probably an overstatement. One encounters too many instances of bidding, irrespective of friendship, to accept this statement as a valid generalization; the interviewee who made it had just lost a sale through the friendship device. He was one of six qualified bidders in a medium-size sale where bidding was intense. Bidding proceeded between two of the six qualified bidders until the bid exceeded appraised price by 75 percent. At this point, one of the two dropped out and a third bidder who had been silent up to then entered the bidding. Again, bidding proceeded until the premium amounted to 80 percent, whereupon the second of the original two bidders dropped out, leaving the third as high bidder and winner of the sale. The interviewee who might have entered the bidding at this point stated privately that he would have liked to have taken the sale for an additional bid of as much as 5 dollars per thousand board feet. He was, however, unwilling to compete against the high bidder or one of the other six qualified bidders because of friendship and business relationships. He feared that profitable business associations might be sacrificed if he entered into competitive bidding.

In another situation, a potential bidder E owns timberland in the area and sells logs of particular species and grade to potential bidders F, G, and H. The latter are reluctant to bid against their supplier for fear of having their log supply cut off. Yet, in another area involving the same timber owner (bidder E), a potential bidder, when interviewed, stated that he does not hesitate to bid against his partial log supplier. Up to the time of the interview, his bidding practice had produced no undesirable consequences.

A third point in determining the maximum bid relates to the fundamental bidding strategy of bidder A. Several interviewees stated that they wished to make abundantly clear their bidding strategy: to use oral auction bidding as a medium of communication among bidders. One interviewee said: "To discourage competition is our bidding strategy and to show those who try to enter that they haven't got a prayer of getting into this area." The statement was made with reference to outsiders and did not include the firms historically active in the area in question. Another buyer, in explaining his strategy, said that he wanted to "demonstrate that it will *cost* an outsider to come in." Still another strategist attempted to demonstrate that whenever he entered oral bidding competition he would purchase the sale regardless of the cost. This strategy, of course, involves withholding bids from sales of minor interest.

Another bidding strategy is to get a high-bid position either anonymously or without appearing to bid against a friend. As indicated earlier, the qualifying sealed bid preliminary to the oral auction is usually made at the appraised price. But occasionally a qualifying sealed bid significantly above the appraised price will be submitted. There appear to be two reasons for such bidding strategy: (1) By making a more or less vigorous sealed bid above appraised price, a bidder is communicating (in an implicit bargaining sense) a strong desire for the sale, hoping that other bidders will acknowledge his position by refraining from "running him up." (2) Perhaps of greater importance in a market restricted geographically to a few buyers who are well known to one another is the anonymity afforded by the sealed bid. In becoming the initial high bidder through this means, bidder A has not bid against anyone in particular. But any subsequent oral bidder is placed in the position of having to bid against a particular person. A strategy of this kind is effective against some bidders, such as bidder B, but not necessarily against all. For instance, an oral bid may be cast against bidder A by bidder D who is not bothered by the above personal relationship. Once bidder D has moved to become high bidder, however, formerly silent bidder B may quickly bid, thereby placing bidder A in an adverse position.

A fourth unwelcome issue pertaining to the maximum bid is emotion. Occasionally a bidder in desperate need of logs to supply his existing facilities throws caution aside and continues to bid. He may be speculating on an improvement in the lumber or plywood market in hopes that such a development will rescue him from an overbid situation.[4] As he reaches his previously estimated maximum, he is haunted by the hope that another 5-cent bid may win the sale. In at least one instance, emotion without any rational basis dominated. In a particularly heated contest, a bidder who had already won the sale declared with pathetic exasperation, "I raised my own bid five dollars."

There are few qualified and identified bidders in oral auction bidding. When a bidding contest develops, one's bid obviously depends on the bid of another, whose bid in turn is dependent on one's bid, and so on. Whether one bids at all may depend on who else is bidding, which may depend on who else is bidding, and so on. Collusive arrangements, both explicit and implicit, develop in order to prevent runaway bidding. All these behavioral patterns are characteristic of and expected from an oligopsonistic structure. Behavior (conduct) follows directly from structure.

TOKEN-BID SALES

A final type of bidding behavior is of special interest because it suggests either an implicit or explicit agreement among potential buyers. This class of bidding, termed "token bidding," occurs when two or more bidders have met the qualification requirements and have submitted sealed bids at the appraised price. Sales regulations require that tie bids be broken by oral auction bidding. One of the qualified bidders makes a token oral bid, usually 5 cents per thousand board feet and usually on the lowest-volume species. If the other bidders agree to this solution and the resulting allocation of timber, they remain silent and allow the token bidder to be awarded the sale. Thus, for a minimum bid on the minimum-quantity species, the tie bid may be settled at minimum cost to the buyer.

In order further to clarify the general character of the token-bid sale, an illustration is provided in table 23. The appraised price per thousand board feet by species is shown. Sealed bids were submitted at the appraised prices for each species by ten qualified bidder firms. In the oral bidding that followed the posting of

---

4 The presence of the escalator clause in contracts since 1961 takes some of the speculative risk out of fluctuating market values for stumpage, as half of any gain or loss owing to a change in the stumpage price index is assumed by the government in national forest timber sales.

TABLE 23

TOKEN-BID SALE, WILLAMETTE NATIONAL FOREST

Species	Volume (in millions of board feet)	Appraised price per thousand board feet (in dollars)	High-bid price per thousand board feet (in dollars)
Douglas fir	22.4	11.10	11.10
Pine	1.0	6.95	7.00
Noble fir and Shasta red fir	2.5	5.15	5.15
Hemlock and other	4.1	3.15	3.15
Total or average	30.0	9.38	9.38

SOURCE: U.S. Forest Service, "National Forest Advertised Timber Sales, Region 6," 1380 (2400) (Portland, Ore., Oct. 13, 1961), p. 24.

sealed bids, one of the ten competitors raised his sealed bid on the pine (the species of minimum quantity) by 5 cents. The other nine qualified bidders remained silent, whereupon the token bidder was declared high bidder and was awarded the sale. This offering had a total appraised value of $281,380. By a token bid on the minimum-quantity species, the high bidder was awarded the timber at a cost of $281,430, or 50 dollars above the total appraised value. This particular sale was a large one, about six times the average sale size offered in the region. Information from personal interviews indicates that operators normally in the market for federal timber consider most national forest offerings to be bargains at the appraised price.

There are several possible interpretations of the behavior of the nine silent bidders. First, they may have felt that the timber was worth only the appraised value or no more than 50 dollars above it. This judgment may have followed a detailed examination of the offering, or it may reflect the fishing strategy outlined earlier. Second, they may have become qualified bidders only to afford an opportunity to cast a preclusive bid against the possible entry of an outsider. Third, they may have had no interest in the timber but simply wanted to establish that each one individually did not bid against whoever happened to be the high bidder. Fourth, there may have been a prior agreement between some or all of the qualified bidders, and even some nonqualified bidders, which designated the intended buyer in advance. And, of course, a combination of the above factors may have been present.

The token-bid sale is not an isolated phenomenon. In the period 1959–1962, 14.5 percent of all oral auction sales (17.3 percent of all volume sold) in the Douglas fir region may be classified as token-bid sales (see table 24).

Both expense and risk are involved in preparing to bid for national forest timber and in actually submitting a sealed bid. Some bidders minimize the expense, but not the risk, by failing to cruise timber and by neglecting to examine any required road-construction project. For firms meeting the cost and incurring the risk of qualification, it appears improbable that a 5-cent bid would be sufficient to discourage interest in the sale. The behavior pattern characteristic of the token-bid sale suggests the implicit or explicit understanding among bidders which one would expect to find in an oligopsonistic structure.

Summary

This analysis of bidding strategy is intended to provide insight into the complex relationships and behavioral patterns prevailing among bidders in an imperfect market. Because the market for timber is oligopsonistic, each bidder must develop a plan for accomplishing his bidding objectives. Because the structure of the industry varies in different geographical markets and the personalities of the competitors differ, a variety of bidding strategies have developed. The kind of conduct described here is consistent with an oligopsonistic structure.

Seven fundamental decisions that must be made by buyers of national forest timber have been identified. These decisions confront the bidder repeatedly and in different situations. This complex decision-making setting was systematized by use of the flow-charting technique adapted from computer programming.

Bidding strategy is the necessary art of employing one's bargaining power in choosing among alternative courses of action in a manner designed to attain certain objectives. Strategy may be examined at three points in the bidding process: (1) presale bargaining, (2) establishing one's qualifying sealed-bid value, and (3) establishing one's high-bid value(s).

First, in presale bargaining, one may plead one's case with other bidders by proffering a variety of arguments usually based on the "fair play" concept. Alternatively, one may react from a position of power which, when carried to an extreme, extends to threats of retaliation if certain conditions are not met.

Second, in determining one's qualifying sealed-bid values, the normal procedure is to bid the appraised value. But four strategies are present in this approach: (1) Some bids are cast at appraised value, representing a fishing strategy; a bidder passively offers to take one or a series of sales at appraised price on the assumption that the sum of any and all sales obtained by this method represents a satisfactory bargain. (2) A bid at appraised price may reflect an attempt to establish a claim on a future sale by arguing that one refrained from bidding up the successful bidder on the subject sale. (3) A competitor may bid the appraised price in order to establish a low success ratio to serve as the basis for a later plea to other bidders. (4) The commonplace strategy is to obtain the sale as inexpensively as possible (i.e., avoid "leaving money on the table"), but the bidder is prepared to go higher than the appraised price in the oral auction bidding. Alternatively, a sealed bid in excess of the appraised price may reflect either of two additional strategies: communicating one's determination to obtain the sale, or anonymously and impersonally placing oneself in the high-bidder position. This course, in turn, places others who may wish to bid in a position where they must make a "personal" attack (an unfriendly act) on the high-bidder position.

Third, the remaining strategy concerns the extent of oral bids beyond the initial qualifying sealed bid, the issue being the limit of the oral auction bid. One may wish to make a preclusive bid against entry by an outsider. Strategy may follow either of two courses: bids may be cast to make entry impossible at any cost, or bids may be cast to make entry expensive, but possible. In the absence of preclusive intentions, a high-bid value may be set which would yield a fair profit on processing the subject sale. A maximum-bid value may also be set which would allow only variable operating costs to be covered, yielding neither profit nor a residual cash flow for fixed costs. Beyond this point, emotion (irrationality) may rule.

In the token-bid sale, two or more persons become qualified bidders, but the sale is transacted by one bidder casting a token bid, usually on the species of minimum quantity, while the other bidder(s) remains silent. The token-bid sale is of special interest because it strongly suggests the kind of working agreement among bidders which might be expected in an oligopsonistic structure.

CHAPTER 10

Oligopsony in the Timber Resource Market

An empirical study concerned with the behavior of competitors in the markets for federal timber must be conducted within an explicit theoretical framework, which in this instance is the theory of oligopoly. From economic theory testable hypotheses may be derived.

THE THEORETICAL BACKGROUND

Oligopoly theory[1] is admittedly inadequate despite the hundreds of books and thousands of articles which have been written on it. It is concerned with competition among the few sellers of a given product or factor of production. As this study is concerned not with the few sellers but with the few buyers of a factor of production, the discussion should be based on oligopsony theory. There is, however, no separate theory to explain competition among few buyers. Oligopsony has either been ignored or treated only indirectly by extension of oligopoly theory. In his analysis of regional monopoly and oligopoly, Harold Hotelling economized on analysis and verbiage with the following blanket coverage: "If in the following pages the words 'buy' and 'sell' be everywhere inter-

---

[1] Good discussions of the development of oligopoly theory are available in J. K. Galbraith, "Monopoly and the Concentration of Economic Power," in H. S. Ellis, ed., *A Survey of Contemporary Economics* (Philadelphia: Blakiston Co., 1949), and K. W. Rothschild, "Price Theory and Oligopoly," *Journal of Political Economy*, LVII (June, 1947), 299–320. For a detailed analysis and extension of contributions to oligopoly theory by Augustin Cournot, Joseph Bertrand, F. Y. Edgeworth, and Heinrich von Stackelberg, plus Fellner's own important contribution, see William Fellner, *Competition among the Few* (New York: Knopf, 1949). Game theory modifications are given in Martin Shubik, *Strategy and Market Structure* (New York: Wiley, 1960). The most recent important empirical and theoretical contributions by Joe Bain and Paolo Sylos-Labini are reviewed and extended by Franco Modigliani, "New Developments on the Oligopoly Front," *Journal of Political Economy*, LXVI (June, 1958), 215–232.

changed, the argument remains equally valid."[2] Not only has oligopsony theory been ignored, but empirical studies on competition among few buyers are appropriately "few."

The justification for blanket and parallel treatment of oligopsony theory is the fact that the behavior of firms as buyers of productive services or as sellers of products is highly similar. Although the differences are perhaps minor, they should be acknowledged:

1) The analytical devices needed to discuss price-input determination in oligopsony differ in expository form from those needed to discuss price-output determination in oligopoly. The latter is concerned with few interdependent sellers. Price and output are determinate only with specific assumptions about the behavior of other sellers in the oligopoly. The basic analytical data consist of the firm's cost and demand functions. Similarly, in oligopsony price and input are determinate only with specific assumptions about the behavior of other buyers in the oligopsony. But the basic analytical data consist of the production function and factor supply schedules.

2) Markets may be geographically narrower in an oligopsony as compared with an oligopoly. This follows from the proposition that value per unit of weight is normally, but not invariably, greater for final products than for raw materials used to produce the final products. In the absence of discriminatory freight rates, items of relatively low value per unit of weight involve relatively heavy transportation charges and therefore rather circumscribed markets. This second difference between oligopsony and oligopoly may have no analytical significance, but may be, rather, merely a commentary on relevant research procedures. For example, in subnational markets extreme care must be used in developing concentration ratios from the customary statistical sources.

3) Price tends to be the significant variable in oligopsony, whereas in oligopoly nonprice factors, such as advertising, packaging, credit terms, and so forth, are relatively more important variables. The oligopolist frequently sells to consumers whose knowledge is relatively imperfect. On the other hand, an oligopsony, by definition, is made up of few buyers. Outside the framework of a multitude of consumers and within the framework of fewness, buyers tend to be professional, and knowledge of product

---

2 Harold Hotelling, "Stability in Competition," *Economic Journal*, XXXIX (March, 1929), 42.

quality and price is more nearly perfect. A very slight price differential, or other product characteristic that may be translated
into a price differential, is more likely to bring forth volume purchases among knowledgeable buyers than among poorly informed
consumers. This third distinctive characteristic may again have
little analytical significance, but instead may be a commentary on
research objectives. One would hesitate to counsel that less attention be given to nonprice competition in oligopsony than in
oligopoly research when a serious fault in oligopoly theory is that
inadequate attention is given to nonprice competition.

The theory of bilateral monopoly (or bilateral oligopoly with
collusion) is similarly relevant as a theoretical framework for this
study of federal timber markets because, in a given market, few
sellers (or perhaps only one, the Forest Service) confront few buyers.
There are, however, two significant differences, which mean that
bilateral monopoly theory does not provide a useful analytical
framework for the study of oligopsony in the federal timber
market:

1) Bilateral monopoly theory applies only if one buyer faces
one seller, or if two or more collusive buyers or sellers are in complete collusion and operate effectively on the principle of joint
profit maximization. Perfect collusion among buyers is nowhere
apparent in the separate geographical markets for federal timber.
Rather, the situation is one of oligopsony with various degrees of
collusion among buyers.

2) A second point rendering bilateral monopoly inapplicable to
the timber market concerns seller behavior. In bilateral monopoly
theory, the seller tries to maximize monopoly profit by establishing
a quantity of output to be offered at a level that equates his marginal cost and marginal revenue. The Forest Service, however, is
committed to selling an amount of timber given by the allowable-
cut calculation rather than a profit-maximizing calculation. If the
seller is not a profit maximizer, the only element left in bilateral
monopoly which might be applicable to oligopsony is the possibility of joint profit-maximizing oligopsonistic buyers. This latter
provision has been challenged in point 1 above. Hence, the theory
of bilateral monopoly offers no assistance in identifying a theoretical framework for the empirical study of competition in the market for federal timber.

The essence of oligopoly or oligopsony is interdependence
among sellers or buyers, respectively. There is interdependence
among buying units in that one buyer realizes that any course of

action he elects must take into consideration and be dependent upon a course of action followed by his rivals, who, in turn, are aware that any course of action they elect must take into consideration and be dependent upon actions of the first and other rival buyers, and so on. The problem of competition among the few has been authoritatively stated: "The oligopsonist, instead of setting up a demand function, attempts to select a definite price to be paid for the materials and services he buys and a definite quantity to be purchased, which, in combination with one another, are optimal from his point of view. But the quantity he is capable of buying at any given price depends on the prices paid by his competitors, who, in turn, are appreciably affected by what price he pays."[3]

In the absence of a specific agreement or other precise knowledge about how one's rivals will react to one's own initiative in an oligopsonistic market, the buyer may only conjecture about the reactions of his rivals to a given situation. An oligopsonist is uncertain about the shape of the supply function he faces as an individual buyer. Buyers who operate in competitive factor markets at one end of the spectrum, or a monopsonist at the other end, can know the shape of the relevant supply functions, the former because actions of a buyer in competitive markets are unnoticed, the latter because the firm is also the industry.

Agreements among oligopolists or oligopsonists may be either explicit or implicit. An explicit agreement is the result of direct contact and negotiation among the participants, and is unlikely to be in written form. Rather, it is expressed in oral terms and is sanctioned as a gentlemen's agreement. Since collusive agreements are violations of antitrust statutes, they are not enforceable; injured parties would hardly bring court action in the event of breach of agreement. Such action has been brought in at least one instance, however.[4]

Illegality notwithstanding, the existence of agreements to re-

---

3 Fellner, *op. cit.*, p. 11.

4 The plaintiff alleged that an agreement existed whereby the parties would not compete with one another for the purchase of a particular tract of Bureau of Land Management timber, but the defendant did so compete and bid $428,136.50 on timber appraised for sale by the BLM at $314,810.25. A civil action was instituted in which the plaintiff sought $273,000 damages for an alleged breach of contract (*Report of Investigation of the Sale of Government-Owned Timber by the Forest Service, Department of Agriculture and the Bureau of Land Management, Department of Interior*, U.S. Government Accounting Office, Office of Investigations, I-17338 [1953], p. 9).

strain bidding under various conditions is widely acknowledged within the industry: "Representatives of the Forest Service and the BLM stated that they are generally aware that agreements exist between certain operators, often referred to as a 'gentlemen's agreement,' whereby the operators will refrain from purchasing Government timber outside of their respective areas."[5] Although government officials are aware of such agreements, legal proof of their existence is quite another matter. In 1964 the Justice Department brought action against five firms as buyers of national forest timber in the Waldport working circle of the Siuslaw National Forest, charging violation of the Sherman Act.[6] The complaint was dismissed, however, on the basis of inadequate evidence.

An implicit agreement is not preceded by direct bargaining, but is the result of quasi bargaining. It is a kind of spontaneous coordination of interests arising naturally out of a structural situation in which there are few operators. A sophisticated operator tries to "find out from the responses of the other parties what the ultimate consequences of his own patterns of behavior are; and each party tries to discover which of the alternative patterns of behavior results in mutual reactions that are in the nature of a tacit agreement (or convention), and are more favorable from his point of view than any other tacit agreement acceptable to the others."[7] In timber auction markets, quasi bargaining takes place as a buyer gains thorough familiarity with the bidding strategy of his rivals, together with their log input requirements and their inventories of logs and standing timber. The formality of negotiation marks the difference between explicit and implicit agreements, but the results may be the same. Two producers who have for years been operating in the same working circle without bidding against each other in their respective spheres of influence do not need to meet in direct negotiations concerning an upcoming sale. Each is well aware that if one suddenly qualifies and bids against the other, retaliation will follow at the next opportunity, with the result that total timber supplies will remain the same and only the cost of timber will change.

Implicit collusion arises in a market where there are few buyers. Antitrust action, or fear of such action, may discourage and eliminate explicit agreements. But when the buyers who are aware of

---

5 *Ibid.*

6 *United States of America v. Cascadia Lumber Co. et al.*, U.S. District Court for the District of Oregon (1964), CR 64–73.

7 Fellner, *op. cit.*, pp. 15–16.

their interdependent relationship are few, implicit collusion should be expected.

Both explicit and implicit agreements are subject to frequent breakdown and warfare, but disruption occurs more often in implicit agreements whose details are not carefully specified. Periodic breakdown in agreements occurs when outsiders, and perhaps occasionally insiders, test the strength of the beneficiaries of such agreements. A series of token-bid sales indicating the existence of implicit understandings serves as a tempting invitation to others, both insiders and outsiders, who are not among the beneficiaries. As noted earlier, the process of testing agreements forces the participants in a collusive arrangement to make entry by an outsider either impossible or expensive. As a result of successful collusion, the proportion of token-bid sales obtained at no significant premium over appraised price will be relatively high, and the average bid-appraisal ratio will be relatively low. Furthermore, periodic testing of strength may result in occasional high premiums over appraised price paid either by the challenging firm obtaining costly sales or by insiders in costly defense of their position.

If an oligopsonistic market cannot accurately be described as collusive (explicit or implicit), it is in a state of "warfare" to a varying degree. Price and quantity are indeterminate for the firm. The term "competitive" cannot with technical accuracy be applied to a situation of this kind, but should be reserved for a structural situation where there are many buyers (or sellers) and where no one is large enough to appreciably influence price. This classification, however, does not preclude pricing results that approximate the competitive price. In the oligopsonistic situation there is interdependence among buyers; the profit-maximizing behavior of one buyer is dependent upon the behavior of his rival, whose action in turn is dependent upon the behavior of the first buyer, and so on.

A warfare situation may be either long term or short term. The latter result reflects a breakdown in a collusive agreement; the former, the existence of too many producers to be coordinated in a collusive agreement or a substantial excess of milling capacity over normal log supplies. A long-term warfare situation has these results: (1) There will be very few token-bid sales. (2) The average ratio of bid price to appraised price will be relatively high. (3) The structure of the market will probably be quite fluid, with firms making their exit from the market when lumber prices and veneer prices are unfavorable and, in turn, reentering, or with new firms entering under relatively free-entry conditions when final product prices and demand conditions are favorable.

A short-term warfare situation may simply be one of the periodic intervals between agreements which produce a workably collusive market. This type of warfare would be expected to produce a modest proportion of token-bid sales and a sharp distinction in the extent of competitive bidding between periods when a collusive agreement is in effect, on the one hand, and when open warfare exists on the other. Firms that are able to obtain some single-bidder and token-bid sales in a period governed by collusive agreements gain a financial ability to bid relatively high prices when challenged during a period of open warfare.

Price and Quantity Determination in the Federal Timber Market

Market supply elasticity of timber may be analyzed under long-run conditions (fifty to eighty years) and under three short-run conditions: less than one year, one to thirty years, and thirty to fifty years. The supply curve for timber is most elastic in the long run and least elastic in the less-than-one-year short run. But in no "run" does the elasticity-of-supply estimate depart importantly from inelasticity. Similarly, detailed analysis reveals that the demand for timber is also price inelastic.

In my treatment of timber supply, I have ignored quantity responses to price changes which are not sustainable responses. A cyclical recovery in the building materials industry, including lumber and plywood, producing, in turn, a higher demand for and a higher price of stumpage, may bring forth a temporary (unsustainable) increase in timber offered for sale. As an increase in supply in year one comes at the expense of compensating curtailments in year zero or years two, three, and so on, the quantity response is simply an inventory adjustment. Instead, the analysis was restricted to sustainable quantity changes in which price changes cause adjustments in standards of utilization of timber or timberland and therefore sustainable production changes.

Also, the analysis of oligopsony is limited to the federal timber market and to specific timber sale conditions imposed by the Forest Service. While federal timber sales represent only about 40 percent of all log production in the Douglas fir region (1962 basis, see table 9), federal timber accounts for most of the free-market timber sales. Normally, timber in private ownership is logged by the

owner primarily for processing in mills within the same ownership. Some logs (not timber) are sold or traded from private (also
public) log production.

Having estimated market demand and supply functions for
timber (see chaps. 2, 3), we may now join these functions and discuss price determination under three headings: (1) in a geographical market composed of few firms as buyers, with the Forest Service
as seller and with no collusion; (2) in a geographical area where collusion is practiced by the few buyers (a collusive oligopsony); and
(3) for an individual firm in an oligopsonistic market where firms
attempt to operate independently of one another. The third situation is one of interdependence among buyers acting independently.
It differs from the first, which is concerned with market-price determination.

1) Market-price determination in an oligopsony when collusion
is absent may be analyzed with the aid of figure 16. The supply
curve of national forest timber is shown as P_1ES (less-than-one-year
short run) or, alternatively, P_1ES' (one-to-thirty-year short run).
From the previous analysis of the timber supply function it will

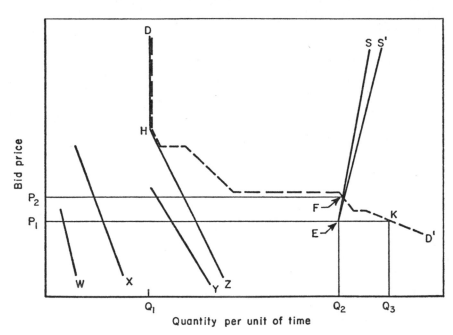

Fig. 16. Market-price determination in an oligopsony when collusion is
absent.

be recalled that the Forest Service may not legally sell timber below the appraised price. This point, indicated by P_1, may alternatively be called the "refusal price." Any quantity of timber may be purchased up to Q_2 at the appraised price, and zero quantity below the appraised price.[8] The *ES* segment of the less-than-one-year supply curve indicates that quantity offered is highly inelastic with respect to price. If the demand for federal timber is greater than the supply (at appraised prices), premium bids will develop, accompanied by a very modest increase in timber supply. The supply curve segment *ES'* indicates that, in a longer period of time (one to thirty years), higher prices bid for timber will bring forth slightly larger additions to supply as formerly submarginal logs and species become supramarginal.

The demand curve for all firms in a noncollusive oligopsony is given as *DD'*. It will be recalled that the industry demand curve is obtained by summing individual firm value of marginal product functions that have been adjusted for substitution among factors in response to changes in factor costs. Individual firm demand curves for timber are shown as *W*, *X*, *Y*, and *Z*. Value of marginal product and marginal physical product curves for any one firm have identical slopes. As firms within a single geographical timber market expand and contract lumber output, their effect on the national lumber market is too small to influence the price of lumber. The wide vertical range of the demand curve from *D* to *D'* should be acknowledged as an illustrative liberty. As it is based upon partial equilibrium analysis, the range of allowable price and quantity variation is quite limited. The *DH* segment of the demand curve, however, is not based on marginal productivity analysis, but instead reflects a position that may be taken by firm *Z*. It is the result of one firm standing ready to purchase quantities up to OQ_1 at very high bid prices, if necessary, to prevent entry by outsiders.

Joining the industry demand and less-than-one-year supply functions, price equilibrium is given as P_2, reflecting intersection point *F*. Price P_2 rations a nearly fixed quantity of resources among competing buyers. The second function of a higher price, to stimulate an increase in the quantity offered, is of modest importance even within a longer time span. The market equilibrium price P_2

---

[8] If a series of timber stands offered for sale by the Forest Service receive no bids, appraisal procedures would probably be reexamined and appraised prices lowered. "No-bid" sales of national forest timber occur only infrequently. Data available for the period January 1, 1964, through June 30, 1965, show 42 no-bid sales out of 1,748 offerings, or 2.4 percent.

should be understood as an average price. Some firms, by luck or through possession of market power, may obtain timber at the appraised price or another price between P_1 and P_2. Correspondingly, other firms obtain some timber sales at prices in excess of P_2.

2) Market price may also be determined for a given geographical area characterized by few buyers who are able to practice a degree of collusion. The above section is concerned with market equilibrium in the absence of collusion among individual firms. Such firms, however, should be aware that a large premium over appraised price (P_2 minus P_1) does not bring forth a large additional quantity of timber, but represents, instead, an inducement to collusion. By introducing cooperation among bidders, it would obviously become possible to obtain approximately the same quantity of timber at P_1 rather than at P_2. The necessary ingredient to produce this effect is the coordination by individual oligopsonists of their bidding behavior, with the result that the structure of the oligopsony takes on the characteristics of a monopsony, that is, a single buyer.

The objective of coordinated conduct would be joint cost minimization with respect to timber. Price would have to be reduced to P_1. Joint profit maximization introduces yet other requirements, including an allocation of timber among participating firms in such a way that marginal costs among several plants are equated. Further, profits among participating members would have to be pooled and redistributed in accordance with principles chosen by the participants. Fellner argues that such a redistribution would reflect the bargaining power of oligopsonists.[9] While there is abundant evidence that the oligopsonistic timber markets in the Douglas fir region include many arrangements to minimize the cost of acquiring federal timber, there is no evidence that any agreements exist to produce unqualified joint profit maximization.

A resource cost–minimizing monopsonist would calculate a marginal factor cost function for his timber purchases. Such a marginal cost curve would be identical with the P_1E segment of the supply curve, as shown for quantities less than or equal to OQ_2. Within a framework of a less-than-one-year short run (the supply curve P_1ES), slight supply increases are shown corresponding to very large price increases. As there is a sharp corner in the supply curve at point E,

9 Fellner (*op. cit.*, pp. 24–33) discusses at length the determining factors pertaining to the distribution of profits arising out of collusion. He also has an extensive discussion of joint profit maximization and its limitations (*ibid.*, chaps. 4–8).

the marginal factor cost curves become discontinuous at point E. Further, as the higher prices relate to all volumes sold in response to more intense bidding activity, the marginal costs of bringing forth slight supply increases would be very high. Whether one reasons with a very short-term supply function, P_1ES, or with a longer-term function, P_1ES', there is no intersection of the demand curve (adjusted value of marginal product function for the buying monopsonist) and a marginal factor cost function. Resource cost minimization would therefore lead a monopsonist or collusive oligopsonists to demand OQ_2 and to restrict bidding to the appraised price P_1. The magnitude of the transfer of wealth from public to private control is approximated by the difference between P_1 and P_2 multiplied by the quantity P_2F (for the less-than-one-year short run).

With a monopsony or collusive oligopsony price P_1 and quantity OQ_2, an allocation problem arises. If the price system were allowed to perform the allocation function, P_2 would exclude firm W from the market. The factor demand function of firm W (its value of marginal product function) is indicated in figure 16. Similarly, firms X, Y, and Z would demand somewhat less timber at P_2 than at P_1. At the collusive oligopsony price P_1, firm W is in the market, and firms X, Y, and Z would like to have a larger supply of timber. The total quantity demanded at P_1, in the absence of allocation restrictions, is given by point K (OQ_3). At the low price P_1, quantity demanded, EK, must be eliminated by oligopsonistic devices. There are many alternative methods of equating supply and demand at P_1. For example, firms W, Y, and Z may elect to eliminate firm X from the market by "paying him off" (buying him out). As the quantity demanded by firm X at P_1 is approximately equal to the quantity EK, such action would solve the allocation problem so long as this static situation remains. As another alternative, each member of the oligopsony may agree to curtail input requirements by a fixed percentage of their present input. As yet another and perhaps more realistic alternative, the scarce timber supply might be rationed on the basis of hard bargaining reality, with the weakest firms being forced to accept the heaviest cutbacks in timber supplies.[10] Although there are many alternative means of nonprice

---

[10] This interpretation is consistent with Fellner's view of bargaining. For a contrary point of view that "in bargaining, weakness may be strength," see T. C. Schelling, "The Strategy of Conflict: Prospectus for a Reorientation of Game Theory," *Journal of Conflict Resolution*, II (Sept., 1958), 244–249.

allocation, the essential factor remains that an effectively collusive oligopsony carries with it the necessity of allocating scarce timber among the members of the oligopsony.

The model of a collusive oligopsony discussed above implies perfect collusion. In the Douglas fir region, however, there are no observable instances of perfect collusion. Instead, in areas of restrained competition (to be identified later) agreements do not take in all the industry members and, furthermore, are imperfectly observed.[11] Complete participation requires that all firms operating in a single geographical area, plus other firms that could profitably purchase, cut, and transport timber outside the area, be included in the agreement. Within the Douglas fir region this objective probably cannot be realized, and intensive personal interviews suggest no serious attempt at complete participation. Imperfect observance leading to distrust of agreements is common. The experience of one sawmill owner dependent upon federal timber illustrates this point. The millowner, whom I shall identify as bidder A, was driving to a timber sale in company with a gyppo logger. In the course of the conversation (explicit bargaining), the gyppo logger said, "Let me bid on this one and you take the next." Bidder A consented to this explicit agreement in restraint of bidding. In the course of bidding for the first sale, the gyppo logger was outbid and lost the sale to a third party. On a later day, as the two were driving to the second sale, which by prior agreement was bidder A's sale, the gyppo logger reaffirmed, "This is your sale. I won't bid unless you drop out." The sale proceeded to a relatively high bid price, when bidding ceased, leaving bidder A as the high bidder. The gyppo logger, who had previously agreed to remain silent, then commenced bidding and bid up bidder A by an additional 2 dollars per thousand board feet. Bidder A, reporting the incident to me, said: "This was my first and last deal. I won't have any part in further deals. I'll bid what it is worth to me and no more. Let others do the same." Imperfect observance of this type is probably to be expected in an industry often characterized as ruggedly individualistic and among firms with a relatively short time horizon.

3) In exploring the question of market-price determination for an individual firm in a noncollusive oligopsony, the objective is to identify the problems faced by a noncollusive firm in a situation characterized by interdependence among producers. The particu-

11 These two types of departures from perfect collusion are identified and elaborated by Joe S. Bain, *Industrial Organization* (New York: Wiley, 1959), p. 273.

lar problem may be illustrated by examining what we have called "interdependence among producers acting independently."

In figure 16, two supply curves were identified for the purpose of discussing industry supply and demand equilibrium. From the point of view of an individual firm, however, the essence of the oligopsony is that the firm's supply function cannot be identified except on the basis of specific assumptions about the behavior of other firms. An individual profit-maximizing entrepreneur, in considering a possible course of action, needs to know the price effect of his demand for more or less timber input. A buyer in perfect competition is so small that his additional demand for input has no appreciable effect on market price. Similarly, a monopsonist, because he is the single buyer, need not be concerned about the behavior of other buyers. By definition, they do not exist. The oligopsonist, on the other hand, must be concerned about the reaction of rivals when he asserts a demand for a larger share of a nearly fixed supply. If a prior agreement stipulates that other producers will withdraw from the market, there is no problem. A collusive oligopsony is equivalent to a monopsony.

The dilemma facing the oligopsonist in a noncollusive situation may be resolved by making specific assumptions about the behavior of other buyers. For example, a buyer may assume (1) that his rivals will make way for his additional demands and that his own higher bid will not be challenged, or (2) that his rivals will resist his own demands for a higher share of the input and that his bids above appraised price will be matched, plus a "little bit," until all rival bidders have exhausted their bidding ability. The latter procedure is a costly one to follow because, in a subsequent sale, the rivals enter the auction without the burden of a high-cost prior purchase.

An assumption may resolve the problem facing the oligopsonist, but the assumption is not necessarily a correct one. The supply curve derived by conjecture may not correspond to the supply curve that actually appears. A conjectural supply curve in a noncollusive oligopsony is indeterminate except by assumption, and the assumption may be erroneous.

Assume that firm X, whose value of marginal product function is shown in figure 16, is a highly profitable producer and has a strong desire to expand production. The value of marginal product functions (see fig. 16) indicate that firm W would drop out of the market for national forest timber before P_2 is reached. The price P_2 cannot possibly be a profit-maximizing price for any producer so long as the average cost of acquiring national forest timber remains at P_2. If firm W should permanently leave the industry, the market equilibrium price would remain at P_2. The bidding behavior of firm X could not be justified from a profit-maximizing point of view unless the higher price should lead to the withdrawal of a second firm or of a substantial future reduction in the demands of either firm Y or firm Z. If a substantial and permanent reduction in capacity did occur, and, further, if firm X could correctly assume that new entry would not take place, the equilibrium price would return to point E and the bidding pattern of firm X (wherein prices were bid up to P_2) might be justified in the long run. The answer to this profitability calculation is a function of the time pattern of future log inputs and prices and the discount rate, with probability calculations being attached to all variables.

THE COURNOT MODEL

A characteristic of the federal timber market which distinguishes it from other oligopsony markets is that most sales are conducted on the basis of oral auction bidding, preceded by sealed bids normally submitted at appraised price. Tie sealed bids must be resolved by oral bidding. One characteristic of homogeneous oligopsony—identical prices—is therefore not a characteristic of the federal timber market. Oral bidding begins from the sealed-bid prices. When several firms are qualified to bid, a common practice is for one qualified bidder, bidder A, to make a token bid above the appraised price (that is, to raise the appraised price usually 5 cents per thousand board feet on the species of minimum quantity). This bid is shown as point L in figure 17. Bidder A may have been previously selected by some or all of those qualified to bid in

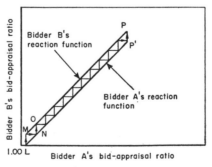

Fig. 17. Bid-price reaction functions.

the instance of an explicitly collusive oligopsony. If the conditions of the explicitly collusive agreement are honored and there is no internal defection by parties to the agreement or external challenge from bidders not party to the agreement, point L will be the high bid price and bidder A will be declared the winner.

An agreement in restraint of competition may, however, be based on quasi bargaining (implicit bargaining) rather than on explicit bargaining. Whereas explicit bargaining requires direct contact and negotiation among the parties concerned, quasi bargaining may produce collusive results very similar to those produced by explicit bargaining, but without direct contact among bidders. Instead, quasi bargaining rests on understandings gained as a result of observations in prior bidding contests and on thorough knowledge of log requirements, inventories, character of processing facilities, and so forth, of rival firms. But quasi agreements resulting from quasi bargaining are less reliable than explicit agreements resulting from explicit bargaining. Although oral bidding under quasi agreements may still begin with a token bid, the parties to the agreement have less confidence that a second bid will not be cast above the token bid placed by bidder A.

Even when a sale takes place in complete absence of any explicit or implicit agreement, the initial bid may still be a token one. If there is no agreement, or if an agreement, either explicit or implicit, exists but has been broken internally or ignored by bidding from external sources, successive higher bids will be cast. The bidding pattern that may develop is suggested in figure 17. The initial token bid cast by bidder A is shown at point L. Bidder B (or C or D, etc.) may follow with a higher bid, perhaps at point M. A first bid beyond the token bid indicates one of two developments: (1) Bidder B may not have moved fast enough to beat bidder A in casting a token bid. Bidder B, in raising the bid, may simply be "feeling out" bidder A, hoping that he, now aware of bidder B's interest in the sale and perhaps knowing of B's need for the timber in question, will withdraw. If bidder A fails to withdraw and, instead, casts his own second bid, thereby communicating a strong intention to buy the timber offered, bidder B may withdraw. Therefore, a bid by bidder B may simply indicate that continued or initial quasi bargaining is taking place in the course of the sale proceedings. (2) The bid at point M by bidder B may, on the other hand, indicate a warfare situation. This circumstance may develop even though an agreement (explicit or implicit) exists, or in the complete absence of any kind of mutual understanding. If bidder A is seriously interested in the sale, he then casts his second bid, perhaps at point *N*. In the event of a warfare situation, presumably bidder B follows with a bid, perhaps at point *O* where he matches bidder A's bid plus offering a little more. Alternate bidding between two or more parties in a warfare situation would be expected to proceed somewhat along the stair-step path shown in figure 17, terminating at some point *P*. In this kind of "instantaneous interdependence," the alternate buying prices bring forth immediate reaction bids, and no timber is sold at transitional bid prices short of *P*.

The terminal position of bidding (point *P*) will be reached when a bid price has been arrived at which exceeds the maximum bid of all bidders except the high bidder. Point *P* is indeterminate, as a variety of motives may be influencing the bidders and a variety of calculations may be followed to indicate one bidder's maximum.

The type of bidding outlined in figure 17 is similar to the oligopoly model originated by Cournot and modified by Bertrand.[12] The stair-step bidding is based on the assumption that a high bid cast by one party will obtain the entire volume offered for sale. At all points prior to point *P*, similar assumptions are made by alternative bidders, all of which prove to be incorrect. The line *MP* may be interpreted as bidder B's price reaction fuction. A vertical line drawn from any bid cast by bidder A, such as bid *L*, to any point on line *MP* indicates a matching bid plus a little more, which may obtain the sale at a minimum cost. This point would either maximize A's profit or minimize his loss up to the point where variable costs may still be covered. Similarly, the parallel line *NP'* may be interpreted as bidder A's price reaction function.

The Price and Allocation Leadership Functions

As identical final bids are not permitted and as the high bidder is awarded the entire timber contract, there is no application of the price leadership principle in the auction market for federal timber.[13] Similarly, the leadership equilibrium position that Fellner elaborated from the Cournot-Bertrand models does not apply, for the high bidder is awarded the entire timber volume offered and

---

12 See Fellner, *op. cit.*, pp. 55–86.

13 Although the high bidder is awarded the entire timber volume offered for sale, the volume may be subsequently split among several interested persons after the standing timber has been logged. This process of selling or trading some of the logs from a given sale is a standard procedure, particularly among medium-size or small operators who do not have fully integrated operations located nearby.

the second-high bidder receives nothing in the original award. Departing from the price leadership principle, the point P' in figure 17 may optimize the position of bidder A, despite failure to obtain the timber. By bidding up the price of timber and "dumping" the sale on bidder B, the winner's financial position may be weakened. The impaired position of bidder B resulting from obtaining a high-cost sale, or perhaps successive high-cost sales, will improve the relative strength of bidder A, providing he is not in a weak timber position. This may be to A's advantage in any future test of strength.

Nevertheless, in certain rather unique situations there may be a leadership position to be fulfilled in allocating scarce timber among competing suppliers. Within a narrow geographical area that is rather well organized, where milling capacity significantly exceeds the timber supply, certain buyers may take a leadership position in allocating timber and enforcing the agreed allocation. If the allocation machinery should fail, open warfare would probably result. As allocation agreements must be enforced in order to avoid bidding warfare, the leadership position must be held by a firm or firms whose economic position is strong. Enforcement requires an ability to take four kinds of reprisal action: (1) If the recalcitrant firm is a millowner, the leader(s) must have the power to deny such firm access to either timber or logs in sufficient quantity to keep his mill in operation. (2) Again, if the recalcitrant firm is a millowner, the leader(s) must have power to ensure that the cost of any timber or logs obtained by the recalcitrant firm precludes profitable operations. (3) If the recalcitrant firm is a gyppo logger, the leader(s) must have the power to ensure that he will be denied logging contracts by firms operating within the area. (4) Whatever the economic function of the recalcitrant firm, the leader(s) must have power to prohibit sale of unwanted logs from such firm to mills in the area.

The power to take effective reprisal action is derived from two sources: (1) A firm or firms in an allocation leadership position must be financially able to buy a given timber sale regardless of the cost. This power is necessary if a recalcitrant firm is to be denied access to sufficient quantities of timber. (2) The leader(s) must have access to alternative sources of timber so that he (they) may dump timber on the recalcitrant firm at relatively high prices. A series of such sales would have either of two consequences: a firm being disciplined would be forced into bankruptcy, or short of bankruptcy, it would be forced to come to terms with the allocation leader(s).

As the supply of national forest timber in a given geographical area is highly inelastic with respect to price, it is immediately obvious that competitive bidding above the appraised price simply transfers wealth from the bidder to the government (and thus to other taxpayers) and does not produce additional quantities of timber. At the same time, the process of bidding up the price of timber allows the price system to allocate scarce timber supplies among those firms able to make the necessary high bids. Because the quantity supplied is highly inelastic at any price above the appraised price, profit maximization for firms operating within any given geographical area gives clear signals. Profit maximization requires cost minimization, and the minimum cost is the appraised price. It is virtually unthinkable that sophisticated buyers of federal timber would be unaware of the requirements of cost minimization in their timber purchase program. Being aware of the requirements of cost minimization and being able to do something about it are, however, two quite different matters. Where milling capacity exceeds timber supplies, as appears to be a persistent feature in the Douglas fir region,[14] cost minimization requires an agreement among bidders, and, consequently, allocation of scarce timber by means other than the price system. If bidding were restricted to a predetermined set of qualified bidders, such as exist in the Grays Harbor Federal Sustained Yield Unit, then collusive arrangements would be easily established. If entry is not precluded by legislation, however, any potential bidder may become a qualified bidder and thus attempt entry into a given geographical market. With entry into the bidding arena almost costless (if a bidder neglects to cruise the timber and estimate the cost of any required road construction), it becomes difficult, if not impossible, to consistently maintain a record of minimum cost purchases. Since entry persists as a continuous possibility, the parties to a collusive agreement cannot maintain consistent and infallible control over their costs. With free entry, Fellner's position concerning the efficiency of collusion becomes an overstatement. He maintains that oligopolists frequently do reach an agreement, and that, when this happens, "the parties will surely not be indifferent to the size of the pie that they are now dividing. Jointly, they have the size of the pie under control."[15] With free entry into auction markets, the parties to a collu-

---

14 See John Fedkiw, *Forest Industry Capacity, Production and Available Log Supplies in the Douglas-Fir Subregion,* U.S. Forest Service Research Paper PNW-11 (Portland, Ore., 1964), p. 5.

15 *Op. cit.,* p. 33.

sive agreement cannot be sure that they have the size of the pie under control. This is true even though all parties to the agreement abide by its terms.

The need to allocate timber among competing users when the price system is rejected requires various degrees of formal understandings. Some geographical areas are subdivided into spheres of influence. If one well-established and entrenched firm normally operates within a very restricted area, quasi agreements acknowledge his prior claim to any timber sales taking place within such restricted area. Parties to the quasi agreement would normally include other well established firms within the same working circle. They may be expected to abide by such an agreement because they also attempt to maintain a claim on other spheres of influence. A breach of such a quasi agreement would leave the violator open to retaliation. Where spheres of influence are well recognized, there is obviously little need for formal agreements to allocate various timber sales. In other situations, where spheres of influence are not established by custom and where more than one firm may be expected to compete for a given timber sale, an understanding that confers upon one such bidder the right to buy a specified timber sale might necessitate a parallel agreement on allocation of logs from the specified sale. The logs may be allocated by differing mill characteristics. Thus, a veneer plant, a gang headrig dimension sawmill, and a band headrig sawmill cutting for high-value lumber might claim logs having separable and identifiable characteristics. Allocation might thus be assisted by differing mill needs among several potential bidders. If the potential bidders are firms having integrated operations, an allocation agreement might specify that bidder A will obtain sale X in its entirety and bidder B will obtain subsequent sale Y in its entirety.

SUMMARY

The theoretical framework serving as a guide to the empirical study of oligopsonistic markets and from which I have derived many of my hypotheses is oligopoly theory. There is no separate oligopsony theory, and, for several reasons, oligopoly theory cannot be transferred without modification. First, the tools of analysis differ between product markets and factor markets. Second, markets in which oligopsonists buy tend to be geographically narrower than markets in which oligopolists sell. And, third, price is a more significant variable in the former, whereas nonprice competition is relatively more significant in the latter. On the other hand, the essence of oligopoly theory—the idea of interdependence and consequent explicit or implicit agreements—transfers intact to the oligopsony situation.

Drawing on the earlier analysis of supply and demand elasticities, we studied price determination under three different sets of assumptions. Effective collusion would result in a transfer of wealth from public to private control in an amount depending on the difference between the appraised price of timber and the noncollusive equilibrium price. Effective collusive pricing, in turn, requires not price leadership, but allocation leadership. The allocation leader(s) must have available several kinds of reprisal action as a prerequisite to effective allocation leadership. The ability to take reprisal action, in turn, requires that the leader(s) be in a strong financial position and have a secure timber reserve. In the two succeeding chapters, hypotheses derived from economic theory are tested against the record of timber sales in the Douglas fir region.

CHAPTER 11

Competition for Federal Timber: Sale Basis

The objective of the analysis contained in chapters 11 and 12 is to appraise the performance of competitors in the markets for national forest timber. The first major question is: How competitive, or noncompetitive, are national forest timber sales? A second major question is: To what extent do large firms possess market power in the national forest stumpage market? A series of minor questions follow. How important is the number of qualified bidders as a factor accounting for the degree of competition? What is the effect of economic size of the buyer on the degree of competition for any given sale? How effective are barriers to entry (sale size and road-construction requirements) in limiting competition? Finally, does sale type (oral auction or sealed bid) affect the extent of competition? In this chapter, analysis is based on individual timber sales. In chapter 12, the analysis shifts to sales grouped by geographical markets.

This analysis of the bidding record for federal timber is based on timber sales by the Forest Service.[1] The extent of the published record differs by time period. Excellent data are available for the period 1959–1962.[2] All the relevant data available on individual timber sales have been coded on IBM cards. As a minor and insignificant exception to the above statement, a few sales have not been coded if the published record is obviously in error. Thus, the data to be analyzed are based upon nearly 100 percent coverage of the published national forest timber sales in the Douglas fir region for

---

[1] "National Forest Advertised Timber Sales, Region 6," U.S. Forest Service, 1380 (2400) (Portland, Ore.).

[2] Beginning in 1963, and to some extent in November and December of 1962, established economic relationships were upset as the result of a devastating hurricane that struck the Douglas fir region on October 12, 1962. The vast timber blowdown forced a rapid acceleration in timber sales.

1959–1962. The published record, however, is not a complete listing of national forest timber sales. Very small sales of less than $2,000 in value are not part of the published record. Although numerous, such sales represent an insignificant part of the total volume sold.

Study of the published record was supplemented by approximately 140 interviews with persons directly concerned in the process of bidding for federal timber. About three-fourths of the interviews were with buyers of federal timber; the rest were with timber sale administrators, mainly those affiliated with the Forest Service.

SALES CLASSIFIED BY DEGREE OF COMPETITION

Sales may be classified as competitive or noncompetitive. Noncompetitive sales are subclassified by number of bidders active in a given sale. As competitive sales are not subclassified, there are three degrees of "competitiveness" among recorded timber sales.

1) First among noncompetitive sales is the one-bidder sale. The selling procedure adopted by the Forest Service for oral auction sales requires that anyone intending to bid for a given timber sale must first become qualified as a bidder by submitting a sealed bid at or above the appraised price and by tendering a specified minimum cash deposit. As a sealed bid cannot be submitted after the sale commences, those who fail to enter are thereby excluded from oral auction bidding. In most instances, qualifying sealed bids are submitted at the appraised price for each species of timber to be sold. If only one bidder is legally qualified, the offering is awarded to that bidder at his bid price, normally the appraised price.

2) The second class of noncompetitive sales I have termed token-bid sales, in which two or more qualified bidders participate but show no evidence of serious bidding. Serious bidding may be defined as a bid price exceeding the appraised price by not less than 0.5 percent, or, alternatively, as a ratio of bid price to appraised price greater than 1.00 rounded to the nearest 0.01. When competition exists among bidders, several bids would be cast by alternative bidders, and, as a result, the ratio of amount bid to the appraised value would significantly exceed 1.00. On the other hand, where cooperative arrangements exist among bidders, there is evidence only of minimal bidding or of no bidding above appraised price. Bidding does not normally carry the bid price as high as 0.5 percent above the appraised price. Hence, defining "serious bidding" in this way makes it possible to quickly separate those

sales indicative of cooperative agreements and understandings among bidders from obviously competitive sales. In the absence of significant competitive bidding, notwithstanding the presence of two or more qualified bidders, token-bid sales are here classified with noncompetitive sales.

3) The third class of timber sales includes all those not accounted for in the noncompetitive group. Competitive sales, therefore, may be defined as all oral auction sales having two or more bidders where the ratio of bid price to appraised price is greater than 1.00 rounded to the nearest 0.01.

ECONOMIC SIZE CLASSES OF BUYERS

The record of timber sales also facilitates classification by economic size of the buyer. For this purpose, a category called "large firms" has been defined as comprising the twenty largest lumber-producing firms, the twenty largest plywood-producing firms, and the eight largest timberland owners in the Douglas fir region as of the year 1960. Lumber production, plywood production, and timber ownership outside the Douglas fir region are excluded in identifying membership in the large-firm group. As several firms are in two categories and a few are in all three, the combined list includes only thirty-six firms. Of these thirty-six, seven did not buy national forest timber in the four-year period 1959–1962. Thus there are twenty-nine large firms included in the category as described above. They do not have this status as a result of the quantity of national forest timber purchased. Indeed, the largest firm, Weyerhaeuser Company, supplies most of its raw-material needs from its own timber resources and is, in fact, a very small purchaser of national forest timber.

The second class of buyers comprises "small firms" or "all other buyers," meaning all buyers other than those belonging to the large-firm group. Small firms consist principally of lumber, veneer, and plywood mills and gyppo loggers. The term "gyppo logger" is a matter-of-fact reference to firms and individuals whose business is to log timber for others. The gyppo logger occasionally buys timber for his own account, though he may be a *de jure* buyer operating on behalf of and financed by a *de facto* buyer. The *de facto* buyer is commonly a millowner, either lumber or veneer. The use of stand-in buyers imparts some confusion to the classification of "large firms" and "all others," as it is sometimes difficult to know who the *de facto* buyer is.

THE BID-APPRAISAL RATIO

The bid-appraisal ratio is the ratio of the bid price to the appraised price. As present regulations do not permit acceptance of bids for national forest timber at below the appraised price, the minimum bid-appraisal ratio is 1.00. There is no maximum, and it is not uncommon to find bid prices exceeding appraised prices by a multiple of four or five, resulting in bid-appraisal ratios of 4.00 and 5.00.

The bid-appraisal ratio is here used as a common measure of the extent or degree of competition for individual timber sales. As absolute value differs among sales owing to timber quality, its accessibility, any road-construction cost the bidder must bear, distance to market, and other factors, neither bid value nor appraised value can be used to compare the extent of competition for various timber sales or to compare absolute values of various tracts. The same appraisal procedure is applied throughout the Douglas fir region. Forest Service employees who are responsible for appraisal are centrally trained and centrally supervised. The bid-appraisal ratio, therefore, offers the best, though by no means the perfect, measure of competition. Sales having a bid-appraisal ratio of 1.00 rounded to the nearest 0.01 have already been defined as noncompetitive sales. All other sales have been defined as competitive, and the degree of competition is assumed to be given by the amount of the premium over the appraised price.

Certain shortcomings in the bid-appraisal ratio should be clearly understood. First, while there is a high degree of central control over appraisal methods, timber appraisers are not infallible; hence, errors in judgment are likely to occur. It is hoped such errors will be small, or, at least, that they will be randomly distributed. To the degree that buyers assume the appraised price represents a constant percent of fair market value for the timber and judge their bidding in terms of the premium over the appraised price, rather than in terms of the absolute bid value, the bid-appraisal ratio is a satisfactory indicator of the degree of competition for federal timber.

Second, when the appraised value is low, whether accurate or not, a small absolute premium over appraised price makes the bid-appraisal ratio (or percent premium over appraised price) relatively high. Thus, it is not uncommon for timber appraised at, say, 3 dollars per thousand board feet to be bid up to 6 or even 9 dollars per thousand board feet, resulting in a bid-appraisal ratio of

2.00 or 3.00. On the other hand, it is most uncommon for timber appraised at 30 dollars to be bid to 60 or 90 dollars per thousand board feet. Therefore, higher bid-appraisal ratios would be recorded for timber appraised at relatively low value. This fault in the bid-appraisal ratio is analyzed at a later point.

Third, the numerator of the fraction occasionally reflects forces other than those considered competitive. For example, some sales are bid up by preclusive, punitive, desperation, or emotional (irrational) bidding. On the other hand, in some sales bidding is restrained by various degrees of collusion. Finally, ignorance of true value may cause bidding to either exceed or fall short of true value. But these forces are present to some degree in many competitive markets and are part of the crucible in which flexible prices are determined.

Although the bid-appraisal ratio is not a perfect measure of degree of competition, it is better than the next-best alternative, the "high bid," or the actual sale price of the timber per thousand board feet. Use of the high bid would be justified if timber sales were homogeneous. In fact, every timber sale differs from the next. For example, as a condition of the sale, the successful bidder normally is required to construct certain logging roads according to standards established by the Forest Service. A costly road-construction job is, in effect, sold with the timber and causes the value of the timber to be less than it would be if no road construction was required. Further, timber differs by quality as well as by species and density. Good-quality timber has greater value not only as standing timber, but also by reason of lower logging cost. In addition, different timber sales differ in value by reason of distance to market: the longer the distance, the higher the transportation cost and the lower the residual value of the timber. The difficulties enumerated above are but a few of the factors causing timber to differ in value from one sale to another and rendering the bid price (high bid) useless for purpose of comparing sales and classes of sales. In view of these difficulties, it is easily conceivable that timber purchased for 2 dollars per thousand board feet will be logged at a loss, whereas timber purchased for 20 dollars will be underpriced. These differences, together with many more, are taken into consideration in the appraisal process. Final product values are estimated, and all processing and logging costs, including the cost of road construction and an allowance for profit and risks, are subtracted to arrive at the estimated fair-market value which becomes

the appraised price. Although both the appraised price and the
high bid are imperfect measures, the bid-appraisal ratio is used as
an index of degree of competition.

The analysis begins with a preliminary exploration of the competitive setting. The "diagnostic" questions raised are formulated
into hypotheses suitable for testing against the accumulated record. The record is examined, first, by tabulations and, second, by
multiple regression analysis.

HYPOTHESES TO BE TESTED

Observations of a number of national forest and Bureau of Land
Management timber sales were preceded and followed by extensive interviews with buyers of federal timber. In addition, the record of bidding for federal timber was scrutinized in a preliminary
manner. Then relevant questions were formulated and testable
hypotheses concerning market behavior and performance were
developed.

The several geographical markets for national forest timber are
not homogeneous. Although they are generally characterized by
few rather than by many buyers, competitive conditions nevertheless run all the way from intense competition in some areas to
patently obvious cooperative arrangements in others. In some instances, neighbors never perform the unfriendly act of bidding
against one another, whereas in others they seem to take particular
delight in bidding up the price of federal timber. For example,
in one instance when two firms were competing for badly needed
timber, a third bidder, entering into the fact and the spirit of the
bidding, cast a series of small bids. As the bid price approached a
100 percent premium over the appraised price, the two serious bidders fell silent, whereupon the sale was awarded to the third bidder
who was seen to lower his head and heard to murmur, "My God."

From material presented earlier, it is apparent that firms differ
widely in size, financial strength, and owned timber resources. Bidders for federal timber range all the way from several firms within
the exclusive "Big Two Hundred" category down to the small operations involving only family members. The presence of corporate
giants with relatively unlimited resources and economic power
leads to questions concerning the relationship between cost of timber (measured by the premium over appraised price), on the one
hand, and buying power (based on the economic size class of the
bidder), on the other.

The possibility of effective barriers to entry arises from differences in sale size and road-construction requirements. The total value of single national forest timber sales ranges all the way from a few hundred dollars per sale up to values in excess of a million dollars. Given the wide range of financial resources represented by timber buyers, and the probability that many potential timber buyers are poorly financed, large sales with accompanying high road-construction costs may represent effective barriers to entry for the less well-financed segment of the industry. One difficulty was alleviated by the Small Business Act of 1958, which provides for loans to small businesses for road construction.

Within a single geographical area, intense interest is expressed in some sales by many bidders, while only passive interest is expressed by a few, and often one bidder in sales closely related in time and general characteristics. The same observation holds among areas. Intense competition is usually characteristic of sales having many bidders. When there are only a few bidders, an apparent degree of cooperation appears to exist, and bidding frequently is limited to token proportions.

National forest timber sales are of two types, each exhibiting different behavioral implications. Most sales are transacted under oral auction procedures, all of which require a sealed bid as one of the qualifying requirements. About 12 percent of the sales and 3 percent of the volume sold, however, are within the category of sealed-bid sales where oral auction bidding is not permitted. Bidding strategy will obviously differ between these two sale types; one of them allows the bidder to see and assess his competition before casting his final bid, whereas the other does not. The sealed-bid mechanism offers the Forest Service an opportunity to attack the collusive bidding that springs from definitive knowledge about the identity of one's competitors at a given sale.

Our preliminary exploration leads to certain questions that may be diagnostic with reference to departures from the competitive model. These questions may be phrased as hypotheses that can be tested against the record.

The first diagnostic question is: Do large firms, as defined above, have enough buying power to secure federal timber sales at lower costs than their smaller competitors? As the price per thousand board feet of timber is a kind of catchall variable, the cost referred to here is the premium over appraised price.

An oligopsony in the timber-buying market consists of a few firms of varied size. A given geographical oligopsony may embrace a very few of the large firms (though usually only one) in the large-firm group. Further, it may include a few additional firms that are large within the limits of a small geographical area, but not large enough to be included among the Big Twenty lumber producers, the Big Twenty plywood producers, or the Big Eight timberland owners. And, finally, a given timber market normally includes a fringe of small firms consisting of mill operators and gyppo loggers who are regular or potential bidders for federal timber. In an oligopsony with the structure identified here, economic theory would lead one to expect that large firms would possess and exercise buying power, based on their economic size, to obtain needed timber resources at low prices relative to prices paid by smaller competitors. In order to test this theoretical market power of large buyers against observations, the following first hypothesis may be advanced: The bid-appraisal ratio, or the premium over appraised price, varies inversely with the size class of the successful bidder.

The second question suggested by preliminary exploration concerns barriers to entry into the federal timber market. Financial barriers to entry arise from large sales involving a cash deposit and working capital plus a probable heavy road-construction requirement and risk. As the cost of the road-construction requirement increases and the value of the timber offered per sale is higher, the competitive fringe of small firms may drop from the list of potential bidders. The capital requirement for large sales is relatively small, and a federal loan program is available. But some potential bidders (small millowners and gyppo loggers) are still not able to meet the financial requirements of large sales.

In formulating a hypothesis to test this relationship, it must be kept in mind that multicollinearity is to be expected between high road-construction cost and large sale size. Data are available on both variables. The hypothesis may therefore be stated so that either the sale size or the road-construction cost is tested for significance, with degrees of competition measured by the premium over appraised price. The second hypothesis then is: The bid-appraisal ratio, or the premium over appraised price, varies inversely with the volume per sale or the required road-construction cost.

The third question concerns the relationship between number of competitors and degree of competition. Economic theory is clear on the expected relationship. Atomistic competition requires numerous buyers, with the obvious result that collusive covenants among them are both unworkable and unthinkable. As the number of bidders becomes smaller, cooperative arrangements become thinkable but not necessarily workable. If the potential bidders are few, and are known and established in their communities, collusive agreements, either explicit or implicit, become a realistic possibility.

An index listing the number of bidders in each geographical market and the average number of bidders qualified to bid on a series of individual sales is available. Joe Bain has argued that actual entry need not take place for restraint to be exercised on monopoly pricing by a collusive oligopoly; potential entry will restrain pricing to a relatively narrow limit above the competitve price.[3] Bain's argument, however, refers to a situation in which the oligopolists set their price and adjust output in order to make the established price effective. The timber oligopsony does not fit the Bain model, for the supply of national forest timber is fixed by the Forest Service and is based on allowable-cut considerations. The Forest Service then establishes a refusal price (the appraised price) at which the bidding may begin. As potential entrants may be discouraged at the moment they attempt to secure a given timber sale, there is little need for the entrenched oligopsonist to discourage entry at prior sales, which could be done by bidding the price above any existing noncompetitive price advantage. Furthermore, bidding price up in order to establish a "limit price" on entry would force a firm, in a single-bidder sale, to bid against itself.

Using the data on the number of qualified bidders per sale as an index of potential competition by geographical market, the third hypothesis to test the relationship of bidders to degree of competition is: The bid-appraisal ratio, or the premium over the appraised price, varies positively with the number of bidders qualified to bid on given timber sales.

The fourth question concerns the competitive relationships established by oral auction sales, on the one hand, and sealed-bid sales on the other. On an a priori basis we would expect different results depending on assumptions made about the degree of collusive behavior among bidders. Assuming no overt collusion among participants, Sidney Weintraub concludes that if the "participants involved are approximately in the same economic position, there is no reason to expect that the results of oral and sealed-bids should differ substantially over time for each firm will have fairly clear ideas on the bidding capacities and tendencies of its rivals." As-

---

[3] Joe S. Bain, "A Note on Pricing in Monopoly and Oligopoly," *American Economic Review*, XXXIX (March, 1949), 448–464.

suming that costs differ among firms and that, as a consequence, firms place different maximum values on log input, he suggests that "oral bidding is likely to be more conducive to higher prices to the seller than sealed-bids, for in the bidding process, information is obtained by each of the participants about the bid behavior of its rivals."[4]

If, however, it is acknowledged that perfect competition for federal timber may not prevail and that there is instead a degree of collusion, either explicit or implicit, a priori reasoning would lead to opposite conclusions. Where bidders are few and workable agreements exist, oral auction bidding allows the oligopsonist to observe with finality who his competitors are for a given sale at the moment the sealed bids are opened. If sealed bidding (as the initial step in an oral auction sale) reveals that bidders are limited to those who cooperate, one should expect only a tie-breaking bid (token bid). If the Forest Service elects to use the sealed-bid method of selling in areas characterized by minimal competition, uncertainty enters the market. Because a second chance at bidding is precluded by the sealed-bid method, and because it is not possible to know with finality the identity of all bidders or the amounts they are bidding, caution would dictate sealed bids above appraised price by the cooperative bidders. Thus, when competition is minimal and the Forest Service uses sealed bids to combat suspected collusion, one would expect bid-appraisal ratios in sealed-bid sales to exceed those in oral auction sales.

A third possibility exists. When competition is minimal, the Forest Service may not use the sealed-bid procedure for the purpose of eliciting a competitive response, but for any one of a variety of other reasons. When the Forest Service has attempted to use sealed bids in areas suspected of collusive behavior, strenuous objections have been raised by potential timber buyers. In response, the Forest Service has usually retreated.

For the period 1959 through 1962, data showing whether the sealed bid or the oral auction technique was used are available on all reported sales. Based on the assumption (1) that departures from a perfectly competitive model are significant, and (2) that the Forest Service employs the sealed-bid sale to combat suspected collusion, the fourth hypothesis may be thus stated: The bid-appraisal

---

4 Sidney Weintraub, "An Examination of Some Economic Aspects of Forest Service Stumpage Prices and Appraisal Policies," mimeographed report prepared for U.S. Forest Service (June, 1958), p. 98.

ratio or the premium over appraised price shows high values for
sealed-bid sales and low values for oral auction sales.

TABULAR ANALYSIS OF BIDDING FOR NATIONAL FOREST TIMBER

The first major question is: How competitive (or noncompetitive)
are national forest timber sales? Based on data for national forest
timber sales in the Douglas fir region, table 24 shows the characteristics of competitive and noncompetitive oral auction timber sales
in the period 1959–1962. Of the 2,340 sales completed, 17.6 percent
were uncontested or were one-bidder sales. These sales, smaller
than average, accounted for only 10.2 percent of the total volume
sold. Token-bid sales, strongly suggestive of collusion, accounted
for 14.5 percent of the sales and, larger than average, for 17.3 percent of the volume sold. The remaining sales, 67.9 percent of the
total number, were competitive; they represented 72.5 percent of
the volume sold. Noncompetitive sales therefore, accounted for
approximately one-third of the sales and more than one-fourth of
the total volume sold. The average bid-appraisal ratio by definition
is 1.00 for all noncompetitive sales. A wide difference exists in cost
of timber between sales that are noncompetitive and sales characterized by significant bidding competition. For the competitive
sales, the average premium over the appraised price is 63 percent.[5]
Thus a sharp distinction exists between competitive and noncompetitive sales, together with a marked cost differential.

Table 24 also reveals that the average number of bidders differs
significantly among the three classes of sales. Again, by definition,
the uncontested sales are one-bidder sales. The average number of
bidders per sale in token-bid sales was 3.06, whereas it was 5.28 in
competitive sales. The uncontested one-bidder sales were of relatively low volume, and, correspondingly, fewer had a road-building

---

[5] Although the adequacy of the appraisal process is not the central concern of this
study, I may point out that competitive bidding that results in a bid price 63 percent
over appraised price raises serious doubts about the accuracy of the appraisal method.
Table 24 shows that the average premium bid over appraised price for all sales is 46
percent. As buyers may plan on balancing high-cost sales against sales obtained at
the appraised price, the average premium for all sales may provide a better indication of market value or competitive price. If the competitive price is as much as 46
percent above the appraised value, which is intended to represent the fair market
value, and if appraisal methods are uniformly applied throughout the Douglas fir
region, one must conclude that the Forest Service consistently underappraises the
fair market value of timber. This conclusion has also been reached by others (see
"Federal Timber Sales Policies," U.S. House of Representatives, Thirty-first Intermediate Report of the Committee on Government Operations, 84th Cong., 2d. sess.,
House Report no. 2960 [Washington, 1956], p. 24).

TABLE 24

Characteristics of Competitive and Non-competitive Oral Auction Timber Sales in the Douglas Fir Region, 1959–1962

Type of sale	Number of sales	Percent of sales	Volume sold a	Percent of volume	Average bid-appraisal ratio	Average number of bidders per sale	Average volume per sale a	Percent of sales requiring road construction	Average road construction cost for sales requiring construction (in dollars)
Noncompetitive	752	32.1	3,129,357	27.5	1.00	1.00	...	...	...
One-bidder	412	17.6	1,157,286	10.2	1.00	1.00	2,852	59.9	41,077
Token-bid	340	14.5	1,972,071	17.3	1.00	3.06	5,746	75.4	69,545
Competitive	1,588	67.9	8,258,607	72.5	1.63	5.28	5,206	71.8	59,941
Total b	2,340	100.0	11,387,964	100.0	1.46	4.20	4,872	70.2	58,625

a In thousands of board feet.

b Excludes sales to Simpson Timber Company in the Shelton Cooperative Sustained-Yield Unit.

SOURCE: Developed from quarterly reports of U.S. Forest Service, "National Forest Advertised Timber Sales, Region 6," 1380 (2400) (Portland, Ore.).

cost requirement attached. The road-construction cost, when present, was relatively light. When sales are classified by type of competition, the first documentation of multicollinearity between sale size and road-construction requirement appears.

Data shown in table 24 also indicate that the number of bidders is positively correlated with degree of competition, as suggested in the third hypothesis. Competitive sales show a high premium over appraised price and also, clearly, a larger average number of bidders. In sum, table 24 provides evidence relating to the hypotheses, pertinent information about the magnitude of the two classes of noncompetitive sales relative to competitive sales, and other characteristics of oligopsony in the federal timber market.

To the second major question—Do large firms have a position of market power in the national forest timber market?—an affirmative answer could be given if the record showed that large firms obtained their stumpage at a significantly lower cost than small firms. Table 25 shows bid-appraisal ratios and other competitive characteristics for oral auction sales in 1959–1962 in the Douglas fir region, classified as those purchased by large firms and those purchased by all other buyers. Large firms obtained a disproportionately large share of their total input in one-bidder sales, and also acquired a disproportionately large share of the token-bid sales. In total, the large firms obtained 34.2 percent of their total national forest timber under noncompetitive conditions, paying no significant premium over appraised price. In contrast, smaller firms obtained only 25.5 percent of their total national forest timber under similarly advantageous conditions.

Small firms purchased a larger share of their total volume under competitive conditions and, in many instances, under intense competition. Thus, 74.5 percent of all national forest timber purchased by small firms was classified as competitive in the period under discussion. The average premium paid in these competitive sales was 68 percent over appraised price. In contrast, large firms paid only a 43 percent premium over appraised price for a smaller share in the competitive category. Small firms therefore suffered two disadvantages: (1) they acquired a smaller share of the timber sold under noncompetitive conditions with no significant premium over appraised price; and (2) for the larger share they acquired competitively, they paid a relatively high premium. Expressed in terms of the overall bid-appraisal ratios, small firms paid a weighted average premium over appraised price amounting to 51 percent, whereas large firms incurred a premium of only 28 percent.

TABLE 25

COMPARISON OF COST AND OTHER CHARACTERISTICS OF ORAL AUCTION TIMBER
SALES TO LARGE[a] AND SMALL[b] FIRMS, DOUGLAS FIR REGION, 1959–1962

Type of sale	Volume sold[c]	Percent of volume	Average bid-appraisal ratio	Average number of bidders per sale	Average volume per sale	Percent of sales requiring road construction	Average road-construction cost for sales requiring road construction (in dollars)
Noncompetitive							
One-bidder							
Large firms	291,164	11.3	1.00	1.00	4,502	68.7	69,263
Small firms	866,122	9.8	1.00	1.00	2,531	58.1	34,594
Token-bid							
Large firms	588,205	22.9	1.00	2.91	8,022	88.6	87,294
Small firms	1,383,866	15.7	1.00	3.10	5,160	72.1	63,931
Competitive							
Large firms	1,692,350	65.8	1.43	4.80	7,454	84.2	76,011
Small firms	6,566,257	74.5	1.68	5.36	4,841	69.7	56,785
Total							
Large firms	2,571,719	100.0	1.28	3.72	7,014	82.2	77,330
Small firms	8,816,245	100.0	1.51	4.29	4,483	68.0	54,531

a Large firms include the twenty largest lumber producers, the twenty largest plywood producers, and the eight largest timberland owners. Purchases by the Simpson Timber Company in the Shelton working circle under a co-operative sustained-yield agreement are excluded from consideration.

b Small firms are all buyers other than large firms as defined above.

c In thousands of board feet.

SOURCE: Developed from quarterly reports of U.S. Forest Service, "National Forest Advertised Timber Sales, Region 6," 1380 (2400) (Portland, Ore.).

The differential cost of national forest timber to purchasers classified by economic size is a critical statistic. The analyst must therefore be relatively certain that the premium differential shown above is not the result of chance fluctuations owing to wide variations in the bid-appraisal ratio found among many national forest timber sales.

The T-test may be used to ascertain the significance of the difference between the two bid-appraisal ratios. Based on the null hypothesis that there is no difference between the weighted average value of the bid-appraisal ratio for big firms and the same value for smaller competitors, and using the 5 percent confidence level, the T-test yields these results:

Small Firms	*Large Firms*
$S_1^2 = \dfrac{\Sigma f X_1^2 - \overline{X}_1^2}{N_1'}$	$S_2^2 = \dfrac{\Sigma f X_2^2 - \overline{X}_2^2}{N_2'}$
$= \dfrac{24{,}981{,}844 - (1.51)^2}{8{,}821{,}190}$	$= \dfrac{4{,}699{,}491 - (1.28)^2}{2{,}554{,}859}$
$= 2.832 - 2.280$	$= 1.8394 - 1.6384$
$S_1^2 = .552$	$S_2^2 = .201$

$$S_D = \sqrt{\frac{S_1^2}{N_1} + \frac{S_2^2}{N_2}}$$

$$= \sqrt{\frac{.552}{1981} + \frac{.201}{359}}$$

$$= \sqrt{.000279 + .000560}$$

$$= \sqrt{.000839}$$

$$S_D = .02896$$

$$T = \frac{\overline{X}_1 - \overline{X}_2}{S_D}$$

$$T = \frac{1.51 - 1.28}{.02896}$$

$$T = 7.94$$

The T-test reveals that at the 5 percent confidence level the null hypothesis must be rejected. There is a significant difference in the premium over appraised price paid by large and small firms for timber purchased from the national forests in the Douglas fir region.

The data shown on the premiums paid by economic size class are based on prices bid for national forest timber—the numerator of the bid-appraisal ratio. The prices actually paid for such timber may not correspond precisely with the bid prices for two reasons. First, the final buying price is subject to a price escalator provision whereby stumpage rates are adjusted up or down by 50 percent of the difference between the base period price index and a current price index for stumpage. If the stumpage price index should increase by 2 dollars per thousand board feet from the base period, determined by the date of the sale, the actual price paid would be increased by 1 dollar above the bid price. Similar adjustments are made if the stumpage price index should decline. The escalator provision has applied in the Douglas fir region only since the spring of 1961. Adjustments made in the stumpage price as a result of changes in the stumpage price index presumably are randomly distributed between large and small firms. Thus there is no reason to suspect that changes made in the premium over appraised price would significantly effect the premium differentials by economic size class shown above.

Second, a process called "rate redetermination" is required in all national forest timber sales contracts when the operating period, including road construction, requires more than four full operating seasons.[6] Through this process, timber is reappraised after the required passage of time, and a new price is established for the remaining volume not yet cut and paid for. The redetermined stumpage rate is independent of the bid price charged on the volume processed prior to redetermination. In large sales, competitive bidding thus determines the price of only the minimum volume that must be removed prior to rate redetermination. The minimum volume appears to vary between 40 and 60 percent of the total volume in large sales and averages 50 percent of the total volume.

The effect of rate redetermination may be illustrated by a hypothetical example. Consider a sale under the following circumstances: (1) total volume estimated and actually produced equals

---

6 "Forest Service Handbook," U.S. Forest Service, sec. 2423.8.

20 million feet; (2) bid price exceeds appraised price by 100 percent; (3) rate redetermination takes place when 50 percent of the total production has been removed; and (4) no basic changes occur in the underlying economic data affecting stumpage value during the life of the contract up to the point of rate redetermination. Under these circumstances, rate redetermination would normally restore the original appraised price for the second half of total log production. Ten million feet would be sold at a 100 percent premium over appraised price as given by the bid price, and the remaining 10 million feet would be sold at the redetermined rate which, in the example, would equal the appraised price. The final cost of the timber would involve, not a 100 percent premium over appraised price, but a 50 percent premium.

Table 25 shows that, on the average, sales acquired by large firms were substantially larger than sales acquired by smaller firms. If large sales tend to be concentrated among large firms, then downward adjustments owing to rate redetermination would reduce the premiums paid by large firms more than they would reduce premiums paid by smaller firms. Whereas the escalator factor appears to have no significant effect on the differential premiums by economic size class, the rate redetermination factor would have differential effects, so that the premium advantage enjoyed by large firms is even greater than the very significant differentials shown in table 25. Any adjustment in the apparent premiums associated with economic size of the buyer would involve a large clerical burden. We can be quite certain of the direction of the error arising out of failure to make a rate redetermination adjustment in the data. It is felt that the additional accuracy in the precise amount of the differential would not be worth the clerical burden. The analysis here is therefore based entirely on published bid prices and not on actual prices, which differ owing to operation of the escalator provisions and the rate redetermination process. The reader, however, is asked to keep in mind these two qualifications.

On the basis of this information, the first hypothesis—that the bid-appraisal ratio or the premium over appraised price varies negatively with the size class of the successful bidder—may be accepted. Although table 25 and the statistical test of significance establish the fact that large firms obtained timber under advantageous conditions relative to their smaller competitors, they do not establish net relationships between the bid-appraisal ratio, on the one hand, and several explanatory variables on the other. For example, it is not known whether large firms obtain their timber under relatively low premiums precisely because they are large, or because they operate under conditions of fewer bidders, or because they operate in working circles that are generally noncompetitive, or for other reasons. A multiple regression analysis (given at a later point) is useful in attempting to separate the influence of several variables to obtain measures of net relationships.

Table 25 reveals other sale characteristics when sales are classified by size of buyer. Consistent relationships are found throughout the data. For example, in all three competitive classes, larger firms obtain larger sales; a higher percentage of the sales they obtain have a road-building requirement; and, if road construction is required, the cost is higher in sales obtained by large firms. This evidence tends to support the second hypothesis, that large sale size and heavy road-construction requirements may serve as barriers to entry. Such barriers would be effective only against small and rather poorly financed potential bidders. Further documentation of this point must also await regression analysis.

There is a clear difference in the intensity of competition, as indicated by the average number of bidders per sale, for sales acquired by large firms, on the one hand, and for those acquired by smaller firms, on the other. The average number of bidders was 2.9 in token-bid sales acquired by large firms, and 3.1 in those acquired by smaller firms. Even for competitive sales, there is a difference in the degree of competition between the two economic size classes. Large firms found an average of 4.8 bidders per sale in competitive sales, whereas small firms found an average of 5.4.

Based upon the assumptions that the market for national forest timber shows significant departures from perfect competition, and that sealed-bid sales are employed by the Forest Service to combat suspected collusion, the fourth hypothesis asserts that premiums over appraised prices would be higher in sealed-bid sales than in oral auction sales. The data in table 26 suggest that the hypothesis is not tenable. The weighted average bid-appraisal ratios for sealed-bid and oral auction sales in 1959–1962 were 1.42 and 1.46, respectively. The difference between them is not statistically significant. The net relationships between bid-appraisal ratio and sale type, along with other independent variables, are explored in multiple regression analysis.

Table 26 also reveals that sealed-bid sales accounted for slightly less than 10 percent of all national forest timber sales, and for only 2.5 percent of total volume sold. The average sale size chosen for

TABLE 26

COMPETITIVE CHARACTERISTICS OF ORAL AUCTION AND SEALED-BID SALES IN THE
DOUGLAS FIR REGION, 1959–1962

Type of sale	Number of sales	Percent of sales	Volume sold[a]	Percent of volume	Average volume per sale[a]	Weighted average bid-appraisal ratio
Oral auction	2,340	90.5	11,387,964	97.5	4,872	1.46
Sealed-bid	245	9.5	294,497	2.5	1,202	1.42
Total	2,585	100	11,682,461	100	4,524	1.46

[a] In thousands of board feet.

SOURCE: Developed from quarterly reports of U.S. Forest Service, "National Forest Advertised Timber Sales, Region 6," 1380 (2400) (Portland, Ore.).

sealed-bid selling was relatively small. The average sealed-bid sale was only 1,202 thousand board feet, compared with 4,872 thousand board feet in oral auction sales. This information suggests that sealed-bid sales are not intended to frustrate collusive arrangements, but rather are selected on some other basis related to sale size.

REGRESSION ANALYSIS OF BIDDING FOR NATIONAL FOREST TIMBER

The auction market for national forest timber is a complex one involving a multitude of possible relationships among several variables. By use of multiple regression analysis, it is possible, in a sense, to untangle the complex relationships and establish net regression of observed bid-appraisal ratios on the relevant independent variables for which statistical data are available.

For analytical purposes, the statistical model used is that of stepwise multiple linear regression.[7] The dependent variable in the regression analysis is the bid-appraisal ratio for each sale in the Douglas fir region in the period 1959–1962. Nine independent variables are tested against this dependent variable for statistical significance. The independent variables are:

1) Number of bidders per sale (X'_1). Data for this variable are given by the number of bidders legally qualified to bid by virtue of a sealed bid accompanied by the required cash deposit. The number of bidders per sale has been identified in published records on timber sales from 1959 to date. The prime sign in X'_1 indicates that a logarithmic transformation of number of bidders has been employed. On an a priori basis, one would expect a curvilinear relationship between the number of bidders and the bid-appraisal ratio. One-bidder sales are transacted at a bid-appraisal ratio of 1.00, for a single qualified bidder would not rationally bid against himself in an oral auction sale. On occasion, a one-bidder sale is in fact transacted at a price significantly above appraised price. It happens when a sealed bid is cast above appraised price, suggesting an error in judgment by the bidder who apparently was convinced of impending oral auction opposition. When only one

---

[7] The regression programs chosen for this analysis are BIMD no. 34, which is available for inspection at the Western Data Processing Center, University of California, Los Angeles, and the "80-Series Multiple Linear Regression System," 1620 Users Group Membership Code no. 5076. The programs were processed on an IBM 7090 computer at the Western Data Processing Center and an IBM 1620 computer at the University of California, Santa Barbara, respectively.

bidder is qualified to bid and his sealed bid exceeds appraised price, the premium serves no purpose other than to transfer wealth from the bidder to other taxpayers. In a majority of the sales for which two bidders have qualified, the bidding is significantly in excess of appraised price because of the high probability that some two-bidder sales will be heatedly contested. For successively higher numbers of bidders, however, the same rate of increase cannot be expected. Some increase in bid-appraisal ratio follows from the fact that cooperative arrangements among bidders are more difficult to maintain as the number of bidders increases. Therefore, the bid-appraisal ratio would tend to continue its upward movement but at a decreasing rate. I have chosen a logarithmic function to represent this curvilinear relationship between the number of bidders and the bid-appraisal ratio.

2) Economic size class of buyer (X_2). Two size classes of successful bidders have been identified and defined above. They are large firms and all firms other than those classified as large.

3) Road-construction cost per sale (X_3). Construction costs are shown in dollars per sale. Some of the smaller sales do not require road construction.

4) Sale size (X_4). The size of each sale is given in thousands of board feet, log scale.

5) Appraised price per thousand board feet (X'_5). The appraised price is an average of all species weighted by volume per species. As previously noted, very high bid-appraisal ratios may be found among sales having a very low appraised value per thousand board feet. The relationship between appraised price and bid-appraisal ratio, however, should not be linear, but instead should be curvilinear and convex to the point of origin. At successively higher appraised values, the error discussed previously in the bid-appraisal ratio should result in a sharp drop in average bid-appraisal ratios followed by further reductions, but at a continuously decreasing rate of decrease. To represent the expected relationship, a logarithmic transformation of the appraised price is used in the regression program.

6) Housing starts per month (X_6). This variable is the seasonally adjusted monthly value of nonfarm residential housing units started. Because my present concern is with competition for federal timber, I am not interested at the moment in the cyclical variation that may be associated with various levels of housing starts. I am interested, however, in determining the net relationships for independent variables that have competitive significance. I have,

therefore, introduced certain additional variables such as housing starts in order to identify and neutralize any significant effect they may have on the bid-appraisal ratio.

7) Douglas fir lumber price index (X_7). This is a price index for Douglas fir, dimension, construction, 25 percent standard, BLS series 08-11-22.14. This variable represents another possible cyclical relationship that has no special interest at the moment to this study of competitive conditions. It is introduced for the reasons outlined in connection with X_6.

8) Sale type (X_8). The sale type consists of oral auction or sealed-bid sales classifications.

9) Time (X_9). This variable, like variables X_6 and X_7, is introduced in order to determine whether a linear secular trend in bid-appraisal ratios is present.

The critical limits for acceptance of any given independent variable are defined by the 5 percent fiducial or confidence level. The final equation derived as a result of the stepwise multiple linear regression program is

$$Y = 2.19 + .8881X'_1 - .083X_2 - .00001X_4 - .9569X'_5,$$
$$\quad\quad\quad (.0306) \quad\quad (.028) \quad\quad (.000002) \quad\quad (.0402)$$

where Y is the bid-appraisal ratio, X'_1 is the logarithmic value of number of bidders, X_2 is the economic size class of the successful bidder, X_4 is average sales size, and X'_5 is the logarithmic value of appraised price. The standard errors of each regression coefficient are given in parentheses. All variables pass an analysis of variance test for significance at the 5 percent confidence level.

The coefficient of multiple correlation for the above multiple regression equation is $R_{YX'_1X_2X_4X'_5} = .60$. The coefficient of determination is $D_{YX'_1X_2X_4X'_5} = .36$; it indicates that the four variables identified here as having a significant relationship to the bid-appraisal ratio account for 36 percent of the original variability in the dependent variable. The standard deviation of the bid-appraisal ratios for all 2,585 sales transacted in 1959–1962 is $S_Y = .60$ ratio points. When the bid-appraisal ratio is estimated on the basis of the four independent variables shown in the above equation, the standard error of estimate becomes $S_{YX'_1X_2X_4X'_5} = .49$ ratio points.

The coefficient of correlation given above is not particularly high; correspondingly, the improved reliability of estimates based on four independent variables rather than on a simple average of the bid-appraisal ratios is not vastly improved. Our interest, however, is not in the highest possible coefficient of multiple correlation. Rather, we are interested in determining whether or not select variables having competitive consequences are significantly related to observed differences in the bid-appraisal ratio among several sales. Thus, I have established the significance of each of the variables identified in the multiple regression equation.

Because the coefficient of multiple determination indicates that only 36 percent of the total variability in the dependent variable has been accounted for, there are additional variables not included among the nine independent variables tested which are unaccounted for and which represent important determinants of the outcome of a given timber sale. Data are not available, however, on additional variables that I would like to include in the equation. Further, certain important determinants are not quantifiable under given measurement techniques. For example, it is quite likely that one important determinant in the vigor of bidding for a given sale is the personality of each individual bidder and the human relationships among bidders. A single bidder, possessing a desire for a specific timber sale, may bid vigorously when opposed by an outsider but refrain entirely from bidding when opposed by a neighbor and friend. Further, the degree of need for logs at a given point in time is also a determinant of the vigor of bidding. Perhaps the psychological attitude at the moment occasionally influences premium bidding over appraised price. One's personal assessment of future events, such as, for example, the probability of getting a future timber sale, may influence bidding at any given time. Finally, the existence of deals among bidders and the probability estimations of their being successfully completed influence bidding vigor.

The relationships shown in the regression equation may be clarified by reference to the two graphs that plot the independent variables against the bid-appraisal ratio. Figure 18 shows the curvilinear slope of the number of bidders per sale for large and small firms. When there is only one bidder, the bid-appraisal ratio is almost invariably 1.00. If there are two bidders, and if the average appraised price and the average sale size are both held constant at their mean values, the best estimate of the bid-appraisal ratio for large firms is 1.15, or 15 percent above appraised price. Correspondingly, the best estimate of the bid-appraisal ratio for all buyers other than large firms is 1.23, or a 23 percent premium over appraised price. By means of the regression equation all other variables, except the number of bidders, may, in effect, be held constant, and the behavior of the bid-appraisal ratio for either large

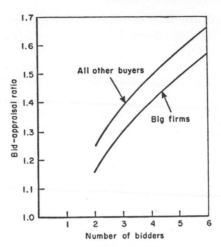

Fig. 18. Net regression lines showing bid-appraisal ratio by firm size
computed from logarithm of number
of bidders.

firms or their smaller competitors at various levels of number of
bidders may be examined. As hypothesized and specified by the
logarithmic function, the bid-appraisal ratio increases rapidly from
one to two bidders and continues to increase thereafter, but at a
reduced rate. All independent variables except the economic size
of the successful bidder may be held constant. When the number
of bidders qualified at a given sale is three, when the average sale
size is held constant at its average value (4,524 thousand board feet),
and when the weighted average appraised price per thousand board
feet is held constant at its arithmetic mean ($20.11), a given sale
purchased by a large firm would result in a 30 percent premium
over appraised price; if purchased by a smaller firm, it would produce a 38 percent premium over appraised price.[8]

One may object that the treatment given the number-of-bidders
variable does not in fact establish a regression relationship beyond
what has already been fixed by the definitions employed. One-
bidder sales are noncompetitive and normally have bid-appraisal
ratios amounting to 1.00. Given the facts that many sales have more
than one bidder and all competitive sales by definition have not

---

[8] Caution should be used in applying these estimates to a point in time outside the
1959–1962 period. Such an application is valid only if the underlying conditions that
prevailed in 1959–1962 also prevail in other periods.

only more than one bidder but bid-appraisal ratios in excess of 1.00, a positive relationship between the number of bidders and the bid-appraisal ratio is inevitable. The analysis does not, therefore, clearly establish a positive relationship between bidders and bid-appraisal ratio for sales having more than one bidder. In order to meet this objection, a separate regression analysis has been made for competitive sales only. Similar results appear, however. The same four variables are significant. The number-of-bidders variable enters the equation with an F value of 168.2. As the critical value is $F_{.95} = 3.84$, there can be no reasonable doubt about the significance of number of bidders in accounting for variability in the bid-appraisal ratio.

The multiple regression equation based on all reported timber sales may be further clarified by reference to figure 19, where the sale-size variable has been introduced and the economic size class has been repeated. If the appraised value and the number of bidders at their average values are held constant, the bid-appraisal ratio declines as average sale size increases. This result is in accord with the second hypothesis. Relatively large sales (8 million feet) tend to be accompanied by a bid-appraisal ratio averaging .08 ratio points below the relatively small sales (1 million feet).

A regression line representing the appraised price (X'_5) is not shown graphically, as this variable has no competitive significance. Its inclusion in the regression equation allows its effect on the bid-appraisal ratio to be held constant so that the more important competitive relationships may be studied independently of the effect of variations in the appraised price.

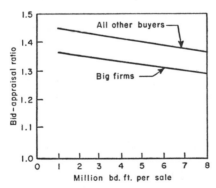

Fig. 19. Net regression lines showing bid-appraisal ratio by firm size computed from volume per sale.

The multiple regression equation permits identification of the hypotheses that are tenable. The first hypothesis asserted that the bid-appraisal ratio, or premium over appraised price, varies negatively with the size class of the successful bidder. Table 25 shows that large firms do in fact incur a significantly lower premium for national forest timber purchases than do smaller firms. The difference is .23 ratio points in the bid-appraisal ratio (a bid-appraisal ratio of 1.28 for large firms and 1.51 for small firms). By means of the foregoing regression equation it has been established that the net relationship between buyer size class and the bid-appraisal ratio, after account has been taken of the number of bidders per sale, the sale size, and the appraised price, is a differential of not .23 but .08 ratio points. Some of the larger difference, which in fact exists, may be accounted for by differences in number of bidders, in sale size, and in average appraised price. Again, table 25 shows that sales acquired by large firms average fewer bidders and greater volume per sale. The regression equation reveals that the bid-appraisal ratio is positively correlated with the number of bidders per sale and is negatively correlated with sale size. Thus, some of the 23 percentage points difference in premium paid by large firms compared with smaller buyers is related, not to economic size of buyer, but to other variables included in the regression equation and, perhaps, even to additional variables not part of the equation. The first hypothesis, asserting a negative relationship between bid-appraisal ratio and size class of successful bidder, is therefore tenable.

The logical evidence in support of the second hypothesis—that the bid-appraisal ratio or premium over appraised price varies negatively with volume per sale or a road-construction cost requirement—rests on financial requirements that serve as barriers to entry and affect smaller firms that are potential bidders for public timber. This hypothesis suggests that a high degree of multicollinearity should be expected between sale size and road-construction cost. The simple coefficient of correlation between volume per sale and road-construction cost confirms the expected degree of multicollinearity: $r = +.88$. With a high degree of multicollinearity, one would not expect both variables to enter the equation. Rather, when one or the other variable enters, the remaining variable becomes insignificant. In fact, when sale size enters the equation, the slope of the coefficient of regression for X_4 is negative, as suggested in the hypothesis. An analysis of variance test shows that

the reduction in total variability in the dependent variable resulting from the entry of X_4 is significant at the 5 percent confidence level. The second hypothesis is therefore tenable.

The third hypothesis asserts that the bid-appraisal ratio, or premium over appraised price, varies positively with the number of
qualified bidders. The principal regression equation, based on all
sales, establishes a clearly significant positive relationship, which
is further supported by an analysis based on competitive sales only.
Again, significance is clearly established. The third hypothesis is
tenable.

Although appraised price (X'_5) enters the regression equation,
this variable has no analytical significance with respect to competitive conditions. Rather, it indicates and acknowledges a fault in
the measure chosen as the dependent variable, the bid-appraisal
ratio. Its entry with a negative sign in the regression equation indicates that higher bid-appraisal ratios are correlated with lower
values of appraised price. Having measured the influence of appraised price, this error factor is held constant and, within the
limitations of the linear model, the effect of any given variable on
the bid-appraisal ratio may be seen (figs. 18, 19).

The variables that failed to enter the multiple regression equation are also of interest. The failure of road-construction cost (X_3)
to enter has been ascribed to multicollinearity with sale size. Of
special import is the failure of sale type (X_8) to enter the regression
equation. The fourth hypothesis, suggesting that sealed-bid sales
produce a higher bid-appraisal ratio than oral auction sales, is
based on the assumptions (1) that there are significant departures
from the competitive model in specified geographical areas, and
(2) that the Forest Service would attack this problem with tools
that include the sealed-bid type of sale. Table 26 presents evidence that no significant difference exists between the bid-appraisal ratios for the two sale types. When net relationships are
considered, there continues to be no significant difference. It should
be pointed out, however, that when sale size and other variables
are taken into consideration, the sign of the coefficient of regression
is as expected; that is, sealed-bid sales are associated with higher
bid-appraisal ratios. Table 26 also includes evidence that raises
doubt concerning the validity of the second assumption, suggesting instead that sealed bid sales are used for purposes other than
to elicit a higher degree of competition in a noncompetitive geographical area. Sealed-bid sales are generally quite small relative

to oral auction sales. It is evident that the Forest Service has not consistently used sealed-bid sales as a means of combating suspected collusion, but for other reasons.[9]

The time variable (X_9) also fails to enter the equation, indicating that there is no net linear trend in the bid-appraisal ratio over the period 1959–1962. The rejection of linear trend must be interpreted cautiously. The time period under study is too limited to draw conclusions with respect to a secular trend in the dependent variable. Had significance been present, I could not assert with confidence that it represented a secular trend rather than cyclical or irregular variation.

The remaining variables that fail to enter the regression equation are housing starts (X_6) and an index of Douglas fir lumber prices (X_7). These variables are introduced, not because they have

---

[9] After identifying areas in which timber was not being sold at competitive prices, the Comptroller General of the United States recommended that federal agencies "use sealed bidding in their respective timber management areas where situations such as those noted by us exist, with the objective of fostering competitive sales conditions" ("Report to the Congress of the United States," Comptroller General of the United States [Feb., 1965], p. 20). In replying to this recommendation, the Forest Service clarified its position concerning sale type: "The objective is to employ a procedure which will result as far as possible in equitable competitive conditions among all classes of bidders. Other things being equal, the established prevailing practice in the Region, sub-Region, or locality should be preferred. Departures from customary procedure may be made to facilitate community stability or to facilitate National Forest administration" ("Forest Service Handbook," sec. 2431.55). The dominant consideration appears to be conformity with local preference: "In the application of the policy on choice between auction and sealed bidding, the Forest Service has given considerable weight to local practices which are functioning satisfactorily. Thus in the Eastern United States, sealed bidding is the accepted practice. Auction bidding is seldom used. In the Pacific Northwest, auction bidding is the expected means for offering timber. . . . The key difference between the situation in the Eastern United States and the Pacific Northwest is the degree of dependence of established mills on purchase of National Forest timber. In the East, there are typically alternate sources of timber supply. In the Pacific Northwest, many mills close to the National Forest have virtually no other source of raw material. The basic difference between auction and sealed bidding is that in sealed bidding surprise is always a possibility. For dependent established enterprises, the possibility of surprise is regarded as uncertainty and a threat to stability. Auction bidding renders surprise ineffective in the determination of an award. It substitutes a test of need and strength." It is conceded that "auction bidding permits the members of a collusive ring to either preclude an outsider from purchasing an offering or to raise the price to the point where if he does purchase it, it will be financially disastrous. It is quite clear that sealed bidding procedure should be used where such abuse of the auction bidding procedure has developed" (letter from Orville L. Freeman, secretary of agriculture, to Congressman William L. Dawson, chairman, Committee on Government Operations, House of Representatives [June 10, 1965]). The Secretary objected, however, to the Comptroller General's identification of collusive areas, and indicated that defining areas subject to collusive agreements constitutes a major problem.

special significance for a study of competition, but rather to take into consideration any effect they may have on the bid-appraisal ratio. The analysis indicates that within the limited four-year period there is no significant cyclical effect; hence, these variables may be neglected.

SUMMARY

In about one-third of the sales of national forest timber in the Douglas fir region over the four-year period 1959–1962, noncompetitive conditions prevailed; competition entered into the remaining two-thirds. The premium in competitive sales exceeded that in noncompetitive sales by 63 percent. Noncompetitive sales included token-bid sales, which strongly indicated collusive behavior among buyers. The spread in bid-appraisal ratios between competitive and noncompetitive sales was so wide (63 percent) as to cast serious doubt on the accuracy of the appraisal process. Given the large premium over appraised price for competitive sales, appraised price cannot reasonably be equated with fair market value.

With respect to market power, there was a significant difference in cost of timber between large and small firms. Large firms paid an average premium of 28 percent over appraised price, whereas the average premium for small firms was 51 percent.

With the aid of multiple regression, four hypotheses relating to the extent or degree of competition for timber were tested; three were accepted. First, a significant negative relationship (net) was found between the economic size class of buyers and the extent of competition as indicated by the bid-appraisal ratio, confirming a net market power position of large firms. Second, a significant negative relationship was found between the extent of competition and average sale size or average road-construction cost: the larger the sale size and the road-construction cost, the lesser the degree of competition (the lower the bid-appraisal ratio). Third, the extent of competition is a positive logarithmic function of the number of bidders active in any given sale. Obviously, a one-bidder sale is noncompetitive. But sales having two or more bidders show the same positive net relationship.

The hypotheses tested and accepted are derived from economic theory. The findings are consistent with the oligopsonistic structure identified in Part II. On the other hand, a fourth hypothesis—that sealed-bid sales are associated with higher bid-appraisal ratios—was rejected. Although the relationship is not statistically significant, the sign of the coefficient of regression is as expected.

CHAPTER 12

Competition for Federal Timber: Geographical Area Basis

The market for timber is a narrow one, geographically speaking. The physical terrain, together with the existing highway system, tends to create circumscribed markets identified by drainages or combinations of drainages. An individual buyer tends to identify with the area in which he normally operates and to refer to it as "my area." Buyers not normally purchasing timber within a given geographical area are treated as outsiders, and are not welcomed by insiders. Timber sales are recorded by national forest and by smaller regions called working circles. Working circles usually correspond to drainages and provide a rough approximation to what may be treated as individual markets for national forest timber.

The objective of this chapter is to test certain hypotheses that may explain observed differences in degree of competition among working circles. Of particular interest are: the number of qualified bidders in each market, the importance of large firms as timber buyers in individual timber markets, and barriers to entry.

COMPETITIVE CONDITIONS BETWEEN GEOGRAPHICAL AREAS

The Douglas fir region may be analyzed in terms of forty-three separate working circles (geographical markets), not including the Shelton working circle. Timber sales within each working circle have been recorded for the four-year period 1959–1962. For each working circle, a new measure, called the "percent competitive," can be computed. This measure is a ratio whose numerator is the volume sold under competitive conditions and whose denominator is the total volume sold, whether competitive or noncompetitive, by working circle. Only oral auction sales are considered.

The forty-three different national forest timber markets vary widely in degree of competition. A frequency distribution showing the number of working circles classified by percent competi-

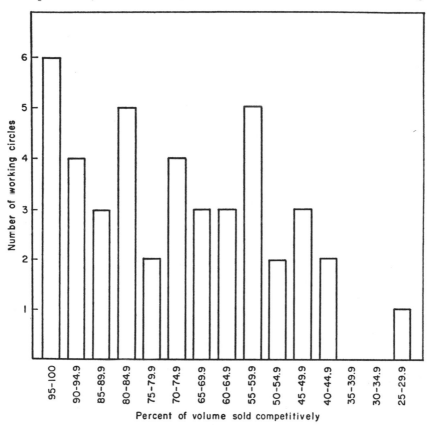

Fig. 20. Number of working circles classified by percent of total volume sold under competitive conditions, 1959–1962.

tive is presented in figure 20. Six working circles are intensely competitive, with 95 to 100 percent of all volume sold being sold under competitive conditions. On the other extreme, only 28.4 percent of one working circle's total volume sold is classified under competitive conditions. The median percent competitive is 73.2 percent. Thus, there is a wide variation in degree of competition prevailing among the several geographical markets.

Homogeneity among working circles can be tested for by means of chi-square analysis. The question may be phrased as follows: May the 2,340 oral auction sales transacted in forty-three Douglas fir region working circles be regarded as coming from a single population that is homogeneous with respect to the competitive-noncompetitive classification, or does the division of sales into com-

petitive and noncompetitive groups vary significantly among
working circles? A definitive answer is provided in table 27. The
discrepancy, in the aggregate, between the observed and theoretical frequencies is $X^2 = 272.58$. At the 5 percent level of significance, $X^2_{.95} = 55.76$. The level of X^2 is so high that one may accept,
with great confidence, the hypothesis that percent of total sales
varies significantly among working circles.

If more than 95 percent of the volume is sold competitively, the
distinction between competitive and noncompetitive sales is of
little importance. The fact that less than 5 percent of the sales are
transacted at appraised price leads to the conclusion that the difference in cost of timber between competitive and noncompetitive
sales is of little consequence. It does, however, become an item of
considerable importance when the share of noncompetitive sales
becomes significant.

Two questions of equity immediately arise in the latter situation. First, there is an equity question among individual firms
operating within a given geographical market. If noncompetitive
sales are concentrated in a few established firms, these firms attain
an unfair advantage in their competitive relationship with other
firms. Their unit timber cost is lower. All lumber and plywood
firms sell in highly competitive markets. In turn, all firms must
compete for quality resources, including labor as well as timber.
On the other hand, if noncompetitive sales are equally distributed
among all buyers within a given working circle, the question of
equity should disappear within the confines of a single market.
Such is not the case, however.

Second, the question of equity also arises among working circles.
Figure 20, indicating a wide variation in degree of competition
among geographical areas, immediately suggests that operators located within intensely competitive working circles are at a disadvantage relative to operators within noncompetitive working
circles. This disadvantage is independent of the degree of efficiency
which operators are able to achieve in their normal manufacturing
and logging operations. Yet, all producers within the Douglas fir
region compete in roughly the same highly competitive markets
in selling lumber and plywood. Thus evolve questions of equity
among producers, both within a given working circle and among
working circles, arising from the fact that some timber is sold at
appraised price whereas a residual quantity is sold at a premium
averaging 63 percent above appraised price. The proportion differs
widely among geographical areas.

The nature of the competitive circumstance that produces vast

TABLE 27

TEST OF HOMOGENEITY[a] BETWEEN OBSERVED AND THEORETICAL FREQUENCIES IN WORKING CIRCLES CLASSIFIED ACCORDING TO DEGREE OF COMPETITION

	Sales						
	Noncompetitive			Competitive			
Working circle	f_o	f	$\dfrac{(f_o-f)^2}{f}$	f_o	f	$\dfrac{(f_o-f)^2}{f}$	Total
Soleduck	7	10	0.90	25	22	0.41	32
Quilcene	10	10	0.00	22	22	0.00	32
Quinault	26	15	8.07	20	31	3.90	46
Glacier	6	9	1.00	22	19	0.47	28
Skagit	5	5	0.00	10	10	0.00	15
Baker River	4	8	2.00	20	16	1.00	24
Suiattle	2	7	3.57	19	14	1.79	21
Darrington	9	16	2.06	41	34	1.44	50
South Fork Stillaguamish	7	8	0.13	18	17	0.06	25
Skycomish	10	6	2.67	10	14	1.14	20
Snoqualmie, Cedar River, Green River[b]	2	4	1.00	11	9	0.44	13
White River	6	10	1.60	24	20	0.80	30
Mineral	9	5	3.20	6	10	1.60	15
Packwood	21	20	0.05	41	42	0.02	62
Randle	11	22	5.50	56	45	2.69	67
Spirit Lake	7	5	0.80	8	10	0.40	15
Lewis River	1	10	8.10	30	21	3.86	31
Mount Adams	30	23	2.13	42	49	1.00	72
Wind River	13	15	0.27	33	31	0.13	46
Canyon Creek	6	9	1.00	21	18	0.50	27
Hood River	1	9	7.11	28	20	3.20	29
Clackamas-Sandy	22	58	22.34	160	124	10.45	182
Hebo	27	21	1.71	39	45	0.80	66
Waldport	24	28	0.57	63	59	0.27	87
Mapleton	76	36	44.44	37	77	20.78	113
South Santiam	55	32	16.53	45	68	7.78	100
North Santiam	28	22	1.63	39	45	0.80	67
McKenzie	35	45	2.22	105	95	1.05	140
Lowell	17	25	2.56	62	54	1.19	79
Oakridge	60	52	1.23	102	110	0.58	162
Cottage Grove	22	19	0.84	36	39	0.23	58
North Umpqua	45	49	0.33	108	104	0.15	153
South Umpqua	33	32	0.03	66	67	0.01	99
Coquille	17	9	7.11	12	20	3.20	29
Rogue River (Siskiyou)	19	15	1.07	28	32	0.50	47
Chetco	15	9	4.00	12	18	2.00	27
Josephine	27	28	0.04	60	59	0.02	87
Applegate	9	6	1.50	10	13	0.69	19
Ashland	12	8	2.00	13	17	0.94	25
Butte Falls	7	10	0.90	23	20	0.45	30
Rogue River	9	22	6.55	61	48	3.52	70
Total	752	752	192.32	1,588	1,588	80.26	2,340

[a] Test of homogeneity: $X^2_o = \Sigma \dfrac{(f_o-f)^2}{f}$

$$= 192.32 + 80.26$$
$$X^2_o = 272.58$$
$$X^2_{.95} = 55.76$$

[b] Three small working circles combined.

differences in percent competitive among working circles can be identified. Three reasons, which may account for differences among timber markets, are readily apparent.

First, if the total annual log supply in a given market is approximately equal to or even exceeds the normal milling capacity of the market, the proportion of transactions at approximately the appraised price would presumably be high. One would expect some timber to be sold at appraised price under one-bidder conditions. Further, if two or more bidders qualify on a given sale, bidding would presumably be limited to a few percentage points above appraised price. This situation would follow from knowledge of the fact that additional timber sales would soon be offered with minimal bidding interest.

Second, a minimal degree of competition, paired with a milling capacity consistently lagging somewhat behind log supplies, might also prevail in an area characterized by regular increases in timber offered for sale within the timber market. Within the Douglas fir region as a whole, the secular trend over the years 1951 through 1962 in quantity of national forest timber offered for sale was upward. The linear trend in volume sold increased annually by about 200 million feet. Offsetting this increase in national forest timber (plus increased sales of other publicly owned timber) was an approximately equal decline in private timber harvested annually. The net result for the entire Douglas fir region was an approximately constant volume of log production from all sources in the period 1951–1962. These relationships, however, applied to the Douglas fir region as a whole; within individual timber markets there were instances of increasing and decreasing total timber volume available annually.

Third, another situation that might lead to evidence of minimal competition is one where relatively few buyers have a normal milling capacity in excess of the total log supply available within an individual market. Unrestrained competition would normally lead to relatively high premiums over appraised price. The function of competition in a situation of this kind would be to ration the relatively scarce timber by means of the price system, with the result that timber would be allocated to the highest bidders who presumably are also the most efficient operators. By this impersonal process, the least efficient producers would be unable to obtain timber, or would be able to do so only at prices that would not allow profitable operations; eventually, such producers would be forced to withdraw from the market.

When potential bidders for timber are few rather than many, it becomes possible for the few to allocate scarce raw material through various working agreements and understandings. When such agreements are effectively policed by the members, bidding is restrained, bidders take turns as buyers, several producers within the area receive less timber than they would like to have at prevailing prices, and, finally, some inefficient producers are able to continue operations. This situation is one of oligopsonistic markets characterized by explicit or implicit agreements among buyers; a relatively high volume of token-bid sales would be evidence that it exists. One would not necessarily expect to find a large number of single-bidder sales because the rules of selling national forest timber require that all bidders who want to cast an oral auction bid must first qualify by a scaled bid and a cash deposit. A party to a collusive agreement may want to be qualified, whether or not he was the previously selected buyer, in order to be able to cast a preclusive bid during the auction. Such action may be necessary in order to prevent an outsider's entry into the area. Timber markets where competition is clearly restrained can therefore be identified by a relatively high proportion of token-bid sales.

It is conceivable that a given working circle or group of working circles may show a large volume of timber sold under noncompetitive conditions and with minimal premiums on competitive sales without evidence of collusive behavior. These results could stem from consistent overappraisal by the Forest Service and general awareness of overappraisal by bidders in the specific area. Appraisal procedures and practices are, however, subject to a high degree of central coordination. Further, the large average premium paid for competitive sales relative to noncompetitive sales precludes equating the appraised price with fair market value; instead, it indicates substantial underappraisal. An occasional appraisal may be faulty or overestimated, but a series of noncompetitive sales are indicative of noncompetitive conditions resulting from one of the above three conditions, rather than consistent overappraisal in a specific working circle.

In several working circles in the Douglas fir region the existence of collusive agreements is suggested by a relatively high proportion of token-bid sales. One of these may be scrutinized in order to identify its general characteristics, and to determine whether the beneficiaries are few in number or include all qualified bidders. In the Mapleton working circle, one of the largest volume markets in the Douglas fir region, 503 million board feet of timber were sold in 113 separate oral auction sales in the period 1959–1962. Of this total, 36 percent of the volume and 30.1 percent of the sales fell within the token-bid category. The bid-appraisal ratio for the Mapleton working circle was 1.17. The average number of bidders was relatively low, 2.42 bidders per sale. These bidding characteristics may be compared with Douglas fir region averages as shown in table 24. For all competitive characteristics, the results cited for the Mapleton working circle indicate a relatively low degree of competition.

Of the 34 token-bid sales in this working circle, 24 were of the nickel-bid variety, in which a tie bid can be resolved at minimum cost to the buyer. In addition, 42 sales were transacted under single-bidder circumstances, representing 83.4 million board feet, or 16.6 percent of all oral auction timber sales within the working circle. Thus, only 37 of 113 sales were competitive. Only 47.6 percent of the total oral auction volume sold fell within the competitive category. Whereas all single-bidder sales and all token-bid sales were obtained at appraised price or at an insignificant premium over appraised price, the purchasers of timber sold competitively within the Mapleton working circle paid a premium averaging 35 percent over appraised price.

The beneficiaries of token-bid sales are rather few. For example, the separately identifiable qualified bidders in the Mapleton working circle numbered fifty-three. Twenty of the fifty-three actually made direct purchases, and only ten succeeded in obtaining token-bid sales. One of these sales was unimportant because the volume sold was minuscule. All the remaining nine token-bid sales were to well-established firms. Seven had operations within the boundaries of the working circle and two were strong outside firms. The largest buyer of the token-bid sales was U.S. Plywood Corporation, which is one of the twenty largest lumber producers, one of the twenty largest plywood producers, and one of the eight largest timberland-owning firms in the Douglas fir region. It obtained five token-bid sales totaling 42.1 million board feet, or 45 percent of its total timber purchases within the Mapleton working circle. The remaining buyers of a significant volume of token-bid sales, though relatively large producers in the Mapleton area, are not large enough to be included in the large-firm category.

In the Mapleton working circle, then, token-bid sales were not spread equally among all possible bidders; rather, they were concentrated among relatively few bidders. Further, the buyers of token-bid sales tended to be large and well-established firms operating within the local timber market. Clearly a question of equity arises among producers within a given market. A second question of equity exists among individual timber markets and the producers operating therein.

There is a considerable difference in degree of competition among the forty-three Douglas fir region working circles. Earlier analysis of individual timber sales suggests that the wide variation in bid-appraisal ratios among individual timber sales is a positive function of the number of bidders and a negative function of average sales size, the economic size class of the buyer, and the appraised value per thousand board feet. The analysis here is concerned, not with individual sales or the bid-appraisal ratio for each sale, but rather with separate geographical timber markets and the percent of total volume sold under competitive conditions in each market. Can observed variations among working circles be explained in terms of variables similar to those used with reference to individual sales?

Hypotheses To Be Tested

In testing for certain relationships that may account for the variability in degree of competition among several working circles, four hypotheses may be advanced. The first suggests that the degree of competition is a positive function of the number of bidders active in each working circle. Economic theory holds that when the number of buyers is small, the possibility of effective collusion among them is great. Conversely, when there are many potential buyers, cooperative arrangements are futile and hence are not attempted, or, if attempted, they cannot be effectively policed and maintained. A measure of the number of potential bidders by working circle is not available; however, a measure of the number of bidders qualified to bid on a given sale is available. From these data, the average number of bidders qualified to bid on all oral auction timber sales by working circle can be computed. The latter value may then be used as an index of bidder activity.

In working circles with very few bidders, many one-bidder sales, which by definition are noncompetitive, are found. As the average number of bidders increases, sharp increases occur in the percent competitive. With subsequent increases in the average number of bidders, a continued increase in the percent competitive would be expected, although at a reduced rate. Hence, a logarithmic transformation of the average number of bidders may be used as the first variable (X'_1). The first hypothesis to be tested is: The percent competitive varies positively with the logarithmic value of the average number of bidders by working circle.

The second hypothesis asserts a negative relationship between the relative importance of large firms in given working circles, on the one hand, and the degree of competition on the other. The desired measure of the second independent variable is a measure of the economic importance of large firms. The closest approximation to this desired measure is the share of total volume of national forest timber purchased by large firms within each working circle, expressed by a ratio whose numerator is the total timber volume purchased by large firms and whose denominator is the total volume sold to all bidders in oral auction sales. This measure is termed the "percent big." The second variable (X_2) differs from the large-firm–small-firm variable used in the analysis of individual sales, where the buyer was either included in or excluded from the big-firm group.

The logic supporting this hypothetical relationship rests on the proposition that large firms have a degree of market power as buyers of federal timber that enables them to obtain timber at a cost advantage. They purchase a larger share of timber in one-bidder and token-bid sales. The greater the importance of large firms in given working circles and the larger the share of timber sales they acquire, the smaller the percentage of total sales under competitive conditions. Further, large firms may exert a moderating influence on the kind of competition which occasionally erupts into wild bidding. The method of testing the second hypothesis cannot, of course, separate these two influences, nor can it establish a causal relationship between this or any other independent variable and the dependent variable. The second hypothesis to be tested is: The percent competitive by working circle varies inversely with the percentage of national forest timber purchased by large firms relative to all other firms, that is, with the percent big.

The third hypothesis asserts a negative relationship between the average volume per sale (X_3), or, alternatively, the average road cost for sales requiring road construction (X_4), on the one hand, and the percent competitive on the other. The logic here is identical with that suggested earlier for individual timber sales. It rests upon the concept of barriers to entry. Yet the relationship within the geographical area framework is more tenuous than that within the individual sale framework. In individual timber sales, one sale with modest volume or modest road-construction cost is distinguished from another sale with large volume and heavy road-construction cost. On the basis of geographical area, average volume or average road-construction costs in one working circle are compared with the same measure in other working circles. The barrier-to-entry relationship is by no means as clear in the latter as in the former.

A high degree of multicollinearity exists between average sale size and average road-construction costs. It is not clear before measurement takes place which factor will be more significant with respect to the dependent variable. Whichever factor is of greater significance, its entry into a regression equation automatically reduces the other to insignificance. The third hypothesis to be tested is: The percent competitive by working circle varies inversely with average sale size or average road-construction costs.

REGRESSION ANALYSIS OF THE BIDDING RECORD

The hypotheses enumerated above may be tested as before by the technique of stepwise multiple linear regression. Using the 5 percent fiducial or confidence level, we arrive at a multiple regression equation with two significant independent variables: the logarithmic value of the average number of bidders, X'_1, and the percent big, X_2. The regression equation is

$$Y = 47.65 + 52.26X'_1 - .28X_2.$$
$$(14.12) \qquad (.11)$$

The standard error of each regression coefficient is given in parentheses. The coefficient of multiple correlation $R_{YX'_1X_2} = .59$, and the coefficient of multiple determination $D_{YX'_1X_2} = .35$. While the first and second hypotheses are accepted, the third, involving the average sale size or the average road-construction cost, is rejected.

An objection may again be raised to the selection of data for use in the regression equation: In an attempt to explain observed differences in the relative importance of number of competitive sales by working circle, the average number of bidders for all sales may not give a proper index of numbers of bidders by working circle. This objection has merit, for the larger the number of one-bidder sales in any given working circle, *ceteris paribus*, the smaller the percent competitive and the average number of bidders per sale. The procedure is used because it provides a somewhat more accurate estimate of percent competitive. The objection may be met by using as an index of number of bidders by working circle the average number of bidders only in sales having two or more bidders. The following significant equation is derived:

$$Y = 51.11 + 42.76X'_1 - .302X_2.$$
$$(17.73) \qquad (.120)$$

Again the first and second hypotheses would be accepted, and the third rejected. Hence the objection is irrelevant insofar as acceptability of the hypotheses is concerned. The second equation accounts for a smaller share of the observed total variation. The coefficient of multiple correlation for the second regression equation is $R_{YX'_1X_2} = .45$, and the equation accounts for only 20 percent of the observed total variation.

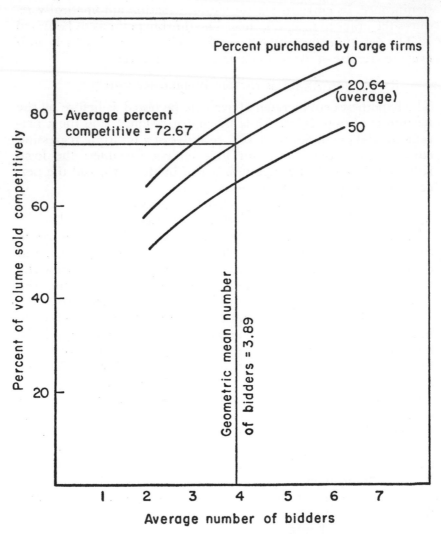

Fig. 21. Net regression lines showing percent competitive computed from average number of bidders and select values of percent of volume purchased by large firms, based on working-circle data.

The relationships given mathematically in the original multiple regression equation may be clarified graphically (see figure 21). When the number of bidders is at its geometric mean value of 3.89, and when there are no large firms operating in a given working circle, the best estimate that can be made for percent competitive is 78.47. When large firms acquire 50 percent of the total volume sold in a given working circle, the best estimate that can be made for percent competitive is 64.42. On the other hand, when the average percent big is held constant at its arithmetic mean value of 20.64, and when the average number of bidders by working circle is 2, the best estimate of percent competitive is 57.58. As the average number of bidders increases to 6 while the influence of large firms is held constant, the best estimate of percent competitive becomes 82.52.

SUMMARY

The analysis based on geographical timber markets permits a new dependent variable to be employed: the percentage of sales sold under competitive conditions by geographical markets. The percent competitive differed widely among the forty-three separate markets analyzed; some were highly competitive while others were noncompetitive. Equity questions arise as a consequence of the disparity in competitive conditions among buyers in different areas.

Through multiple regression analysis, certain factors associated with the observed difference in degree of competition were explored. Particular interest is centered in the market power of large firms. A statistically significant inverse relationship exists between the percentage of total national forest timber sales volume acquired by large firms and the percentage of volume sold competitively by geographical markets: the greater the importance of large firms as timber buyers, the smaller the percent competitive. A positive relationship between the average number of qualified bidders for sales within geographical markets and the percent competitive also exists: the larger the average number of bidders, the larger the percent competitive. Other variables tested are not statistically significant. The regression analysis indicates that 35 percent of the observed variation in percent competitive by geographical markets may be explained by the importance of large firms as timber buyers and by the average number of qualified bidders.

CHAPTER 13

Bidder Futility and the
Market Power of Large Firms

Large firms obtain national forest timber for a significantly lower premium (28 percent) over appraised price than do small firms (51 percent). Multiple regression analysis shows that the significant buying advantage favoring large firms persists when the relationship between firm size and bid-appraisal ratio is measured net of number of bidders, average sale size, and appraised price per thousand board feet. Finally, firm size is significantly related to the degree of competition in forty-three different geographical markets for federal timber within the Douglas fir region. When the volume of federal timber purchased by big firms is large, the percent of total volume sold competitively tends to be low.

These data document the conclusion that large firms possess a significant degree of buying power in the market for federal timber and raise this question: What factors in the structure of the timber industry and in the behavior of firms in the industry account for the observed relationship between firm size and premium over appraised price? Regression analysis is capable only of establishing relationships, not of affirming a line of causality from independent variables to the dependent variable. Causal relationships may be established, however, by a priori reasoning.

DIRECT FORCES LEADING TO MARKET POWER

Two kinds of forces lead to market power: direct and indirect. The direct forces are also of two kinds: (1) barriers to entry resulting from sale size and road-construction cost, and (2) timber-ownership factors. Small firms in the lumber industry, whether gyppo loggers or small mill operators, are notoriously poorly financed. Bidding for federal timber requires that a deposit accompany the initial bid. The minimum deposit is approximately 5 percent of the sale value, but the maximum deposit is $100,000. Financial requirements also include operating capital not only for logging operations but for road-construction obligations as well. Although the capital requirements are modest and federal loans are available to assist in financing road construction, many small firms are so handicapped financially that bidding on large sales with accompanying heavy road-construction costs is precluded.[1] Yet it does not follow that the number of bidders per sale varies inversely with sale size. The record of timber sales from 1959 through 1961 indicates precisely the opposite relationship, that the average number of bidders increases with sale size. The significant factor is that bidders for small sales characteristically are nondisciplined small mill owners and gyppo loggers, whereas bidders for larger timber sales include larger operators whose time span of operations is longer and who are more accustomed to cooperative arrangements and observance of established spheres of influence.

Joe S. Bain's "barriers to entry" concept needs some modification for application to the timber market because it is essentially quantitative. Bain evaluates the condition of entry by the "extent to which established sellers can persistently raise their prices above a competitive level without attracting new firms to enter the industry."[2] There is no discussion of the qualitative factor—the character of the potential entrant firm and its propensity to join in collusive agreements. In timber markets, barriers to entry arising from sale size and road-construction requirements preclude the in-and-out small gyppo logger and the poorly financed small mill operator, but they do not restrain well-financed medium and large firms. The former group are generally more inclined to rugged individualistic market behavior. The latter generally are more permanent in their communities and are more inclined to enter cooperative agreements with other established firms in the same geographical market. While large sale size and road-construction requirements do not restrict entry quantitatively, they do discriminate qualitatively.

A second factor in the direct forces leading to significant market

---

[1] A recent survey of the problems of small lumber companies operating in western Oregon, seeking to determine the factors inhibiting firms as buyers of federal timber, reveals that very small sawmills give first priority to "sales too big" as a barrier to successful acquisition of federal timber. Small mills also frequently list "access road requirements" and "shortage of funds" as factors that limit their ability to acquire federal timber (Franklin Y. H. Ho, *Small Lumber Companies in Western Oregon* [Portland: University of Portland, 1963], p. 65).

[2] Joe S. Bain, *Barriers to New Competition* (Cambridge: Harvard University Press, 1956), p. 3.

power for large firms arises from the ownership of timber resources. Firms having a large volume of timber held in fee ownership enjoy a degree of flexibility in timber buying which allows them to be selective. Such firms are in a position to reject high-cost sales and to restrict their purchases to sales that are, for various reasons, less severely challenged. A firm without timber resources under its control may frequently have to decide whether to purchase a given timber stand regardless of cost or to cease operations. Facing this unpleasant choice, profit-maximizing or loss-minimizing firms will rationally bid up the price of timber, if necessary, beyond the point that allows profit and even beyond the point that allows the buyer to cover his fixed cost. Many, though not all, large firms are in a favored position with respect to timber ownership. The eight largest timberland-owning firms are automatically included in the category of large firms, and thereby enjoy a degree of flexibility arising from timber ownership.

INDIRECT FORCES LEADING TO MARKET POWER: THE CONCEPT OF BIDDER FUTILITY

Indirect forces may contribute to the market power of large firms. Approximately 140 interviews with persons involved in buying federal timber reveal that most small operators have a high degree of respect for the economic power of their large competitors, accompanied by a feeling of futility in regard to competing with large firms for specific timber sales. This sense of what we may call "bidder futility" on the part of small operators seems to be rooted in at least four factors.

First, the superior location of some, but not all, well-established and entrenched large firms influences bidding ability. Location of milling facilities may be a significant advantage in bidding for federal timber. The location of milling facilities near the boundary of a national forest minimizes log transportation costs. At the same time, rail charges for transporting finished products to national markets normally are identical for mills located within a reasonable bidding area with respect to any given national forest. One example will illustrate the point. In the Oakridge working circle in the Willamette National Forest, the Edward Hines Lumber Company and Pope and Talbot, Inc., have obvious locational advantages with respect to Oakridge working circle timber. Each firm is located near the exit of substantial federal timber holdings in two different ranger districts. Other operators normally competing for Oakridge timber are located downriver toward the Eugene-Springfield area. Downriver mills have to haul logs about 40 miles farther than either Hines or Pope and Talbot, paying an estimated 3 to 5 dollars more per thousand board feet for transportation, which increases the average stumpage cost of Oakridge timber by 15 to 25 percent. Rail freight rates, on the other hand, are identical for lumber shipments from Oakridge and from the Eugene-Springfield area to all major market centers.

The locational advantage in itself does not directly explain why large firms obtain federal timber at lower costs than their smaller competitors, resulting, in turn, in a lower percent competitive where large firms operate. An indirect relationship, however, may exist. Noting the locational advantage of entrenched firms, others not possessing this advantage appear to develop a feeling of bidder futility that results in their reluctance to challenge entrenched firms. It should be noted that not all large firms are advantageously located with respect to federal timber.

Second, road ownership influences bidding ability. Ownership of a private logging road leading from a forest to processing facilities enables a firm to use off-highway log transportation. Larger logging trucks may be used which haul approximately 85 percent greater volume per load and at the same time avoid certain highway user taxes. Firms owning substantial quantities of timber and timberland frequently construct private roads in order to achieve these advantages, though only at substantial investment and maintenance costs. Presumably, however, savings exceed costs and yield at least an adequate return on the investment. If no comparable public roads are available, the Forest Service negotiates user rights on private roads on behalf of potential bidders other than the owner of the private road. If milling facilities are so located as to require use of public highways, log weights must meet the more restrictive public highway requirements. If alternative public roads are available, bidders other than the owner of a private logging road may not be given the opportunity to use the private road. In this event, the higher log hauling weights must be foregone; in addition, a more circuitous route may have to be used. Road ownership, perhaps in conjunction with locational advantage, may therefore give certain firms a bidding advantage. When these firms are large, as they frequently are, bidder futility may again develop, so that favored firms are less frequently challenged by others.

Third, the superior economic power of large firms and the respect for such economic power may further contribute to bidder futility among smaller firms. There are at least three important characteristics of superior economic power: (1) Some, but not all, large firms have substantial reserves of timber often acquired before the post–1940 rapid increase in stumpage value, or perhaps acquired subsequently at relatively advantageous terms. In at least one instance, the net cost of timber reserves was further reduced by liquidation at favorable prices of a portion of recently acquired timber. The net effect was that timber reserves retained were held at low stumpage cost. A firm owning low-cost timber is in a position, if necessary, to bid the prices of federal stumpage up to levels that would be ruinous for other firms. A financially secure firm, whether its security is due to ownership of low-cost timber reserves or other reasons, always has the option of attacking its less fortunate competitors by surrendering a portion of its profits derived from strength advantages. Frequent use of this power, however, may be inconsistent with profit maximization. An occasional flexing of economic power, resulting in a high-cost sale, can be offset against low-cost logs from the company's own timber reserves and against other federal timber purchased at appraised price or nearly so. The reality of this situation and knowledge of it by smaller firms contribute to bidder futility and thus to the observed differential cost of timber favoring large firms. This point is separate and distinct from the flexibility advantage previously noted as a direct force leading to the cost advantage possessed by big firms.

2) Superior economic power may also be based on a more secure financial position. Financial resources may be strong owing not only to financial reserves, but also to greater borrowing power. Some large firms have access to capital markets at the prime rate of interest.

3) Superior economic power may arise from diversified and more stable sources of income. Large firms may enjoy a substantial and stable income from pulp and paper production, plywood production, mineral production, and the like.

4) Finally, bidder futility may be the result of the capital gains tax law and the manner of its administration. For the timber-owning firm, a federal timber sale acquired at high cost is not entirely without a favorable aspect. The high price paid can be submitted as evidence for a higher fair market value claimed for the company's own timber. In the process of calculating its capital gains tax, the higher the fair market value assigned, the larger the

income classified as capital gain, and the smaller the income classified as ordinary income. In effect, the income is shifted from the 48 percent[3] tax category to a maximum 25 percent category. Smaller firms owning little or no timber cannot realize comparable benefits from a high-cost purchase.[4] Therefore, the capital gains tax may contribute to the small operator's feeling of futility in challenging a large entrenched firm.

A negative point must also be discussed. Relative efficiency favoring large firms apparently is not a factor contributing to bidder futility. The relative inefficiency of large firms is widely discussed and acknowledged in the industry. Economies of plant and firm scale are examined in chapter 1. Although the data are not entirely satisfactory, the evidence suggests that the penultimate plant size class (60,000 to 140,000 feet per eight-hour day) rather than the largest size class is the most efficient, and that no economies (net) flow from multiplant firms in the lumber industry. The opposite appears more likely to be true—that there are net diseconomies of multiplant firms in lumber production.

The four possible factors listed above support the concept of bidder futility which makes small firms reluctant to challenge large firms in bidding competition. The same argument, however, does not prevent small firms from challenging one another. If bidder futility is a valid concept, three results would be expected: (1) fewer bidders would be registered (qualified) to bid on sales purchased by large firms; (2) a lower proportion of the sales obtained by large firms would show evidence of challenge by other bidders; and (3) when challenge takes place for sales obtained by large firms, the degree of challenge as indicated by premium over appraised price would be lower.

The record confirms all three points. Table 25 shows that an average of 4.29 bidders were qualified to bid on sales obtained by small firms, whereas only 3.72 bidders were qualified on sales obtained by large firms. Bidders frequently know before sales take place whether or not a large firm in the geographical market expects to obtain a given sale. Within a given geographical area, sub-

---

[3] The 1964 corporate income tax rate, including surtax, was 50 percent. It became 48 percent in 1965.

[4] A long-term capital gain may be claimed on federal timber purchases if the time requirement is met and if a gain over cost can be shown. The magnitude of the benefit is small, however, when compared with the capital gain position of large timber-owning firms.

areas are occasionally staked out by large firms and identified as within their spheres of influence. On the second point, the four-year record shows that 74.5 percent of the volume (69 percent of the sales) obtained by small firms were subject to significant challenge, whereas 65.8 percent of the volume (62 percent of the sales) obtained by large firms were challenged. On the third point, when sales were effectively challenged, small firms as high bidders were bid up 68 percent, whereas the large firms were bid up only 43 percent.

A final word of caution is in order. Bidder futility is not a universal phenomenon; it is felt more by some small firms than by others, and by still others is apparently totally ignored. Dominant firms are occasionally called upon to demonstrate their dominance, a process that may be extremely costly. As an example, the recent timber cost record of Pope and Talbot in the Oakridge working circle may be cited. Conditions were stable for the three years 1959 through 1961. Pope and Talbot purchased 27.6 percent of all their timber volume under one-bidder conditions, whereas small firms purchasing timber in the same working circle obtained only 7.9 percent of their volume in one-bidder sales. In addition, Pope and Talbot purchased 45.7 percent of their total volume in token-bid sales, whereas smaller firms obtained only 22.8 percent of their volume in this way. Pope and Talbot thus bought only 26.7 percent of their total volume under competitive conditions, with a bid-appraisal ratio of 1.35. In sharp contrast, small firms acquired vastly more (69.3 percent) of their volume under competitive conditions, and at a slightly higher bid-appraisal ratio (1.38). The overall bid-appraisal ratio for Pope and Talbot for all oral auction sales acquired in the Oakridge working circle during the three-year period was 1.12, compared with 1.25 for smaller firms. The tranquillity in this working circle abruptly ceased when, on June 26, 1962, a very large sale (20 million feet) was offered at oral auction. Pope and Talbot's desire to obtain the sale was challenged by a small firm, Camac Veneer of Springfield. The Pope and Talbot initiative was successful, but only at a bid-appraisal ratio of 3.37. For timber originally appraised at $85,770, Pope and Talbot bid $289,105, or $203,335 in excess of the appraised value. On the following day another relatively large sale (16.3 million feet) was offered in the same working circle. Again, Pope and Talbot's need for the timber was in conflict with another potential buyer, Natron Plywood Company of Eugene. As before, Pope and Talbot prevailed in the oral auction, but at a bid-appraisal ratio of 2.01. Pope and Talbot was forced to bid $297,275 to obtain timber appraised at $148,100. The cost to this large firm of demonstrating dominance within its sphere of influence for these two days in June totaled $352,510 above the appraised price of the timber purchased. Pope and Talbot's vigorous bidding in response to outside challenge not only demonstrated the firm's willingness to make great financial sacrifices in order to prevail, but served to reinforce the previously observed bidder futility attitude of small firms. Pope and Talbot obtained both timber sales and demonstrated its dominance, but its recorded premium over appraised price increased eleven fold from 12 percent in 1959–1961 to 136 percent for all its Oakridge purchases in 1962.

I do not know what motivated two relatively small firms to challenge the large, well-entrenched firm of Pope and Talbot. It is possible that smaller firms exploit the position of entrenched firms and their necessity to protect their respective spheres of influence. A "mischievous" challenge of this kind could be presented by either an "inside" firm or an "outside" firm. A firm within a given geographical market would be unlikely mischievously to exploit the position of the dominant firm, unless it had access to a source of timber for its own needs independent of and secure from retaliation by the entrenched firm. Without such security, the challenger would know that retaliation would surely take place, and that the entrenched firm, particularly if it owned a substantial amount of timber reserves, would be more likely to survive a competitive war than would the challenger. If an inside firm is dependent on public timber, as it usually is, it must "live" in the timber market with its "permanent" rivals, and it is most unlikely to present a mischievous challenge. The outside firm has the added disadvantage of heavy log transportation costs for any timber sale it may obtain in a challenge. Further, if the large firm has several plants located in nearby areas, it may retaliate against the outsider in its area without bearing the same heavy transportation burden for any sale it obtains. The multiplicity of markets in which large firms operate as buyers improves their ability to retaliate and to protect themselves against any kind of challenge. Mischievous challenge, though it may occasionally take place, could be a hazardous game. There is no information to indicate whether, or to what extent, mischievous challenge is practiced.

An attitude of bidder futility is based on real economic facts

of competitive life. It may also be reinforced by "the lively ima-
ginations of small enterprises that contemplate the passive strength
of a large rival."[5] But real or imagined, the strength of large firms
appears to engender bidder futility in many small firms, and thus
to make them avoid confrontations with large firms.

Summary

The observed market power of large firms in public timber auction
markets springs from both direct and indirect forces. Among the
former are barriers to entry into the auction market and timber
ownership. The barriers to entry consist of sale size and/or road-
construction requirements. Large sale size, usually accompanied
by heavy road-construction costs, precludes small and poorly financed millowners and gyppo loggers and limits bidding to the
more adequately financed and usually well-established large firms.
Furthermore, large firms are usually, but not always, substantial
owners of timber resources that enable them to be more selective
in their purchase policy and avoid high-cost sales.

Among the indirect forces that help to explain the market power
position of large firms is bidder futility. Four factors appear to
create a feeling of futility among potential buyers which leads
them to avoid a confrontation with their larger rivals. The first
source of bidder futility is the superior location of some large firms.
A mill location close to the exit of a national forest reduces log
transportation costs but has no effect on rail freight rates to the
important lumber markets. Second, ownership of private logging
roads on privately owned timberland adjacent to a national forest
may substantially lower log transportation costs. Third, large firms
normally possess superior economic power arising from ownership
of historically low-cost timber reserves, a secure financial position
including access to low-cost credit, and diversified and more stable
income. Fourth, large firms have significant advantages in capital
gains treatment of income from timber ownership. When bidder
futility exists, large firms are less frequently challenged in timber
auction markets than are their smaller rivals. Bidder futility, in
turn, contributes to the market power of large firms. Negatively,
there is no evidence to support the point that large firms are more
efficient than smaller firms; hence, relative efficiency apparently
does not add to the bidder futility attitude.

---

[5] Corwin D. Edwards, "Public Policy and Business Size," *Journal of Business,*
XXIV (Oct., 1951), 288.

CHAPTER 14

Performance in Resource Management and Lumber Production

In chapters 11 and 12 the performance of firms as buyers of national forest timber was discussed. The appraisal of other aspects of performance in the lumber industry is complicated by the absence of a satisfactory norm or standard by which performance may be judged. The requirements of satisfactory performance should be suitable for objective rather than subjective judgment so that different researchers examining the same industry with respect to performance and applying the same set of criteria will reach the same conclusion.

The literature on industrial organization reveals that there are no quantifiable performance criteria. An appraisal of performance in the hard-surface floor-covering industry shows that "to date, economic theory has not supplied precise, meaningful, and widely accepted norms of performance for all of the essential dimensions of behavior in given industrial situations. Thus, the assessment of workability of competition in various industries is likely to be influenced materially by value judgments."[1] Workable competition may be accepted as a standard for antitrust analysis and policy, "but it grows increasingly evident that the operating features and properties of 'workable' defy identification except in terms that beg the question. . . . The fact is that the concept, workable competition, is not particularly workable."[2]

The attempts made to set forth criteria of satisfactory perfor-

---

1 Robert F. Lanzillotti, *The Hard-Surface Floor-Covering Industry* (Pullman: State College of Washington Press, 1955), p. 149.

2 Ben Lewis, "The Social Responsibility of Big Business," testimony before the Senate Committee on the Judiciary, 1959, reprinted in Edwin Mansfield, ed., *Monopoly Power and Economic Performance* (New York: Norton, 1964), p. 100.

mance have been concerned almost exclusively with judging oligopoly rather than with judging a competitive structure. The tendency has been to appraise a competitive industry by assumption: "No one seriously disputes that if concentration is low and firm numbers are large, competition (in the absence of collusion) will be effective."[3] Industries with a competitive structure normally are assumed to show satisfactory performance, and appraisal efforts have been diverted primarily to appraising oligopoly structures.

THE CRITERIA OF WORKABLE COMPETITION

Within the last two decades, an extensive literature has been developed concerning the criteria of "workable competition."[4] The statements advanced are usually quite general and nonquantifiable. For example, George Stigler's tentative definition of workable competition, in which he attempts to "illustrate the type of specific criterion" needed to judge workability, lists the following points: "(1) There are a considerable number of firms selling closely related products in each important market area, (2) these firms are not in collusion, and (3) the long run average cost curve for a new firm is not materially higher than for an established firm."[5] Such expressions as "considerable number," "closely related," and "materially higher" are not suitable for objective testing. Nor is it clear whether implicit collusion is covered by the second point, or whether explicit collusion is intended, or both.

The well-known list of structural characteristics indicative of a workable degree of competition, as set forth by Corwin Edwards, is more detailed but, again, it is not suitable for objective testing.[6] While J. M. Clark's pioneering formulations of the concept of

---

[3] Daniel C. Hamilton, *Competition in Oil* (Cambridge: Harvard University Press, 1958), p. 1.

[4] Important contributions to the concept of workable competition are J. M. Clark, "Towards a Concept of Workable Competition," *American Economic Review*, XXX (June, 1940), 214–256; George J. Stigler, "The Extent and Bases of Monopoly," *American Economic Review*, XXXII, Supplement no. 2 (June, 1942), p. 2; Edward S. Mason, "The Current Status of the Monopoly Problem in the United States," *Harvard Business Review*, LXII (1949), 1265–1285; Corwin D. Edwards, *Maintaining Competition* (New York: McGraw-Hill, 1949), pp. 9–10; Joe S. Bain, "Workable Competition in Oligopoly," *American Economic Review*, XL (May, 1950), 35–47; Jesse W. Markham, "An Alternative Approach to the Concept of Workable Competition," *American Economic Review*, XL (June, 1950), 349–361; and J. M. Clark, "Competition: Static Models and Dynamic Aspects," *American Economic Review*, XLV (May, 1955), 450–462.

[5] *Op. cit.*, pp. 2–3.

[6] *Op. cit.*, pp. 9–10.

workable competition have some interesting and unique features, the problem of nonquantifiability remains. Clark's contribution comes as an answer to his pertinent question: "In the light of things we want competition to do for us, what are the features it needs to have which are implied in these objectives?" Identifying three groups of objectives, he gives first priority to "the elements required for progress." As subcategories within this first objective, he again assigns priorities, writing "first comes progress in economical methods of production." This is a reference to technological invention and innovation. Continuing with a second order of priority, he writes, "We want competition to afford customers an amply differentiated range of qualities and types of any given product to choose from." Clark argues that this kind of product differentiation is desired, not for its own sake, but rather as evidence that "producers are exploring." The third order of priority is, "We want new products developed."[7] Thus, product development is desired along with technological improvements.

A second group of objectives identified by Clark is concerned with two subcategories: (1) The benefits of progress should be diffused "to customers in lower prices, or to those who contribute factors of production—chiefly workers—in higher real rewards." (2) Also, the diffusion process should allow a customer to have "considerable confidence that the offerings of different sellers are of approximately equal value, and that he will not be seriously victimized if he fails to shop around."[8]

A third group of objectives for a workable competitive system is concerned with the conditions of competitive rivalry itself. The issue here is not with products and prices, but rather with the human impact of competitive pressures on those who are exposed to them. Clark holds that the benefits of satisfactory progress toward the first two objectives "should not be dependent upon the goodwill and arbitrary decision of private producers, nor on direct governmental order, but on a situation in which normal business motives impel business units (acting independently) to conduct that will tend to further the desired results."[9]

These three groups of objectives are offered by Clark as a reorientation of the traditional framework and a reformulation into dynamic terms. This valued step forward starts out with a state-

---

[7] "Competition: Static Models and Dynamic Aspects," p. 453.
[8] *Ibid.*, p. 455.
[9] *Ibid.*, p. 456.

ment of what we expect competition to accomplish. Like other
statements of workable competition, however, it does not offer a
satisfactory basis for objective measurement. Clark is well aware
of the limitation: "This is admittedly a not-too-precise standard."[10]

A further significant contribution to the workable competition
standard has been given by Jesse Markham. In addition to the
usual standards, Markham suggests that "an industry may be judged
workably competitive when, after the structural characteristics of
its market and the dynamic forces that shaped them have been thoroughly examined, there is no clearly indicated change that can be
effected through public policy measures which would result in
greater social gains than social losses."[11] It is not enough to show
that a given industry has a poor performance record with respect
to one or more criteria; we must also examine the possibility of an
alternative structural form producing an improved result. The job
of appraisal remains both difficult and highly subjective, but the
Markham addendum offers a useful check against a simple list of
requirements for workably competitive status which may include
some that cannot be met under any structural form.

Performance standards based on the concept of workable competition have been applied almost universally to the oligopolistic
case in order to determine whether the performance results approximate those of a competitive industry.[12] My use of the stan-

---

10 *Ibid.* Clark's statement of objectives appears to be a useful approach to appraising performance, but it is of questionable value as a standard of antitrust policy.
Alfred E. Kahn points out that the workable competition standard "would permit
businessmen to do these things provided they can at some future date, when and if
called upon to do so, demonstrate in any of a great number of possible ways that
the practices produced 'good' economic results" ("Standards for Antitrust Policy,"
Harvard Law Review, LXVII [1953], 28–54, reprinted in *Readings in Industrial
Organization and Public Policy,* ed. R. B. Heflebower and G. W. Stocking [Home-
wood, Ill.: Irwin, 1958], VII, 362). Kahn adds that "economic results are to be used
as a basis for acquittal only: no critic has yet suggested that a poor performance
provides a sufficient basis for prosecution" (*Ibid.,* p. 363).

11 *Op. cit.,* p. 361.

12 Several valiant and serious attempts have been made to apply the standards of
workable competition to specific industries. For example, the steel, cellophane,
and tin can industries do not qualify as workably competitive oligopolies (George
W. Stocking, "The Rule of Reason, Workable Competition, and Monopoly," *Yale
Law Review,* LXIV [July, 1955], reprinted in *Workable Competition and Antitrust
Policy,* ed. G. W. Stocking [Nashville: Vanderbilt University Press, 1961], pp. 149–152).
The Gulf Coast oil-refining industry has been found to be effectively competitive,
though oligopolistic in structure (Hamilton, *op. cit.,* p. 188). The integrated American
oil industry has been deemed workably competitive, except in the crude oil sector,
but it is suggested that no alternative industrial structure would yield better performance results (Melvin G. de Chazeau and Alfred E. Kahn, *Integration and Com-*

dards of workable competition represents a "twist" on the usual approach: I apply the concept and standards of workable competition to an admittedly competitive industry (at the output level), challenging what has been called the "plausible aphorism that there can be too much competition as well as too little."[13] But, I also apply these standards, when appropriate, to the input level for the lumber industry which has previously been identified as oligopsonistic in structure.

This appraisal of performance in the lumber industry is based on an eclectic derivation of the requirements for a workably competitive performance. Basically, Professor Clark's requirements are used. These are modified, however, and the formulations of other writers are employed to meet the particular problems arising from the need to relate industrial structure, conduct, and performance. Any analysis of performance and of the relationship among the three dimensions of industrial organization is plagued by the lack of precise standards and by the inability to quantify the standards. Therefore, we must acknowledge that research concerned with performance does not permit an unequivocal appraisal.

THE THEORETICAL RELATIONSHIP AMONG STRUCTURE, CONDUCT, AND PERFORMANCE

Before beginning an empirical appraisal of performance in resource management and lumber production, theoretical expectations based on present knowledge of structure and conduct are set forth. We may then empirically test our theoretical expectations. Knowledge of the relationship between structure, conduct, and performance is highly significant for antitrust policy. A substantial body of opinion holds that a structural test is an insufficient basis for antitrust action and that evidence of unfair practices (behavioral characteristics) must accompany a permissive structure before application of corrective antitrust action would be appropriate. An empirical study that sheds additional light on the relationship between structure, conduct, and performance thus offers a potentially valuable contribution to the determination of public policy.

---

petition in the Petroleum Industry, Petroleum Monograph Series, vol. 3 [New Haven: Yale University Press, 1959], p. 567. As to the hard-surface floor-covering industry, "On the whole, the record and the dynamic forces shaping that performance would permit classification . . . among the workably competitive industries" (Lanzillotti, *op. cit.*, p. 157).

13 *Op. cit.*, p. 362.

A clear statement of what appears to be a prevailing view and is the basis of modern equilibrium theory is given by Frank Knight:

The argument for individualism, as developed by its advocates from Adam Smith down, may be summarized in a sentence as follows: A freely competitive organization of society tends to place every productive resource in that position in the productive system where it can make the greatest possible addition to the total social dividend as measured in price terms, and tends to reward every participant in production by giving it the increase in the social dividend which its cooperation makes possible. In the writer's opinion such a proposition is entirely sound.[14]

Given a competitive structure and skipping over questions of conduct, then, the expected performance record would be one of maximum economic growth and social justice in distribution. By 1942 Joseph Schumpeter, described by Arthur Schlesinger, Jr., as "a reactionary without illusions" and by Professor Stigler as the "distinguished iconoclast of our profession," was arguing that big business (oligopoly), not atomistic competition, was the true engine of progress: "As soon as we go into details and inquire into the individual items in which progress was most conspicuous, the trail leads not to the doors of those firms that work under conditions of comparatively free competition, but precisely to the doors of the large concerns . . . and a shocking suspicion dawns upon us that big business may have more to do with creating that standard of life than with keeping it down."[15]

An attempt at synthesis was made by Edward Mason in 1947: "It may be said, I think, that large numbers are a sufficient though not a necessary condition of workable competition. . . . The fact that large numbers of buyers and sellers *will* insure workable competition does not mean, however, that such numbers are necessary."[16] Mason holds fast to the classical position but, borrowing from Schumpeter, adds the proviso that oligopoly also may provide the desired performance goals. In this study the proposition

---

[14] Frank H. Knight, "The Ethics of Competition," *Quarterly Journal of Economics*, XXXVII (1923), 579–624, reprinted in Frank H. Knight, *The Ethics of Competition and other Essays* (London: Harper, 1935), p. 48.

[15] Joseph A. Schumpeter, *Capitalism, Socialism, and Democracy* (3d ed.; New York: Harper, 1950), p. 82.

[16] Edward S. Mason, "Competition, Price Policy, and High-Level Stability," paper presented at Second Economic Institute, Chamber of Commerce of the United States, Washington, 1947, reprinted in Edward S. Mason, ed., *Economic Concentration and the Monopoly Problem* (Cambridge: Harvard University Press, 1957), p. 179.

that an industry that is admittedly competitive at the output level has in fact produced the best possible performance record is questioned.

The doubt Schumpeter raised about the classical relationship between structure and performance stimulated a great deal of discussion and research. Recently, research has been primarily concerned with the relationship between firm size, on the one hand, and innovation bringing forth economic progress on the other. The debate has taken place principally in the *Journal of Political Economy*.[17] As yet, there is no clear consensus arising out of the debate. The lack of a consensus may be due to the general nature of the research problem as conceived by the participants. There may be no single generalization that relates industrial structure to performance in innovations. Rather, oligopolistic structure and large-scale research may be suitable for research in one class of industries, whereas small-scale research may be better for another class of industries whose product has a different basic character. Or a distinction by type of progress may be significant. In this regard Willard Mueller has suggested that the large firm may be more successful in improving products and processes than in discovering new products.[18] This position has been elaborated by D. Hamberg: "With few exceptions, the large industrial laboratories are likely to be minor sources of major (radically new and commercially or militarily important) inventions; rather they are likely to be major sources of essentially 'improvement' inventions."[19]

Given the criteria of workable competition and a statement of the theoretical relationship between structure, conduct, and per-

[17] See G. Warren Nutter, "Monopoly, Bigness and Progress," *Journal of Political Economy*, LXIV (Dec., 1956), 520–527; H. H. Villard, "Competition, Oligopoly, and Research," *Journal of Political Economy*, LXVI (Dec., 1958), 483–497; G. Schmookler, "Reply," and H. H. Villard, "Rejoinder," *Journal of Political Economy*, LXVII (Dec., 1959), 628–635; James S. Worley, "Industrial Research and the New Competition," *Journal of Political Economy*, LXIX (April, 1961), 183–186; *The Rate and Direction of Inventive Activity*, National Bureau of Economic Research (Princeton: Princeton University Press, 1962); D. Hamberg, "Invention in the Industrial Research Laboratory," *Journal of Political Economy*, LXXI (April, 1963), 95–115; Edwin Mansfield, "Size of Firm, Market Structure, and Innovation," *Journal of Political Economy*, LXXI (Dec., 1963), 556–576; Edwin Mansfield, "Industrial Research and Development Expenditures: Determinants, Prospects and Relation to Size of Firm and Inventive Output," *Journal of Political Economy*, LXXII (Aug., 1964), 319–340.
[18] Williard F. Mueller, "Major Product and Process Innovations, 1920 to 1950," in *The Rate and Direction of Inventive Activity*, p. 344.
[19] Hamberg, *op. cit.*, p. 95.

formance, what specific performance evidence should we expect to find (1) at the lumber-production level and (2) at the timber-ownership and management level?

First, the highly competitive structure of the lumber industry at the output level would lead us to expect workably competitive performance. There should be clear evidence of economic progress in the form of product and process innovations. Evidence should appear in the form of a relatively high annual increase in productivity (output per man-hour of labor input). Further, we should expect to find evidence that the benefits of economic progress are diffused among consumers in the form of the lowest possible lumber prices and among workers in the form of increasing real wages. Profits should reflect only competitive yields on capital. Further, consumers should be able to enjoy a high degree of confidence in the lumber products offered for sale. Personal economic and political freedom should not be restricted as a result of lumber industry structure.

Second, shifting to the area of timber resource ownership, the modest degree of concentration would lead a theorist in the Knight tradition to expect a relatively inferior performance record. Specifically, one would expect that freedom and opportunity in the use of timber resources might be restricted by the power of large firms. Such restrictions might take the form of restrained multiple-use opportunities. Finally, concentrated economic power always raises a question about political equality. Concentrated economic power arising from concentrated timber ownership may lead to disproportionate political power being exercised by owners or managers of large timber-owning firms.

THE PERFORMANCE RECORD IN ECONOMIC PROGRESS

The theoretical expectations for performance, based on knowledge of structure and conduct, have now been established. We may proceed to examine the record with a view to confirming or rejecting the stated expectations. The discussion of specific points in the performance standard identified above is limited by the available data.

Technological innovations: The record.—Professor Clark suggests that the elements of progress are most important among his dynamic criteria of performance. If an industry has a favorable record of technological innovation, one would expect to find evidence in the form of a steady and relatively favorable rate of improvement in output per man-hour of labor input. John Kendrick's

extensive studies of factor productivity trends in American industry provide a valuable first approximation of the technical pro-
gressiveness of the lumber industry. In his examination of eighty
manufacturing industries operating in the United States from 1899
through 1954, Kendrick found that the average annual rate of
change in output of final products per man-hour of factor input
was 2.2 percent. The lumber industry is near the bottom of the
array. It occupies seventy-fourth position among eighty industries,
and its average annual rate of change is 1.1 percent.[20] This record
suggests that relatively little has been done in the lumber industry
to increase the productivity of labor. The normal means of accomplishing this objective is through the addition and improvement of
capital equipment.

While the lumber industry does not compare favorably with
other segments of American industry in the record of productivity
improvement, a cautious interpretation of the record is necessary,
for the "measures are not precision tools of analysis, but are subject to unknown and probably not inconsequential margins of
error."[21] In addition to possible errors to which Kendrick refers,
the lumber industry must operate on an input factor subject to
constant deterioration in quality. Most of the logs processed in
sawmills today would have been treated as culls fifty years ago and
left in the woods. The same comment, however, may be made about
several other natural resource–based industries. Another handi-
cap under which the timber industry operates is that lumber
manufacturing, unlike some of the more spectacular performers in
productivity improvements, deals with a heterogeneous raw material. No two logs are the same. Even when the log is broken down
into cants, the location of knots and other defects must be taken
into consideration in the process of manufacture. Further, as the
raw material is not a liquid and is not made up of minuscule homogeneous parts, it has not been easily adaptable to modern handling
techniques. Nor is it subject to instrumental testing and feedback
control. With these handicaps, the automation revolution has partially bypassed the lumber industry, and it is not clear that the
fault lies with the industry. It may be the consequence of the basic
character of lumber production.

Whereas the fifty-five-year record of productivity trends places

---

[20] John W. Kendrick, *Productivity Trends in the United States* (Princeton: Princeton University Press, 1961), p. 162.
[21] *Ibid.*, p. 17.

the lumber industry among the least progressive, additional light may be shed on the productivity record by analysis of subperiods within the fifty-five-year trend. In the thirty-eight-year period ending with 1937, output per man-hour first declined and then improved, recording no substantial net change between the initial and final years. From 1937 through 1954, productivity improved modestly at first, and then increased very sharply. The greatest improvement occurred over the very short span from 1948 to 1954. The average annual rate of change for this six-year period was 5.5 percent.[22] Oddly enough, the most serious deterioration in log quality processed through sawmills occurred in the latter years, with the growth of the veneer and plywood industry. Apparently competition from plywood, as well as from other new building materials, stimulated new efforts in the lumber industry to improve productivity (reduce costs).

The Kendrick findings offer documentation of impressions gained through familiarity with the industry. In some isolated instances, it is possible to visit a sawmill that is hardly distinguishable, even in the 1960's, from its counterpart of several decades earlier. Such instances, however, are becoming rare, for the least progressive firms have been forced to withdraw from the industry at a rather rapid rate. The drop-out rate among very small and very large mills has been exceedingly high since the late 1940's. At the same time, among medium and medium-large mills, one senses a new interest in technological innovation.

Research and development activity.—Any new interest in technological innovation has not been manifested, however, in formal research and development investment. The lumber industry has been criticized for its lack of interest in research.[23] Its record of lagging technological progress is partially accounted for by its lack of organized effort in research. Recent studies by the National Science Foundation concerning fifteen major industries, plus eighteen smaller categories of industrial groups, are available. Based upon January, 1961, data for manufacturing as a whole, these studies show 7.8 scientists and engineers per 200 employed persons.

---

22 *Ibid.*, p. 484.

23 Joseph Zaremba, *Economics of the American Lumber Industry* (New York: Robert Speller, 1963), p. 193; F. H. Kaufert and William H. Cummings, *Forestry and Related Research in North America* (Washington: Society of American Foresters, 1955); address given by Robert J. Seidl, manager of research, Simpson Timber Co., before a joint session of the Northwest Wood Products Clinic and the Forest Products Research Society, reported in the *Spokesman-Review* (Spokane), April 26, 1962, p. 6.

The lumber and wood products industry (except furniture) is at the bottom of all fifteen industries and eighteen subcategories, with only one scientist and engineer per 200 employed persons.[24] If the lumber and wood products industry were to employ research personnel in the same proportion as do other manufacturing industries, it would have to increase its present employment of such personnel eightfold.

The research and development interest of the lumber industry relative to other industries may also be judged by examining the record of company-financed research and development expenditures as a percent of net sales. In 1959 the sum spent by the lumber, wood products, and furniture industrial category for research and development amounted to only 0.4 percent of net sales. The average of all fifteen manufacturing industries studied was 1.7 percent; only the textile and apparel industry, with 0.3 percent,[25] fell below the wood products industry. The expenditure figure is a somewhat more useful estimate of research and development interest than is the listing of scientists and engineers, as it is based on company-financed expenditures only. The employment of scientists and engineers includes expenditures financed by government agencies, and, therefore, unduly favors the munitions industries. If data were available on the lumber industry apart from plywood and furniture, however, the comparison would be even more adverse for lumber.

Low research and development expenditures and minor employment of scientists and engineers engaged in research in the lumber industry are related to the relatively low rate of improvement in productivity. The coefficient of correlation between research and development expenditures as a percent of sales and Kendrick's average annual rate of change in total factor productivity is $+.62$.[26]

The lack of interest in research which characterizes the lumber industry is dramatized by John Zivnuska, who points out that one firm in the petroleum industry, Standard Oil Company of California, has a research budget three and one-half times as large as that of the entire lumber industry.[27] Zivnuska's comparison of three

[24] *Scientific and Technical Personnel by Industry, 1961*, National Science Foundation, NSF 63–32 (Washington, 1963), p. 33.

[25] *Research and Development in Industry, 1961*, National Science Foundation, NSF 64–9 (Washington, 1964), p. 44.

[26] Kendrick, *op. cit.*, p. 183.

[27] John A. Zivnuska, "The Future for Wood in a Competitive Market," paper presented at joint meeting of the Puget Sound and Columbia River sections, Society of American Foresters, Longview, Wash., May 4, 1963 (mimeo.), p. 6.

segments of the wood products industry is also of interest: "It can be calculated that the pulp and paper industry is investing $17.10 in research for each thousand cubic feet of wood used; the plywood and related industries $5.75 per thousand cubic feet; and the lumber industry $1.50 per thousand cubic feet."[28]

The evidence of lagging research and development in the lumber industry may be quite misleading for three reasons. First, "not all segments of industry afford equal opportunities for exploiting the results of scientific research."[29] There is no way of estimating the potential of research expenditures in the lumber industry. It is quite possible that from the social point of view additional funds invested in research in the lumber industry would yield a submarginal rate of return and would, therefore, be a waste of the nation's resources. I offer no answer to this possibility, but simply point out that R and D expenditures are correlated with improvements in productivity in the aggregate, and that the lumber industry ranks low in both variables.

Second, most large firms operating in the lumber industry are vertically integrated in several timber-related areas. Research and development expenditures by such firms are centered in areas that appear to management to be the most productive, such as the chemical, pulp and paper, and plywood industries. Thus, although there is very little R and D effort in the lumber industry, some individual firms operating in lumber and related industries frequently have large research budgets.

Third, as Jacob Schmookler has indicated in his controversy with Henry Villard, the National Science Foundation Survey inventory included only hired research and development work carried on by company laboratories and technical groups: ". . . in smaller and medium-size firms, part of the job of scientists, engineers, and executives overseeing industrial operations and marketing often consists of improving products and processes. By contrast, greater division of labor in larger enterprises commonly assigns this task to separate departments. The National Science Foundation Survey was apparently confined to the activities of such departments."[30] It is probably true that in the lumber industry most of the research

---

28 *Ibid.*, p. 11.

29 C. Guy Suits, "Opportunity for Basic Research in Industry," in *Proceedings of a Conference on Research and Development*, National Science Foundation, NSF 58–36 (Washington, 1958), p. 91.

30 Jacob Schmookler, "Bigness, Fewness, and Research," *Journal of Political Economy*, LXVII (Dec., 1959), 630.

in process development is disguised research and is performed informally, but continuously, by the millwright and the owner himself. In all companies except the largest, efforts toward technological improvement are not assigned to a separate department. Surveys of the type carried out by the National Science Foundation would, therefore, understate the importance of research and development for improved technology in industries whose research and development activities are informal.

The performance record in lumber with reference to innovation and in the area of price competition appears to be the converse of that found in the rayon industry. In 1950 it was reported that, whereas the fourteen firms composing the rayon industry oligopoly "do not seem to be willing to engage in price competition when the market is 'normal,' they vigorously compete among themselves in other ways. The rate of technological innovation in the rayon industry has been almost unbelievably high."[31]

Technological innovation by firm size.—In addition to knowing the rate of technological progress for the lumber industry in the aggregate, it would be helpful to have some indication of the relative contribution to technological innovation by small, medium-size, and large firms. By means of a written questionnaire, an attempt was made to identify both the inventor and innovator of technological improvements and the developer of new products. This was a sobering experience. In an industry as "open" as the lumber industry, for most items of technological progress it is virtually impossible to assign originality and to separate invention and innovation from improvement in design. New ideas are communicated rapidly, particularly among the small and medium-size operations. Respondents listed many specific items of technological progress, but were rarely able to identify unequivocally the person or firm responsible for either the invention or its introduction. Furthermore, the more thoroughly one penetrates into the origins of a given invention, the less certain one becomes of the validity of his information. The questionnaire method of developing information about technological and product innovations was not successful. As a substitute, informed opinion was sought through personal interviews. A clear impression was gained that the small and medium-size operations have been the source of most of the technological inventions and innovations, while new products have originated almost exclusively with the large firms.

---

31 Markham, *op. cit.*, pp. 353–354.

A research engineer employed by one of the large firms prepared a four-page discussion of important technological advances, including information on the innovator when possible. Although indicating that large mills have been responsible for some technological innovations, the writer concluded that "the small operator and the manufacturer of equipment for small mills have done most of the actual research in lumber manufacture."[32] A similar view was expressed by the resident manager of one of the largest lumber-manufacturing firms, a man of long experience. He stated that the firm he represented was not experimental; rather, it followed others. He reported that "large companies don't do much in equipment development. Our people are pretty much copiers. We can't afford to take time to get off our treadmill." He continued to describe the "little guys" as "basically tinkerers, glorified millwrights who can put a machine together, try it, make it work and experiment." The owner-operator of a very successful medium-size sawmill held roughly the same point of view: ". . . small guys get ideas and prove them, then the machine companies take over and develop the machinery."

Persons representing firms that manufacture sawmill machines were also questioned about the relationship of innovations and mill size. One of them replied that "small firms are quicker to take new inventions; big firms make longer studies and are slower to react." Another representative of a machinery manufacturing firm spoke with greater force, but expressed approximately the same point of view: "The largest are the least receptive to new ideas. In small firms the boss is a good technician and recognizes value. Large firms require reports on feasibility and go through channels." And, regarding the source of new ideas: "Most new ideas come out of small and medium-size mills." The following statement, though probably considerably exaggerated, reflects a prevailing point of view: "I don't know of any new ideas coming from the larger lumber mills." This viewpoint was partially contradicted by another engineer employed by a machinery firm, who reported that some new ideas concerning constructive equipment improvement on existing machinery come from engineering staffs of large firms. Finally, another engineer concerned with machinery development spoke in the colorful language of the lumber industry: "Large firms are too bureaucratic. Why fight, bleed, and die trying to interest large firms in a new process. Life is too short." These points of view

---

32 Confidential correspondence.

should not be interpreted to mean that large firms do not employ modern techniques. In the words of the plant manager of one of the largest firms, quoted earlier: "In my plant, you can see more modern equipment under one roof than elsewhere, but it's all copied. We didn't invent it."

A notable recent exception to the generalization that suggests a minor role for large firms in technological development and innovation is provided by the Continuous Lumber Testing machine, which mechanically grades lumber for strength, replacing visual grading. The CLT-1 machine was developed as a prototype in research laboratories of the Potlatch Forests, Inc., of Lewiston, Idaho. From the prototype, a machinery firm, Industrial Sciences of Portland, Oregon, developed commercial models.[33] The first commercial model produced was introduced by the Frank Lumber Company of Mill City, Oregon, a medium-large firm. A less elaborate competing model, the Stress-O-Matic, developed by the research laboratory of the Western Pine Association, is now produced and distributed by the Tri-State Machinery Company of Dallas, Texas.[34]

The foregoing comments represent a sample of rather widespread opinion. There seems to be general agreement that a relatively large share of the new ideas for technological innovations come from small or medium-size mills, that machines are often developed by ingenious millwrights, and, when such machinery proves workable, it is further developed by a sawmill machine firm. The role of the large firm appears to be that of copier after others have tried and proven new technological processes. One notable exception is the Continuous Lumber Testing machine developed by one of the largest lumber-manufacturing firms.

Product innovations.—New products in the lumber industry have been minimal. As indicated in the preceding section, most large firms are vertically integrated. Product innovations for such firms may be extensive in industries other than lumber. Strictly within the lumber segment, Pres-To-Logs, end- and edge-glued boards, chips, and glue-laminated beams exhaust the list of significant new products recently developed in the lumber industry.

One may be inclined to list the development of veneer and plywood as the dominant product innovation arising out of the lum-

---

[33] Correspondence with Herbert V. McKean, director of research, Potlatch Forests, Inc.

[34] L. W. Wood, "Machine-graded Lumber," *Forest Products Journal*, XIV (Jan., 1964), 41.

ber industry. The use of veneers, however, can be traced back to Greek civilization, and the first patent covering plywood was issued on December 26, 1865, to John K. Mayo of New York City. The patent description provided the following information: "The invention consists in cementing or otherwise fastening together a number of sheets, with the grain of the successive pieces, or some of them running crosswise or diversely from that of the others. . . . The crossing or diversification of the direction of the grain is of great importance to impart strength and tenacity to the material, protect it against splitting, and at the same time preserve it from liability to expansion or contraction."[35] The cutting of veneer on the Pacific Coast originated about 1890, when a veneer lathe was set up in Tacoma, Washington. Its output, however, was used principally for baskets and fruit packages.[36] The first use of Douglas fir timber in structural plywood can be traced to 1905, when a few Douglas fir plywood panels were exhibited at the Lewis and Clark Centennial Exhibition in Portland, Oregon.[37]

In connection with Pres-To-Logs, development of the machine cannot be separated from development of the product. The Pres-To-Log machine was developed in 1930 by Potlatch Forests, which was and still is one of the largest firms in the lumber industry.

End- and edge-glued boards also have a rather long history. In 1932 the Jones Lumber Company of Portland, Oregon, attempted edge-gluing with a paint brush. At the same time, the threads of this development spread in so many different directions, both forward and backward chronologically, that it is not possible to say unequivocally who the innovator was or when the innovation occurred. There appears, however, to be considerable agreement among knowledgeable persons in the industry that the Weyerhaeuser Company pioneered in improving the process and in developing production of both edge- and end-gluing. This company, it is reported, now accounts for a larger share of end- and edge-glued lumber production than all other sources combined.

Other products important to the lumber industry, such as chips, glue-laminated beams, and tresses, may represent significant innovations. The search for their point of origin, however, appears to be futile. Indeed, structural tresses have been in use for as long as houses have been built of lumber. At some point between then and

---

[35] Thomas D. Perry, *Modern Plywood* (2d ed., New York: Pitman Publishing Corp., 1948), p. 34.

[36] *Ibid.*, p. 40.

[37] *Ibid.*, p. 41.

now, prefabricated tresses and the more sophisticated glue-laminated beams became important products of the lumber industry.

The analysis of research and development expenditures by the lumber industry applies to product innovation as well as to process innovation. Although the comparative record in research and development effort is quite unfavorable to the lumber industry, it would probably be even worse if the R and D efforts of the plywood industry could be separated from the larger industrial category called the "lumber and wood products industry."

The findings from efforts to identify the source of product innovations by firm size are in contrast with those for technological innovations. Whereas small firms perform rather well in technological innovation, large firms, it is widely agreed, account for a disproportionate share of product innovations. One careful observer of product innovations in the wood products industry reported that people at the Madison (Wisconsin) Forest Products Laboratory and at the Pacific Northwest Forest and Range Experiment Station find very little interest in new product opportunities among smaller firms.

In addition to the testimony concerned with new products originating in tax-supported research laboratories, further evidence of large-firm interest in product development is that most of the large lumber-producing firms, which are also important in the plywood industry and as timber resource owners, maintain private research laboratories. The plant manager previously quoted as crediting small firms with most of the technological innovations asserted that in product development "we are the leaders. There is a reverse flow from big to little."

There has already been some speculation about the cause of the observed paucity of new product development in the lumber industry. Joseph Zaremba asserts that the competitive structure of the lumber industry has retarded its flow of technological discoveries. His argument is that any new discoveries are quickly disseminated throughout the industry and that the innovator, with an infinitely small share of the market, is left with only the temporary reward of a head start.[38] Another student of forest economics, John Zivnuska, writes that the lumber industry "might warm the heart of Adam Smith, but it would break the heart of any industrial research director." He holds that the lack of research in the lumber industry "is the direct economic result of [its] fragmented structure. . . .

---

[38] Zaremba, *op. cit.*, p. 196.

The structure of the industry is such that it cannot be an effective competitor in technological competition."[39] The views of Zaremba and Zivnuska are diametrically opposed to the classical position as expressed by Knight.

The rapid dissemination of innovations in the lumber industry suggests that the prime beneficiary is not the manufacturer, but the owner of timber resources, which are in derived demand. Stumpage value is a function of final product values, minus production costs. Whenever valuable new products such as veneer and plywood are introduced (based upon timber resources), the value of stumpage increases. Similarly, technological innovations that reduce manufacturing costs (the chain saw, for example) further enhance the value of stumpage.[40] Because the production cycle for timber is exceedingly long, quasi rents accrue to the timberland owner and may be expected to persist for decades, in contrast with the ephemeral innovator's profit accruing to the mill operator. The more valuable incentive to innovate is thus lodged with the resource owner.

Timber resource management performance.—We have been examining the performance record under the heading of "economic progress." Although this heading normally refers only to technological and product innovations, it appears appropriate to discuss economic progress in timber resource management here.

Studies conducted by the Forest Service constitute the prime source of data for appraising timber resource management. The Forest Service has extensively examined recently cutover timberland and classified performance into productivity classes by ownership groups. Findings for the Douglas fir region are shown in table 28. A nationwide study reveals the same general pattern, leading the Forest Service to the following conclusion: "Productivity of recently cut areas on private lands is directly related to the size class of ownership—the smaller the ownership, the lower the proportion of recently cut land in the upper productivity class."[41] The

---

[39] Zivnuska, *op cit.*, p. 5.

[40] Another kind of technological innovation has the opposite effect, however. A technological improvement that increases the physical output of lumber per unit of physical log input reduces the value of stumpage. This follows from the conclusion that the demand for lumber is inelastic. Thus, a technological innovation that substantially reduces saw kerf will bring about greater lumber output per unit of log input. The decline in lumber price will be greater than the corresponding increase in quantity of lumber sold. Therefore, the residual value accruing to the timber resource owner will decline.

[41] *Timber Resources for America's Future*, U.S. Department of Agriculture, Forest Service, Forest Resources Report no. 14 (Washington, 1958), pp. 237–238.

TABLE 28

PRODUCTIVITY OF RECENTLY CUT COMMERCIAL FOREST LAND IN THE DOUGLAS FIR
REGION, 1953

(IN PERCENTAGES)

Ownership	Productivity class		
	Upper	Medium	Lower
Private			
Small (10-5,000 acres)	59	28	13
Medium and large (more than 5,000 acres)	86	10	4
Public	85	12	3

SOURCE: U.S. Department of Agriculture, Forest Service, *Timber Resources for
America's Future*, Forest Resources Report no. 14 (Washington, 1958), p. 618.

Forest Service studies thus indicate that low-quality performance
is not an industry-wide problem, but rather is centered in small
private ownerships.

The Forest Service analysis of performance is based primarily on
a physical rather than an economic performance standard. The
study was developed by a forest mensurationist assisted by foresters
and forest economists. Foresters are often dedicated by training to
certain silvicultural standards of performance. The physical standards were not supported by economic feasibility studies. It is quite
possible, therefore, that the rate of return on an investment necessary to place a firm in the upper productivity class would be a submarginal rate of return and, hence, an unwise allocation of the
nation's resources. This conclusion requires the assumption that
social costs and revenues correspond to private costs and revenues.

One of the important factors in the experience of David Lilienthal leading him to membership in the "New Competition" school
was his observation of performance by large and small firms in the
area of timber management. Lilienthal observes that

The very best demonstrations of conservation practices and management under private ownership in this country are those on huge forest areas owned
and run by large, and in some cases very big, business. Bigness and prudent,
long-view management of our forest resources have, in recent years, been demonstrated to be consistent and profitable. The latter-day operations of the
Weyerhaeuser interests, in the Northwest, as one example, show the advantages
which size can give in utilizing the skills of professional foresters, chemists and
management engineers in making the very best use of our forests and their
products in ways not known forty years ago.[42]

---

[42] David Lilienthal, *Big Business: A New Era* (New York: Harper, 1952), pp. 125–26.

But Lilienthal's standard of good performance is, of course, not supported by economic data and, like the Forest Service judgment, may counsel economic waste.

On an a priori basis, one might expect the performance of large firms to be more satisfactory than that of small firms because an extremely long-time horizon is required for decision making. As the time needed to grow a timber crop to financial maturity in the Douglas fir region varies from about fifty to eighty years, an extremely long-run point of view is required of the timber resource manager. A middle-aged owner of recently cutover timberland cannot be expected to be vitally interested in the financial return from a crop that probably will not mature until long after his own life, and possibly the lives of his children, have ended. On the other hand, some large timber companies expect to be in the forest products business continuously, and the ability of such firms to perpetually support their investments in pulp and paper mills and other facilities requires sustained yield management. On an a priori basis, one would therefore expect relatively long-range management from the large integrated forest products companies, but not necessarily from the small ownerships.

After examining the evidence on timber resource management performance, the President's Materials Policy Commission attributed the poor performance of small firms to the long-run nature of timber resource investments: "The time element appears to be the chief reason for the wide differences. Commercial forest land in public ownership and that owned by large and medium-size owners is relatively well managed because the owners think in long-range terms. Small holders of forest land often have very different attitudes. . . . The idea of timber as a continuing crop has spread slowly; it involves plans that stretch over one or two generations."[43]

If a workably free market existed in timberland, or if long-term credit were readily available, secured by investments in second-growth timber and supported, in turn, by readily available fire and other insurance, then we might expect a more satisfactory level of timber resource management from small ownerships. With these services available, it would be reasonable for an individual to plant a timber crop, knowing that he could freely liquidate his investment by sale of the immature timber crop within a few years or

43 *Resources for Freedom*, President's Materials Policy Commission (Washington, 1952), I, 40.

meet a pressing financial need by borrowing on his crop. Such facilities are generally not available, however.

The continuing tendency to treat the timber crop as a legitimate area of business investment may be attributed to the gradual disappearance of old-growth timber reserves, to the rather rapidly increasing value of timber resources, and to the spread of knowledge about timber resource management. In his extensive studies of capital budgeting in timber resource management, John Fedkiw concludes: "Timber growing is not yet generally regarded as an income and profit producing enterprise in the same sense as manufacturing or sales. Among the larger integrated wood processing firms, however, there is a distinct trend toward setting it up as a profit center with a separate accounting record."[44]

General agreement is observable in interviews in the Douglas fir region and in published statements[45] that the problem of performance in resource management is one that differentiates performance by firm size in the private sector. Larger private holdings and public holdings seem to show the best performance.

Additional welfare benefits may result from more concentrated timberland ownership. When the timber resources of a given producer are sufficiently large to allow lower-elevation logging during periods of severe weather, a more stable pattern of seasonal employment in logging and lumber operations will likely result. Further, if the economic resources of larger companies allow the construction of all-weather roads to winter logging operations, more stable seasonal employment patterns will again result. Seasonal employment patterns indicate that the largest firm in the lumber industry does, indeed, have a considerably more stable pattern of employment than is found in the lumber industry as a whole. The seasonal employment index for the lumber division of Weyerhaeuser Company shows the lowest employment month to be only 5 percent below the average for the year. In contrast, the employ-

---

44 John Fedkiw, "Capital Budgeting for Acquisition and Development of Timberlands," in *Financial Management of Large Forest Ownerships*, papers presented at the 13th Industrial Forestry Seminar, Yale University, Bulletin no. 66 (New Haven: Yale University, 1960), p. 6.

45 In addition to those quoted above, see Karl William Kapp, *The Social Costs of Private Enterprise* (Cambridge: Harvard University Press, 1950); C. F. Korstian, "Forest Research," in *Renewable Resources*, report to the Committee on Natural Resources, National Academy of Sciences, National Research Council, publication 1000-A (Washington, 1965), p. 33; and O. Harry Schrader, address before the Olympic Logging Conference, quoted in *The Timberman*, LXIII (June, 1952), 61.

ment index for lumber and other wood products in Oregon shows
a normal decline of 25 percent at its lowest month. The same series
for the state of Washington shows a normal decline of 23 percent.[46]
The evidence cited above, although inconclusive, suggests that superior performance both in timber management and in annual employment of labor is positively correlated with size of firm.

DIFFUSION OF BENEFITS FROM ECONOMIC PROGRESS

J. M. Clark suggests that economic progress ought to be accompanied by a diffusion of benefits to customers in terms of lower
prices, and to those who contribute factors of production, chiefly
workers, in higher real rewards. In this section the performance record is examined with respect to (1) the price-output-profit complex,
(2) product quality, (3) the behavior of labor's share of lumber industry income, and (4) economic rents accruing to the owner of
timber resources.

Price-output-profit relationship.—It is easy and agreeable to set
up lower prices to consumers as one goal of a workably competitive
industry. An examination of the record, to determine whether or
not a given industry has performed in the desired manner, again
reveals that no satisfactory norm is available. One might modify
Clark's wording and require the "lowest possible" prices for consumers. Thus, a rising trend in consumer prices for an industry
might still reflect the lowest possible prices. This modification
would thereby take into account a conceptual difficulty, but it
would in no way ease the measurement burden, for we do not know
how low prices might have been.

The behavior of lumber prices shows a relatively inflationary
record. From 1926 through 1963 lumber prices increased 3.6 fold,
but the price increase was entirely accounted for in the much
shorter period 1939–1953. During this period of war inflation and
very rapid expansion in residential construction, lumber prices
increased 3.9 fold. Given the construction-stimulated demand for
lumber, together with an inelastic supply function for lumber, the
observed price increase is to be expected. The absence of "lower
prices to consumers" should not be interpreted as a failure of the
industry to perform in a workably competitive manner; rather, it
is simply the result of supply and demand conditions.

Figure 22 clarifies the performance record for lumber prices.

---

[46] For a discussion of the seasonal character of employment in the Douglas fir
lumber industry, see Walter J. Mead, "The Forest Products Economy of the Pacific
Northwest," *Land Economics*, XXXII (May, 1956), 127–133.

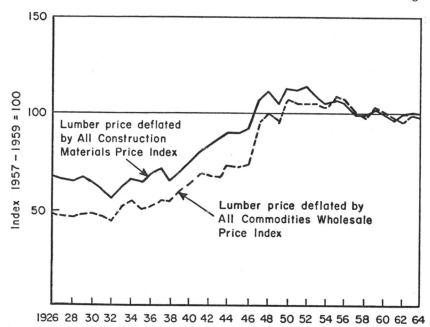

Fig. 22. Lumber price index deflated by All Commodities Wholesale Price Index and All Construction Materials Price Index.

SOURCES: For lumber prices (BLS Code 08-1) and All Construction Materials Price Index: 1926–1960: Housing and Home Finance Agency, *Housing Statistics*, Historical Supplement (Oct., 1961); 1961–1964: Housing and Home Finance Agency, *Housing Statistics*, Annual Data (May, 1965). For All Commodities Wholesale Price Index: Bureau of the Census, *Statistical Abstract of the United States* (Washington, 1965).

Lumber prices are deflated by the All Commodities Wholesale Price Index and by the All Construction Materials Price Index. Over a long span of time, terminating with 1963, lumber prices increased relative to the general price index of wholesale commodities. The price inflation in lumber was more modest, however, when related to all construction materials. Two factors may be suggested to account for this behavior pattern. First, the supply of timber and lumber is inelastic. The supply of some alternative building materials may, however, also be relatively price inelastic, especially under long-run conditions. A second factor of considerable importance is that some competing building materials, including plywood and aluminum, are subject to rapid technological advances. Lacking a clear norm, an examination of relative price movements does not permit a clear appraisal with reference to price performance. Given supply inelasticity and a shift to the right in the construction demand for lumber, a sharp relative price increase should be expected.

The profitability record for lumber manufacturing corresponds closely with expectations derived from economic theory and from knowledge of the highly competitive structure of the lumber industry at the output level. The limited data available are for the period beginning with 1951 and cover the entire lumber industry, rather than the regional industry of primary concern here. The after-tax rates of return on stockholder equity and on sales for lumber manufacturing and all manufacturing are shown in table 29. The record shows no evidence of persistent supracompetitive profits in lumber manufacturing; rather, the opposite condition is suggested. In only one year (1951) of the thirteen years shown were lumber-manufacturing profits higher than those in all manufacturing. This is true whether profits are measured as a rate of return on sales or on stockholder equity. The comparative profit record of performance corresponds closely with theoretical expectations. Clearly, profits are not excessive.

In an oligopolistic industry such as steel, output may be restricted in order to maintain high prices. Oligopolistic behavior may be evident when one examines excess capacity conditions. For ex-

TABLE 29

AFTER-TAX RATES OF RETURN FOR LUMBER MANUFACTURING AND ALL MANUFACTURING, UNITED STATES, 1951–1963

(IN PERCENTAGES)

Year	On sales		On stockholder equity	
	All manufacturing	Lumber and wood products	All manufacturing	Lumber and wood products
1963	4.7	3.1	10.2	8.0
1962	4.5	2.3	9.8	5.6
1961	4.2	1.8	8.8	4.0
1960	4.4	1.6	9.2	3.6
1959	4.8	4.1	10.4	9.3
1958	4.1	2.6	8.6	5.7
1957	4.8	2.3	11.0	4.7
1956	5.2	3.8	12.3	8.7
1955	5.4	5.4	12.6	11.1
1954	4.5	3.3	9.9	6.3
1953	4.2	3.5	10.5	7.1
1952	4.3	4.1	10.3	8.5
1951	5.4	7.3	12.5	13.4

SOURCE: Federal Trade Commission and Securities and Exchange Commission, "Quarterly Financial Report for Manufacturing Corporations," 1951–1963.

ample, it is not uncommon to find 60, or even 50, percent of capacity production in the steel industry concurrent with price increases. Although there is some excess capacity in the lumber industry,[47] lumber producers have no control over price through collective production control. The excess capacity is largely bankrupt capacity rather than restrained output.

Owing to the lack of a suitable norm, the foregoing examination of the price-output-profit relationship has not established conclusively that lumber price performance is either satisfactory or unsatisfactory. There is no evidence to indicate that output has been restricted in order to obtain higher lumber prices. And the profit record has shown no evidence of price exploitation. Instead, it corresponds closely with theoretical expectations derived from knowledge of structure.

Product quality.—J. M. Clark argues that workable competition, as a phase of the diffusion process, ought to create a market in which "a customer may have considerable confidence that the offerings of different sellers are of approximately equal value and that he will not be seriously victimized if he fails to shop around."[48] Apparently a consumer of lumber products cannot enjoy the confidence that Clark's performance standard requires. Most of the lumber produced in the Douglas fir region is grade-stamped before it is loaded for shipment to markets. Recently, however, the use of counterfeit grade stamps has been uncovered. Furthermore, the highly respected weekly report on lumber and plywood, *Random Lengths,* has charged that the recent discoveries of the counterfeit stamps are simply focusing public attention on what has been "an open secret in the lumber industry for years: Through one means or another, much of unmarked low-grade which leaves the mills, acquires the Standard or a Construction grade mark before being nailed up. Or, it is mixed with and substituted for these grades without being marked."[49] According to this report, provisions for enforcement of lumber standards and grading rules are the "responsibility of lumber manufacturers. But, . . . [the provisions] are so inadequate that they can hardly be said to exist."[50] Grave doubts

---

[47] During most of the 1950's the lumber industry carried an average unused capacity of about 15 percent (John Fedkiw, *Forest Industry Capacity, Production and Available Log Supplies in the Douglas-fir Subregion,* U.S. Forest Service Research Paper PNW-11 [Portland, Ore., 1964], p. 5).

[48] Clark, "Competition: Static Models and Dynamic Aspects," p. 455.

[49] *Random Lengths,* Aug. 7, 1964, p. 1.

[50] *Ibid.,* p. 10.

are thus raised as to the degree to which customers may have confidence in the quality of lumber products. One of the merits often claimed for an oligopolistic structure, with name brands that have a trademark value, is that consumers would be protected from quality uncertainty.

Labor's share in the benefits from economic progress.—There is no more suitable standard by which to judge the equity of labor's absolute share in lumber industry income than the level and trend of wage rates in the Douglas fir lumber industry relative to other manufacturing industries. Figure 23 shows that wages in the Douglas fir lumber industry are above the level for all manufacturing. Furthermore, from 1940 through 1962 there was a slight decline in the lumber industry wage rate relative to all manufacturing. Yet,

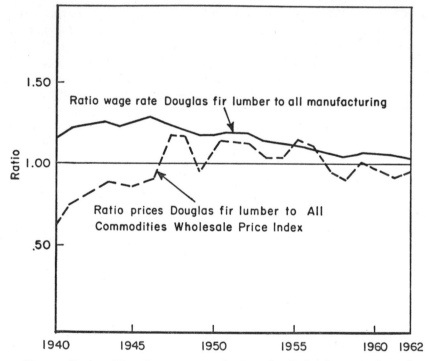

Fig. 23. Ratio of hourly wage rates in Douglas fir lumber-manufacturing industry to all manufacturing, and ratio of Douglas fir lumber prices to All Commodities Wholesale Price Index.

SOURCES: For prices and wage rates in Douglas fir lumber industry: West Coast Lumbermans Association. For wholesale price index (finished goods) and wage rates in all manufacturing: U.S. Department of Commerce, *Business Statistics,* 1963 edition.

the average hourly wage rate in the Douglas fir region increased from 78 cents in 1940 to $2.56 in 1962. Deflating wages by the Consumer Price Index to obtain an index of the trend in real wages, we find that buying power of an hour of labor in the lumber industry increased 52 percent in twelve years, or a compound annual increase in real wages of 3.5 percent. Thus, real wages have improved at a rate approximately equal to the rate in all manufacturing. Whether a different structure would have produced a higher or lower rate of increase is not known.

An examination of the record also permits an appraisal of the relationship between wage rates and profitability in lumber manufacturing. Lumber prices increased rapidly in the immediate postwar period under the impact of a strong demand for housing; the increase was halted in 1951. From that point to the present, lumber prices have fluctuated with cyclical behavior in the construction industry. In figure 23 the relative behavior of Douglas fir lumber prices is compared with the relative behavior of wage rates in the same industry. When lumber prices increase relative to other prices, the wage rate in the lumber industry also tends to increase relative to wage rates elsewhere. Correspondingly, when the relative inflation in lumber prices came to an end in the late 1940's, wage rates in the lumber industry started to decline relative to wage rates in all manufacturing industries. The behavior of relative prices and wages indicates that lumber wage rates evidence a fair degree of flexibility and responsiveness to conditions in the lumber market. When lumber prices increase, presumably lumber profits are attractive. Under these conditions, management is less able to resist wage demands (labor is more successful in obtaining wage concessions). The data suggest that benefits owing to economic progress and higher lumber prices are diffused to workers.

Economic rents accruing to the owners of timber resources.—As noted earlier, most of the benefits from economic progress in the lumber industry accrue to the owners of timber resources. Although timber is a reproducible resource, the production period is so long that quasi rents accrue to the owners of timber resources. Data are not available to show the net profit received by timberland owners, but a useful index is provided by stumpage prices for Douglas fir timber (see figure 8). While lumber prices were increasing nearly fourfold from 1940 to 1964, stumpage prices increased more than sixteen fold. As most of the timber harvested during this period was old-growth timber, there were no production costs in the usual sense. There were, however, carrying charges, in which imputed

interest is dominant. The second most important item in the cost
of carrying timber is property taxes. Economic theory, supported
by the behavior of stumpage prices, rather clearly indicates that the
principal beneficiaries of price inflation owing to a high-level demand for construction, of new product development in the timber-
using industry, and of some technological improvements are the
owners of timber resources. Within the Douglas fir region, ownership of timber resources is approximately equally divided between
public and private ownership.

Summarizing the conclusions about the diffusion of benefits
from economic progress, we find first that very little can be said
with certitude. Standards with which performance may be compared are lacking. Price inflation in lumber products has been
rather intense, but perhaps understandable, in terms of the inelastic supply of timber. The relatively low profit rates for the
lumber industry indicate only competitive returns. Consumers are
not able to place their confidence in the lumber they purchase by
grade rather than by inspection and comparison. In addition, real
wages in the Douglas fir lumber industry have increased approximately in proportion to the increase in all manufacturing industries. Further, wage rates are flexible and respond to favorable, as
well as to unfavorable, conditions of the market for timber. Finally,
most of the benefits resulting from economic progress in the lumber industry accrue to the owners of timber resources.

Freedom and Opportunity

J. M. Clark holds that a workably competitive industry must provide benefits that are dependent neither on paternalistic motives
of private producers nor on direct governmental order, but rather
on a situation that rewards firms for producing the best possible
product and service for the lowest possible price. In an industry
composed of a multitude of independent firms, both buyers and
sellers enjoy what Clark calls a "margin of discretion" in choosing
a course of action.[51]

Defined in this manner, one can scarcely question the existence
of freedom and opportunity at the lumber output level. The issue
arises only at the timber resource level. Where timber in private
ownership is moderately concentrated, the issue of freedom and
opportunity may be raised at two points. First, one might ask if
political equality is in any way impaired by the economic inequal-

---

51 Clark, "Competition: Static Models and Dynamic Aspects," p. 456.

ity arising out of concentrated ownership of timber resources. This condition might have an important bearing on public policy in the area of property taxation. It is conceivable that a large corporation might be the object of adverse legislation or administration because it has few votes. On the other hand, a large corporation possessing concentrated economic power might translate that power into effective political pressure. An instance of either sort may have occurred in the state of Washington with reference to the assessment of timberland for ad valorem property taxes. The Weyerhaeuser Company held approximately 73 million board feet of old-growth timber covering some 2,000 acres in Clark County, Washington. The county assessor established a new and higher assessed valuation on this timber. After appropriate discussion and failure to gain relief, the company announced that owing to the county's timber valuation policy, it would be forced to revise its plan for delayed liquidation and would begin immediately to clear-cut the timber, completing harvest within a two-year period. The company announced that "the change in plans is a direct result of increased property taxes which make it economically impossible for Weyerhaeuser to practice sustained yield forest management in Clark County." Weyerhaeuser held that the "unusual tax situation dictates that the timber be removed."[52]

I will not undertake to judge whether this is an illustration of a public official discriminating against a corporation that has more money than votes or of a major economic power seeking a preferred position. Unquestionably the issue is extremely complicated. What is obviously true is that when concentrated economic power makes a major move, important repercussions may be felt throughout the community. In this instance, repercussions are felt in school finance, employment and payrolls in the community, the level of retail business, and even the job security of an elected county official. Although a large corporation may have few votes itself, it obviously has the power to influence attitudes of others through economic interests. Economic inequality may thus be directly related to the issue of political democracy.

A second issue in freedom and opportunity arising out of concentrated timberland ownership concerns multiple use of timberland. If timberland is widely held in many small ownerships, the many owners obviously have the right of personal enjoyment of their property for such multiple-use objectives as logging, hunting,

---

[52] *Portland Oregonian*, July 2, 1961.

fishing, and camping. In contrast, if timberland is concentrated in a few large ownerships, multiple-use enjoyment may be restricted to fewer people. It appears, however, that multiple-use benefits have been made available to the general public and, further, that these benefits are not, in Clark's words, "dependent on the goodwill and arbitrary decision of private producers." The largest companies, Weyerhaeuser and Crown Zellerbach, for example, have taken the lead in making campsites and hunting rights available to the general public. The Georgia-Pacific Corporation reports that during 1962 approximately 92,000 people participated in picnicking, camping, hiking, hunting, and fishing on company lands made available for public recreation.[53] The company was apparently motivated by the desire to create a favorable public image, which could influence such public policies as property taxation and also deter an irate public where an irresponsible element may resort to incendiary activity in the forests. For whatever reason, multiple-use opportunities still exist, even though privately owned timberland is modestly concentrated.

AN ALTERNATIVE INDUSTRIAL STRUCTURE

If performance is weak, what are the alternatives? By an addendum to the concept of workable competition, Jesse Markham emphasized the availability of promising alternatives. Given the observed pattern of behavior and the performance record of the lumber industry, an alternative structure that may better serve the public interest seems to be available.

Some of the weak aspects of performance identified above may be remedied by a change in structure, whereas other aspects appear impervious and inherent in the nature of the industry. Among the former are (1) lagging economic progress in both technological change and product development, and (2) the market power of large firms in the federal timber market, together with the equity issue resulting from wide price disparities between competitive and noncompetitive sales.

The principal and lasting beneficiaries of economic progress (technological and product development) are the owners of timber resources. Large timberland owners maintain research laboratories concerned with improving timber-growing conditions as well as with technological and product development. Small timberland owners generally do not. And, indeed, the latter would be unlikely

---

[53] *Annual Report* (1962), Georgia-Pacific Corp., p. 13.

to have an economic motive that would justify a private investment of this kind, as the quasi rents accruing to a timberland owner from any given innovation vary in proportion to the size of the holdings. A continuation, and even acceleration, of the present trend wherein commercial forest land is shifted from small to larger holdings would appear to provide additional economic incentive for private research and development investment.

The quality of timber management varies directly with the size of the holding. As small timberland holdings are "blocked up" into large holdings managed by "perpetual" corporations, performance in timber resource management should improve. Therefore a structural change, which appears to be under way, may hasten economic progress and improve the quality of timber resource management.

The present method by which the Forest Service sells timber from national forests creates a wide disparity in price, depending on the presence or absence of competition. As one aspect of this disparity between competitive and noncompetitive sales, large firms have a significant degree of market power. Two alternative proposals are offered to correct this problem.

1) As a minimum, the appraisal procedure should be reexamined and corrected so that it yields an appraised price approximating the market value of timber. It should be clear from the analysis of timber sales (see chap. 11) that the average appraised price falls far short of market value when the latter is determined by competitive bidding. Some of the price discrepancy between competitive and noncompetitive sales, and some of the market power advantage enjoyed by large firms, might be eliminated by more careful appraisal. This step is a procedural change, not a structural one.

2) As a structural change, the method of selling federal timber could be altered.[54] Instead of being sold as heterogeneous stumpage, timber could be sold as more homogeneous logs, sorted by species and grade, in a revitalized wholesale log market. Under this proposal, contractors would log the timber and transport it to concentration yards near an exit to a national forest. At the concentration yard, logs would be debarked and sorted into stacks by species and grades, and specialized (relatively homogeneous) logs would be offered for sale at posted prices. Prices would be determined, not by the present complicated appraisal and bidding procedure, but

---

[54] For a more detailed elaboration of this proposal see W. J. Mead, "A Positive Proposal To Strengthen the Lumber Industry," *Land Economics*, XL (May 1964), 141–152. For criticism and reply see Robert C. Haring and W. J. Mead in *Land Economics*, XLI (Aug., 1965), 290–295.

rather by supply and demand. If a given price for a specific species and grade of log failed to clear the market, the price would be lowered. On the other hand, if demand exceeded supply at a given price, declining log inventories would signal a price increase. Prices would be determined by the necessity to clear the market. Ultimately, what has been called "the law of one price" should prevail; that is, the price of number two Douglas fir sawlogs should be the same in wholesale log markets subject to similar economic conditions. The present elaborate, expensive, and not wholly satisfactory system, whereby timber is appraised "backward" from lumber and plywood, could be eliminated in areas where timber volume is sufficiently large to warrant a wholesale log market. In other nearby areas, the complexity of the appraisal process could be lessened; appraisal could be based on a free market in logs rather than on subsequent final product prices.

A privately owned and supplied log-sorting yard similar to the proposed wholesale log market is now in operation by the Morrison Logging Company on the Olympic Peninsula in Washington. A relatively small quantity of logs (5 million board feet per month) is processed through the sorting yard. To illustrate the different sorts for which markets have developed, hemlock logs are "sorted five ways: local peelers, export peelers, export sawlogs, residuals and pulp logs . . . . Cedar is sorted five ways. No. 1 logs are hauled to Olympia where they are rafted north on Puget Sound to Seattle. Other grades are sold to shingle and shake mills in the Grays Harbor—Olympic Peninsula area." Further, "Logs are often upgraded in the yard by bucking . . . . Peeler logs can be claimed from sawlogs in this manner and each hauled to a different destination."[55] The yard was established in the fall of 1964. It apparently is not only profitable for the enterpriser, but is also advantageous for the region in that timber resource utilization has been improved.

The method of logging under this proposal would not be materially changed. Independent contract loggers currently harvest much of the national forest timber on a contract basis. Contract loggers would continue to serve in this capacity, but a federal agency, rather than a private buyer, would let the contract.

This structural change would entirely eliminate the market power problem along with other problems of price equity between buyers. So long as one price prevailed by species and grade, all

---

[55] *Forest Industries*, XCII (Aug., 1965), 55.

buyers would pay the same price. To the extent that one price prevailed over several geographical markets, the observed inequity between geographical markets owing to differences in degree of competition would also be eliminated. With the timber-buying price advantage of large firms eliminated, independent (single-plant) lumber companies of the present medium and medium-large size would gain a larger share of the log supply. As shown earlier, the optimum size sawmill is a single-plant firm producing from 60,000 to 140,000 board feet per eight-hour shift.

Although this proposal is based on problems arising from an analysis of national forest timber sales in the Douglas fir region, timber from other public agencies (principally the Bureau of Land Management) could easily be incorporated into the proposed wholesale log market. In any event, other sellers of timber would benefit from a revitalized wholesale log market, as appraisal could be based on log prices rather than on lumber and plywood prices.

A very important by-product of this proposed structural change would be amelioration in another area of performance. A problem that has retarded economic progress in lumber production is that mills have historically processed several timber species and a wide variety of log grades. But equipment able to process the largest possible log sizes and lengths would be ineffective and under-utilized when processing small logs. Engineers engaged in sawmill design suggest that mills designed to process logs of more uniform length, diameter, and species would be capable of producing lumber at substantial reduction in costs. In recent years, some progress has been made toward specialization in sawmill input. A reliable wholesale log market would allow further progress toward specialization and efficiency. Competition would force logs into uses that yield the highest possible economic value.

Because all logs obtained through a wholesale log market, as described above, would be bark-free, the supply of bark-free chips suitable for pulp-mill input would be greatly increased. In addition to obtaining economic value from chip sales, benefits would follow from sawing bark-free logs: (1) saw maintenance costs would be reduced as rocks and grit embedded in bark were removed; (2) the probability of spotting spikes would be greater after removal of bark; (3) milling efficiency would be improved because bark-free logs can be handled with more speed; (4) mill clean-up costs would be reduced because bark would not accumulate on the mill floor; and (5) more profitable cuts could be made from a log because the sawyer could "see under the bark." Resource utilization would

be further improved by stimulating such advanced timber management practices as thinning and prelogging. These forest management practices would be encouraged because concentrated
supplies of logs produced from activities of this sort would hasten
the development of reliable markets for such logs. Thus, an active
wholesale log market would allow further efficiency in lumber
production. I have pointed out in this discussion of performance
that technological progress in lumber production has been relatively slow and that lumber prices have increased relative to prices
of competing products. Greater efficiency permitted by the proposed structural change offers a prospect of improved performance.

Thus, we return to the Markham addendum to the concept of
workable competition. The performance record of the lumber
industry, at both input and output levels, leaves much to be
desired. It appears that two structural changes would improve
some aspects of performance. The lumber industry is oligopsonistic
at the input level and highly competitive at the output level, but
it falls short of its potential. It follows that the present structure
must be classified as not "workably competitive" in the sense that
it fails to obtain, to a reasonable degree, the objectives that competition is expected to obtain, and that an alternative structural
arrangement offers promise of more satisfactory performance.

SUMMARY

In this chapter, I have attempted to accomplish the almost impossible task of appraising performance. The analysis suffers from a
lack of precise and quantifiable standards of performance. In their
study of competition in the petroleum industry, de Chazeau and
Kahn, struggling with this same problem, wrote that "performance
tests lack conclusiveness because the potential is unknown. The
record may be good but not half as good as it should have been;
it may be bad, but twice as good as would be likely under any
probable alternative."[56]

On the basis of known structural conditions, we would expect
excellent performance results at the lumber output level to follow
from a highly competitive structure, and questionable performance
results at the timber resource input level to follow from modestly
concentrated timber-resource ownership and an oligopsonistic
structure in the timber market. In many respects, however, precisely the opposite results have been found in both areas. At the

---

[56] *Op. cit.*, p. 55.

lumber output level, progress in technological and product innovations has been poor by comparison with other industries. Research and development interest has been lagging and insignificant. As classical theory would lead one to expect, however, most of the technological changes have originated with small and medium-sized firms. In contrast, the very few product innovations in the lumber industry have generally originated with the largest firms. In both product and technological innovation, large firms appear to be actively engaged in other areas within their sphere of integrated operations, presumably because the marginal return is relatively more attractive in such areas.

Price performance for this highly competitive industry appears to be unsatisfactory. The fault, however, may lie, not with the industry, but with the inelastic supply function for timber and lumber. A rapidly expanding construction demand from 1945 to the early 1950's, in conjunction with an inelastic timber supply, forced a rapid increase in lumber prices. The evidence indicates that consumers may not safely place their confidence in buying lumber by stamped grades. Wage rates are relatively flexible, so that labor shares in both the more prosperous and the less prosperous phases of economic activity. Most of the gains from economic progress accrue, not to labor or to lumber-mill ownership, but to the owners of timber resources.

Freedom and opportunity appear to be secure in the lumber industry. While there is some question about political democracy in a setting of concentrated timber resource ownership, normal market forces apparently motivate large owners to make such resources available for recreational use by the general public. The quality of timber resource management appears to be precisely the opposite from what classical theory would indicate. Quality of performance in timber management appears to vary directly with the size class of ownership.

Overall, moderately concentrated timber resource ownership indicates a higher level of performance in timber management than could be expected from a more atomistic structure of ownership. On the other hand, the competitive structure of the lumber industry at the output level, corresponding closely to the classical model of perfect competition, leaves much to be desired with respect to performance. Knowledge of the highly competitive structure does not allow one to safely predict excellent performance.

The more valid test of performance comes when one asks if an alternative structure could have produced better results. It is impossible to know "what might have been" under other structural conditions. Given the evidence and the deductive reasoning presented above, however, it appears that superior performance would follow if the observed trend toward large-scale timber resource ownership were accelerated and if the federal government merchandised its timber resources in a series of competitive wholesale log markets rather than in the present heterogeneous timber sales. This modification would not only permit firms to achieve greater milling efflicency on the basis of a more homogeneous log input, but it would also lessen, or eliminate entirely, the positions of market power enjoyed by large firms and the inequities resulting from a wide price disparity between competitive and noncompetitive timber sales. In view of the conclusion that present structure and performance fall short of the potential and that two structural changes offer some prospect of improvement, it follows that the present structure must be classified as not workably competitive.

Summary of Findings

In this summary of findings the order of listing corresponds generally to the order of presentation in the text.

1. The optimum plant size for lumber production in the Douglas fir lumber industry, established on the basis of survival data, engineering estimates, and a deductive line of reasoning, is within the range of 60,000 to 140,000 board feet per eight-hour daily capacity. This range includes medium and medium-large mills. A plant at the upper end of the range would employ approximately seventy-five people and incur a capital cost of about 1 million dollars. No clear evidence was found to indicate multiplant firm economies, and, on the basis of deductive reasoning, it was argued that the single-plant firm is optimal. Thus, the Douglas fir lumber industry is a small-scale industry.

2. The demand for lumber with respect to price is within the inelastic range. The dominant factor contributing a degree of elasticity is the possibility of substitution between lumber and alternative available building materials. The closest substitute is plywood.

3. The demand for timber in the Douglas fir region is highly price inelastic. Because lumber's principal competing product (plywood) also requires timber as its major raw material, and because lumber and plywood together constitute the principal market for timber, the demand function for timber must be more price inelastic than the demand function for lumber.

4. The supply of timber with respect to price is highly inelastic in the less-than-one-year short run. As the time period is increased, the supply function becomes more elastic, but even in the long run (defined as fifty to eighty years for Douglas fir region growing conditions) the supply function is held to be relatively inelastic. Elasticity estimates for supply functions are based on sustainable supply increases only, and assume relatively full employment conditions.

5. Although the firm short-run marginal cost function for lumber production is believed to be elastic over a wide range, external diseconomies caused by the inelastic supply function for timber result in a price inelastic industry supply function for lumber (Douglas fir region conditions).

6. Economic concentration in timber resource ownership is low relative to concentration in such resources as copper, alumina, and iron ore. In the Douglas fir region, the Big Four and Big Eight timberland owners account for 26.2 and 34.1 percent, respectively, of all private commercial forest land in the region. The merger movement of the 1950's caused a significant increase in resource concentration. From 1953 to 1960, concentration in timberland ownership by the Big Eight increased from 27.4 to 34.1 percent.

7. An examination of the structure of the federal timber market establishes that the relevant geographical market is very narrow; 92 percent of the volume of timber sold from national forests within the Douglas fir region is processed in mills located within seventy miles of the timber. This limited geographical timber market is the result of a low value of logs per unit of weight. Within any given timber market there are few buyers. The regional average number of qualified bidders in timber sales in the period 1959–1962 was 4.2.

8. Economic concentration in lumber production for the United States lumber industry and for the Douglas fir region segment of it is extremely low. The merger movement of the 1950's, however, coupled with an uncommonly high drop-out rate among very small mills, resulted in a substantial increase in concentration. From 1947 to 1963, concentration in the Big Eight firms increased from 6.4 to 12.4 percent of national lumber production. Nevertheless, lumber remained as one of the most competitive industries in the American economy. A continuation of the drop-out and merger trends, however, would raise the serious problem of maintaining effective competition in the limited markets for federal timber.

9. Barriers to entry into lumber production are minimal relative to other important segments of American industry. The only meaningful entry barrier is in timber supply. The supply of free-market federal timber in the Douglas fir region is vast. Relevant geographical markets are narrow, however, and the timber supply function is inelastic with the result that new entry (net) leads to substantial stumpage price increases. In addition, an entrant may encounter preclusive bidding by established firms.

10. The observed conduct of competitors in the lumber market corresponds closely to theoretical expectations based on the known structure. Lumber prices are market determined. The individual firm faces a horizontal demand curve, and no single firm is able to exert lasting influence on price. Advertising for product promotion is minimal.

11. The gradual depletion of old-growth timber in private ownership and the relative increase of public timber as a source of log input in the Douglas fir region have forced most lumber producers into the public timber auction markets. The oligopsonistic structure, with its complex interfirm relationships, requires that bidders develop a bidding strategy in order to acquire the timber they need. A multitude of alternative bidding strategies are used by firms as they make seven fundamental decisions in the process of bidding for federal timber. Observed patterns of conduct are characteristic of "competition among the few"; that is, conduct follows directly from structure in timber markets. Collusive behavior, either explicit or implicit, is widespread. One of the more interesting types of conduct results in "token-bid" sales, strongly suggesting either explicit or implicit collusion. Where two or more bidders incur the cost and risk of becoming legally qualified bidders, all but one abstain from oral bidding. The sale is then awarded on the basis of a token bid (usually 5 cents per thousand board feet above appraised price) on the minimum quantity species. Of the timber volume sold in 1959–1962, 17.3 percent was sold in token-bid sales.

12. The theoretical framework serving as a guide to the empirical study of oligopsonistic markets, from which I have derived many of my hypotheses, is oligopoly theory. There is no separate oligopsony theory, and, for several reasons, oligopoly theory cannot be transferred without modification. First, the tools of analysis differ between product and factor markets. Second, markets in which oligopsonists buy tend to be geographically narrower than markets in which oligopolists sell. Third, price is a more significant variable in the former, whereas nonprice competition is relatively more significant in the latter. On the other hand, the essence of oligopoly theory—the idea of interdependence and of consequent explicit or implicit agreements—transfers intact to the oligopsony situation.

13. Price determination in timber markets has been considered under three different sets of assumptions. Effective collusion in timber markets would result in a transfer of wealth from public

to private control, the amount depending on the difference between the appraised price of timber and the noncollusive equilibrium price. Effective collusion requires not price leadership, but allocation leadership. Effective allocation leadership requires that the leader(s) be able to take reprisal action against recalcitrant firm(s). Effective reprisal action requires that the leader(s) be able to buy a given timber sale at any cost and have access to alternative sources of timber so that specific timber sales may be dumped on the recalcitrant firm at relatively high prices.

14. Performance in the markets for timber from national forests in the Douglas fir region is subject to serious shortcomings. The wide gap in timber prices between competitive and noncompetitive sales (the former exceeding the latter by 63 percent of the appraised price) casts serious doubt on the accuracy of the appraisal process. In view of the evidence, one cannot equate appraised price with fair market value. Also, the observed gap raises serious equity problems (1) among firms in areas subject to widely differing degrees of competition and collusion, and (2) between timber resource owners (the public) and some timber buyers. Further, the significant buying power of large firms permits them to obtain timber from the national forests at an average 28 percent premium over appraised price, whereas small firms pay an average 51 percent premium. Of the four hypotheses designed to explain the variation in ratios of bid to appraised prices for timber sold in the Douglas fir region and tested by multiple regression analysis, three have been accepted. The ratio of bid price to appraised price for individual timber sales varies directly with the number of qualified bidders and inversely with the sale size and the economic size class of the buyer. The hypothesis asserting that sealed-bid sales would produce relatively high bid-appraisal ratios has been rejected. Sealed bids are not used to combat suspected collusion, but rather for some small sales. The average sale size is 1,202 and 4,872 board feet in sealed-bid and oral auction sales, respectively. These findings, which indicate inadequate performance in the federal timber markets, suggest that similar hypotheses should be tested in other oligopsonistic markets, particularly in natural resources owned by the federal government.

15. When performance in the markets for national forest timber is analyzed on a geographical basis, the percentage of total timber sales transacted under competitive conditions is found to differ significantly by geographical area. In some working circles, more than 95 percent of all volume sold is classified as competitive, and

in six working circles, less than 50 percent of the volume sold is so classified. Of the four hypotheses advanced to explain differences in degree of competition by working circles in terms of the importance of large firms as timber buyers, the average number of bidders, average sale size, and average appraised prices in each working circle, two have been accepted. The percent of total volume sold competitively by working circle varies directly with the average number of bidders and inversely with the percent of total volume purchased by large firms. The latter independent variable is of particular importance. It again reflects the market power of large firms. The larger the volume purchased by large firms, the lower the percentage of volume sold competitively by working circle.

16. Documentation of the market power position of large firms led to an exploration of the causal relationship between firm size and cost of timber. Explanatory factors fall into two groups: (1) direct forces and (2) indirect forces leading to market power positions. Among the direct forces are (a) barriers to entry into the auction market and (b) ownership of timber reserves. Barriers to entry result from large sale size and accompanying large road-construction costs, both carrying capital requirements that preclude bidding by some small and poorly financed firms. A federal credit plan overcomes some of the financial barrier. Ownership of timber reserves allows some large firms to be selective in federal timber purchases, passing up highly contested and costly sales. Indirect forces also help to explain the market power of large firms. The concept of bidder futility, developed from extensive interviews with persons engaged in the bidding process, suggests that four factors create a feeling of futility among some potential buyers, who then avoid a confrontation with their larger rivals. The first source of bidder futility is the superior location of some large and long-established firms. Second, ownership of private logging roads on privately owned timberland adjacent to a national forest may substantially lower log transportation cost. Third, large firms normally possess superior economic power arising from (a) ownership of historically low-cost timber reserves, (b) a secure financial position including access to low-cost credit, and (c) diversified and more stable income. Fourth, large firms have significant advantages in capital gains treatment of income from timber ownership. In 1959–1962 an average of 3.7 bidders competed for sales acquired by large firms, whereas 4.3 bidders competed for sales acquired by small firms. Finally, no evidence was found to support the point that large lumber mills are more efficient lumber producers than

smaller mills; hence, relative efficiency apparently does not add to the bidder futility attitude.

17. Performance at the lumber-production level leaves much to be desired. A fifty-five-year record of productivity shows that the lumber industry is one of the least progressive of eighty manufacturing industries in the United States. Lagging productivity reflects a lack of formal research and development effort in the lumber industry. The data, though incomplete, suggest that small firms have led in technological development, whereas large firms have led in product development. Consumers have not benefited by a decline in lumber prices, either relative or absolute; rather, lumber prices have increased relative to all commodities and to all construction materials from 1926 through 1964. This record may be accounted for in part by an inelastic supply of timber and lumber. Evidence indicates that customers cannot buy lumber products with the confidence that quality corresponds to grade markings. In accordance with economic theory, real wages in the lumber industry increased approximately in proportion to the increase throughout the manufacturing sector of the economy. Further, increases in wage rates in lumber manufacturing reflected market conditions for lumber. Thus, labor shared in greater or lesser profitability. Lumber-manufacturing profits correspond closely with expectations based on the model of pure competition. The principal beneficiaries of economic progress in the lumber industry are timber resource owners receiving quasi-economic rent. From 1940 to 1964, stumpage prices increased sixteen fold.

18. Performance in timber resource management appears to vary directly with size class of the acreage owned. While evidence on the issue of personal freedom and opportunity is inadequate, it appears that large timber-owning firms have made their timberland available for limited public use, so that no serious limitation in multiple use follows from concentration in timberland ownership.

19. Applying the test of workable competition, plus the "Markham addendum," which asks if an alternative structure would have produced more desirable performance than the present structure, I have concluded that the lumber industry is not workably competitive. Two structural modifications would improve performance: (1) Timber resource management would probably be of higher quality if more of the very small timberland ownerships were "blocked up" into additional large ownerships. (2) The observed market power of large firms, and other inequities resulting from the large gap between competitive and noncompetitive sales,

would be eliminated or reduced if federal timber were sold in wholesale log markets rather than as standing timber.

20. As to the relationship between the traditional three categories of industrial organization, conduct (behavior) in the lumber industry follows directly and is predictable from knowledge of structure in both the lumber production level and the timber input level. Satisfactory performance, however, does not follow from competitive structure and conduct at the output level, nor is unsatisfactory performance clearly the result of modestly concentrated timberland ownership. In several important respects, precisely the opposite relationship appears: a competitive structure is associated with unsatisfactory performance, and concentrated resource ownership is associated with desirable performance. In any event, performance cannot be predicted from knowledge of structure in the lumber industry.

Index

Advertising, 130, 267; brand names, 24, 121; outlay, 120–121; packaging, 121; of timber sales, 138
Allowable cut, 56–58, 187
Antitrust policy, 233
Appraisal methods, 135–138, 182, 259–260. *See also* Price, appraised
Appraised price. *See* Price, appraised
Availability: of factors, 33–36; of products, 38, 43–44

Bain, Joe S., 20n, 24, 64, 111, 116, 120, 187, 221
Bargaining. *See* Collusion
Barriers to entry. *See* Entry, barriers to
Bid-appraisal ratio, 182–184, 186–189, 191–192, 193–195, 198–207, 214
Bidding: position, 88; advantages, 114; qualification, 138–139; collusion in, 142, 151, 189, 267; strategy, 142–158, 185, 267; preclusive, 148–150; harrassment, 149; "fishing," 149–150; threats, 152; emotion in, 154–155; token-bid, 155–158, 173, 190, 192, 267; serious, 180–181; futility in, 222–228; "mischievous" challenge in, 227
Bohemia Lumber Co., 106
Booth-Kelly Lumber Co., 86, 104
Bureaucracy. *See* Decision making, managerial
Bureau of Land Management, 57–58

California redwood region: softwood production in, 6
Camac Veneer Co., 226
Capacity: rated, 15; and prices, 54; and log supplies, 212; excess, 253
Capital: theory, 51–52; gain, 113, 224–225, 228; requirements, 115–118, 221
Cascadia Lumber Co., 106
Chicago, Milwaukee and St. Paul Railroad, 86

Clark, J. M., 230–233, 236, 250, 253, 256, 258
Clawson, Marion, 65
Clay, Sir Henry, 20–21
Clemens Forest Products, Inc., 104–105
Collusion, 215; among buyers, 1, 173; in oligopoly, 108; among bidders, 142, 151, 189, 267; quasi bargaining, 163, 173; implicit, 163–164; breakdown of, 164–165; in oligopsony, 169–173, 213; effects of, 188
Competition: in lumber industry, 1; perfect, 77; and price, 127; in sales, 181. *See also* "Percent competitive"; Workably competitive
Concentration, 2; in resource ownership, 78–90, 95–96, 266; in lumber, 98–108, 266; in wholesale distribution, 108–110
Conduct, 127–134, 267; and pure competition, 2
Coos Bay Timber Co., 103–104
Coos Head Timber Co., 105–106
Cost: of production, 22; of timber, 25, 207, 210; short-run, 26–31, 53, 68–69; residential construction, 43–44; of lumber, 44; of labor, 47–48; of transportation, 90–92, 223; of entry, 111–122; of cruising, 144–146; prebid, 146–147; differential, 189, 192–193; of road construction, 199, 204–205, 216–217. *See also* Stumpage, prices
Cournot model, 172–174
Cross elasticity of demand for lumber, 7
Crown Zellerbach Corporation, 59, 258

De Chazeau, Melvin G., 262
Decision making: production line, 22–23; managerial, 24
Demand for lumber: elasticity of, 1, 32, 36, 38–44, 45–46, 50, 71–72, 129, 265; cross elasticity between species, 7; from